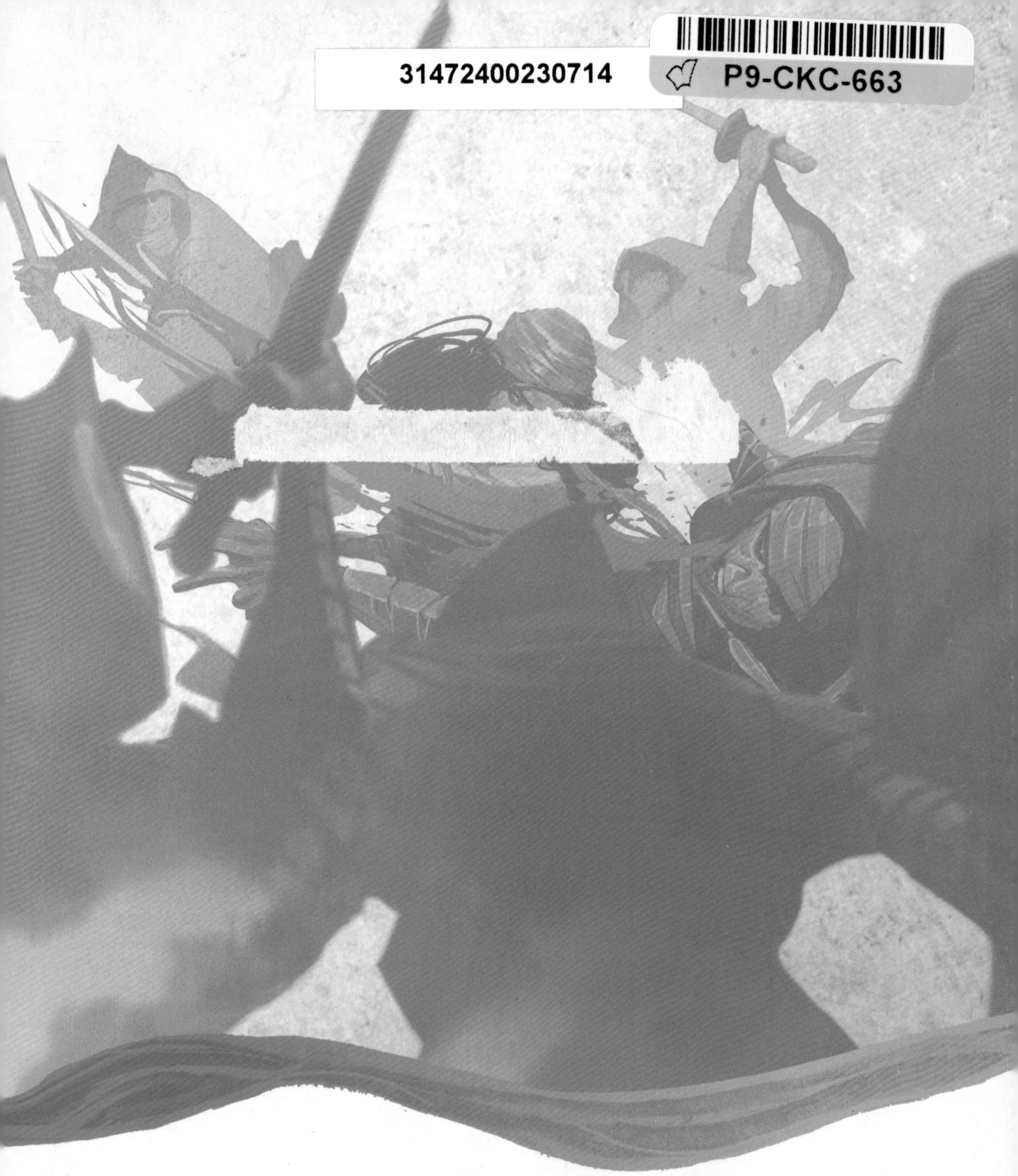

ELEKTRA

ELEKTRA

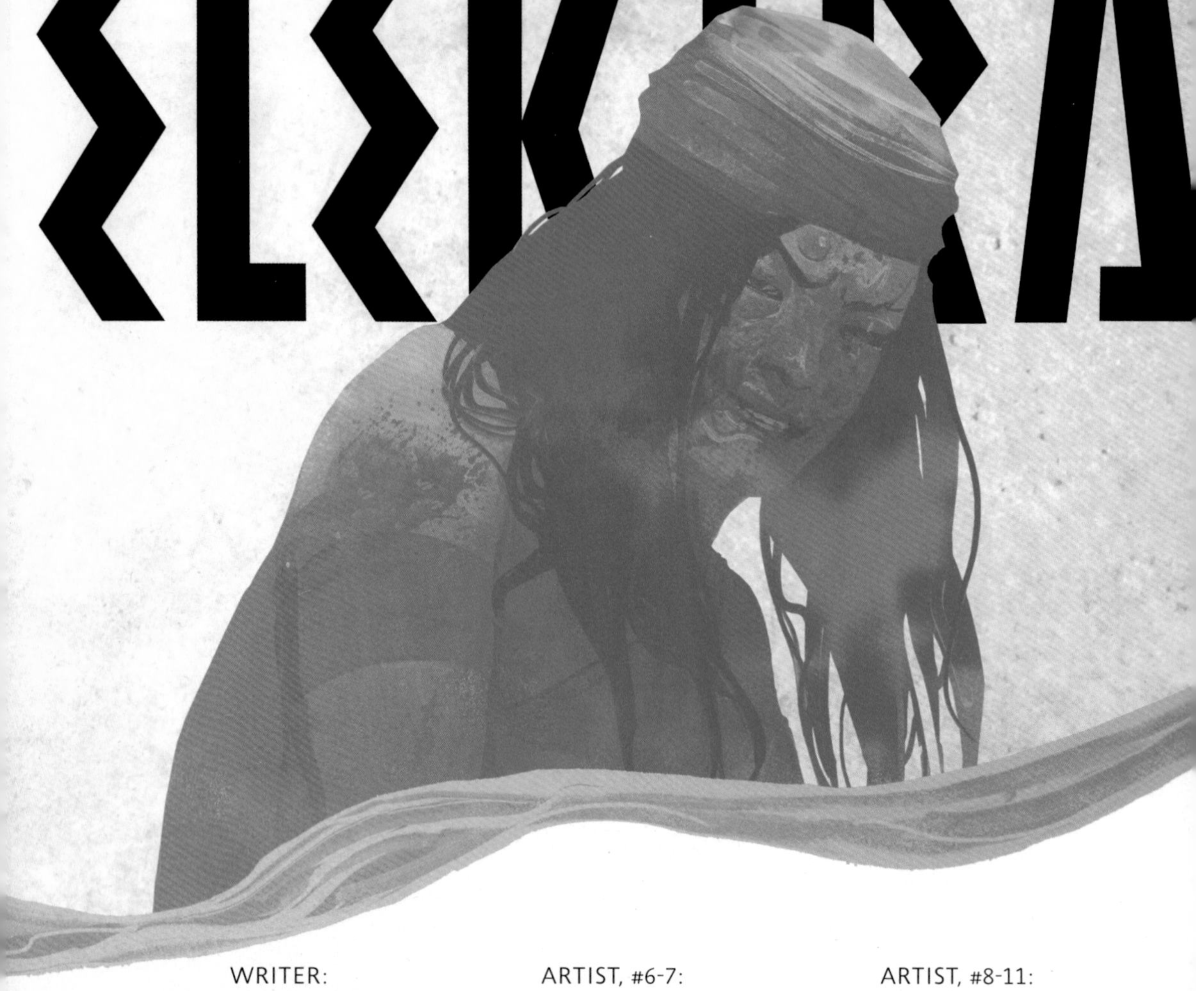

WRITER:
W. HADEN BLACKMAN

ARTIST, #6-7:
ALEX SANCHEZ

ARTIST, #8-11:
MICHAEL DEL MUNDO

COLOR ARTISTS:
ESTHER SANZ (#6-7), **MICHAEL DEL MUNDO** (#8) & **MARCO D'ALFONSO** (#9-11)

LETTERER:
VC'S CLAYTON COWLES
with **MICHAEL DEL MUNDO**

COVER ART:
MICHAEL DEL MUNDO

ASSISTANT EDITOR:
DEVIN LEWIS

EDITOR:
SANA AMANAT

SENIOR EDITOR:
NICK LOWE

COLLECTION EDITOR: **JENNIFER GRÜNWALD** ASSISTANT EDITOR: **SARAH BRUNSTAD**
ASSOCIATE MANAGING EDITOR: **ALEX STARBUCK** EDITOR, SPECIAL PROJECTS: **MARK D. BEAZLEY**
SENIOR EDITOR, SPECIAL PROJECTS: **JEFF YOUNGQUIST** SVP PRINT, SALES & MARKETING: **DAVID GABRIEL**
BOOK DESIGNERS: **RODOLFO MURAGUCHI** & **JEFF POWELL**

EDITOR IN CHIEF: **AXEL ALONSO** CHIEF CREATIVE OFFICER: **JOE QUESADA**
PUBLISHER: **DAN BUCKLEY** EXECUTIVE PRODUCER: **ALAN FINE**

ELEKTRA VOL. 2: REVERENCE. Contains material originally published in magazine form as ELEKTRA #6-11. First printing 2015. ISBN# 978-0-7851-5407-5. Published by MARVEL WORLDWIDE, INC., a subsid of MARVEL ENTERTAINMENT, LLC. OFFICE OF PUBLICATION: 135 West 50th Street, New York, NY 10020. Printed in Canada. ALAN FINE, President, Marvel Entertainment; D BUCKLEY, President, TV, Publishing and Brand Management; JOE QUESADA, Chief Creative Officer; TOM BREVOORT, SVP of Publishing; DAVID BOGART, SVP of Operations & Procurement, Publishing; C.B. CEBUL SVP of Creator & Content Development; DAVID GABRIEL, SVP Print, Sales & Marketing; JIM O'KEEFE, VP of Operations & Logistics; DAN CARR, Executive Director of Publishing Technology; SUSAN CRESPI, Edito Operations Manager; ALEX MORALES, Publishing Operations Manager; STAN LEE, Chairman Emeritus. For information regarding advertising in Marvel Comics or on Marvel.com, please contact Niza Disla, Dire of Marvel Partnerships, at ndisla@marvel.com. For Marvel subscription inquiries, please call 800-217-9158. **Manufactured between 3/6/2015 and 4/13/2015 by SOLISCO PRINTERS, SCOTT, QC, CANA**

10 9 8 7 6 5 4 3 2 1

PREVIOUSLY

ELEKTRA HAS BEEN PURSUING CAPE CROW, A DANGEROUS KILLER BEING HUNTED BY THE ASSASSIN'S GUILD.

NOTORIOUS AND ELUSIVE, CROW HAS MADE A CAREER OUT OF STEALING THE CONTRACTS OF OTHER ASSASSINS. NOW, THEY WANT THE MONEY THEY'RE OWED AND HIS HEAD.

ELEKTRA FOLLOWED HIM ACROSS THE GLOBE, AND SAVED HIS LIFE FROM A BLOODTHIRSTY MADMAN NAMED BLOODY LIPS.

WORKING WITH CROW, HOWEVER, HAS GIVEN THE GUILD A NEW TARGET... ELEKTRA HERSELF.

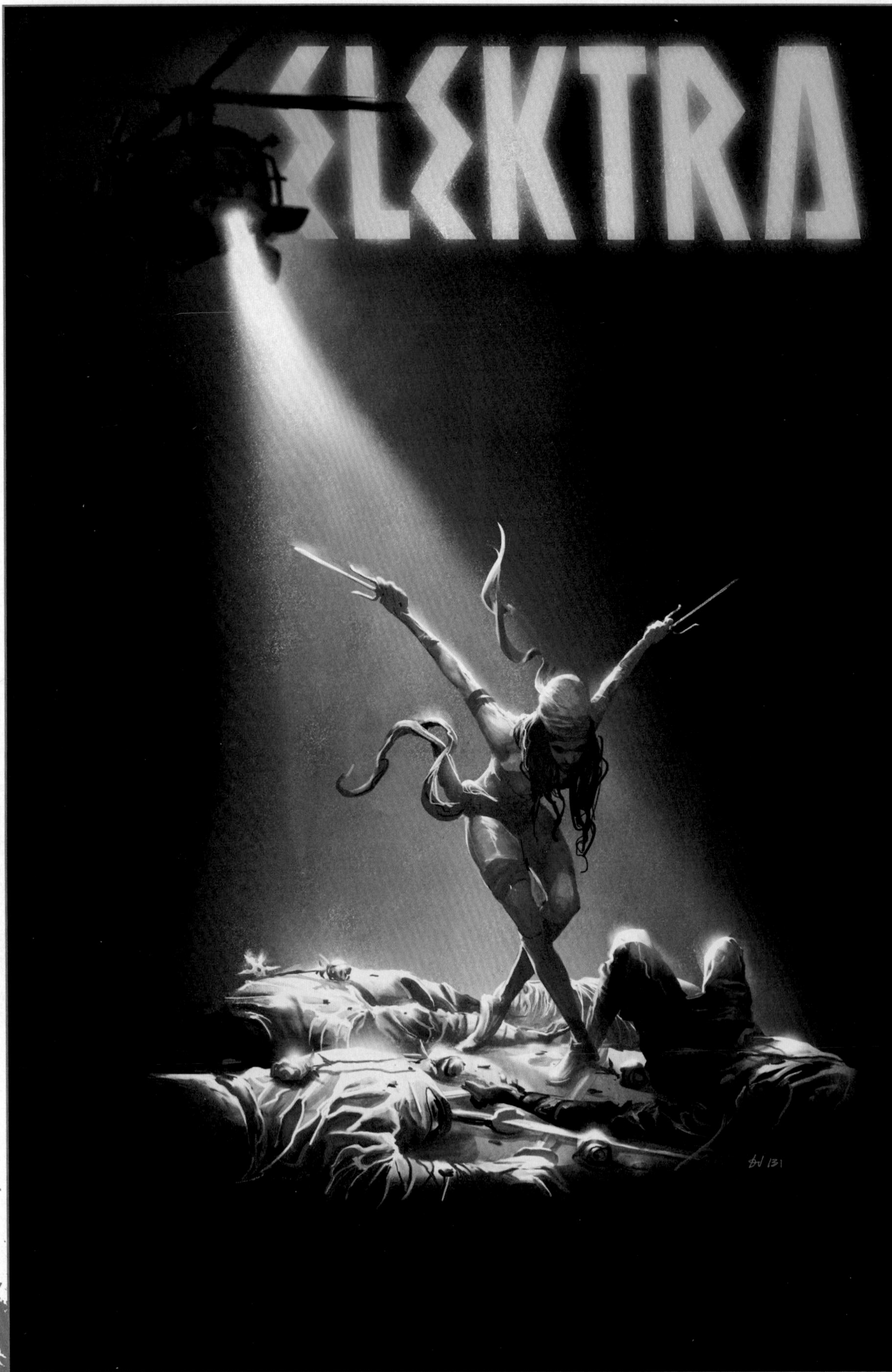
ELEKTRA

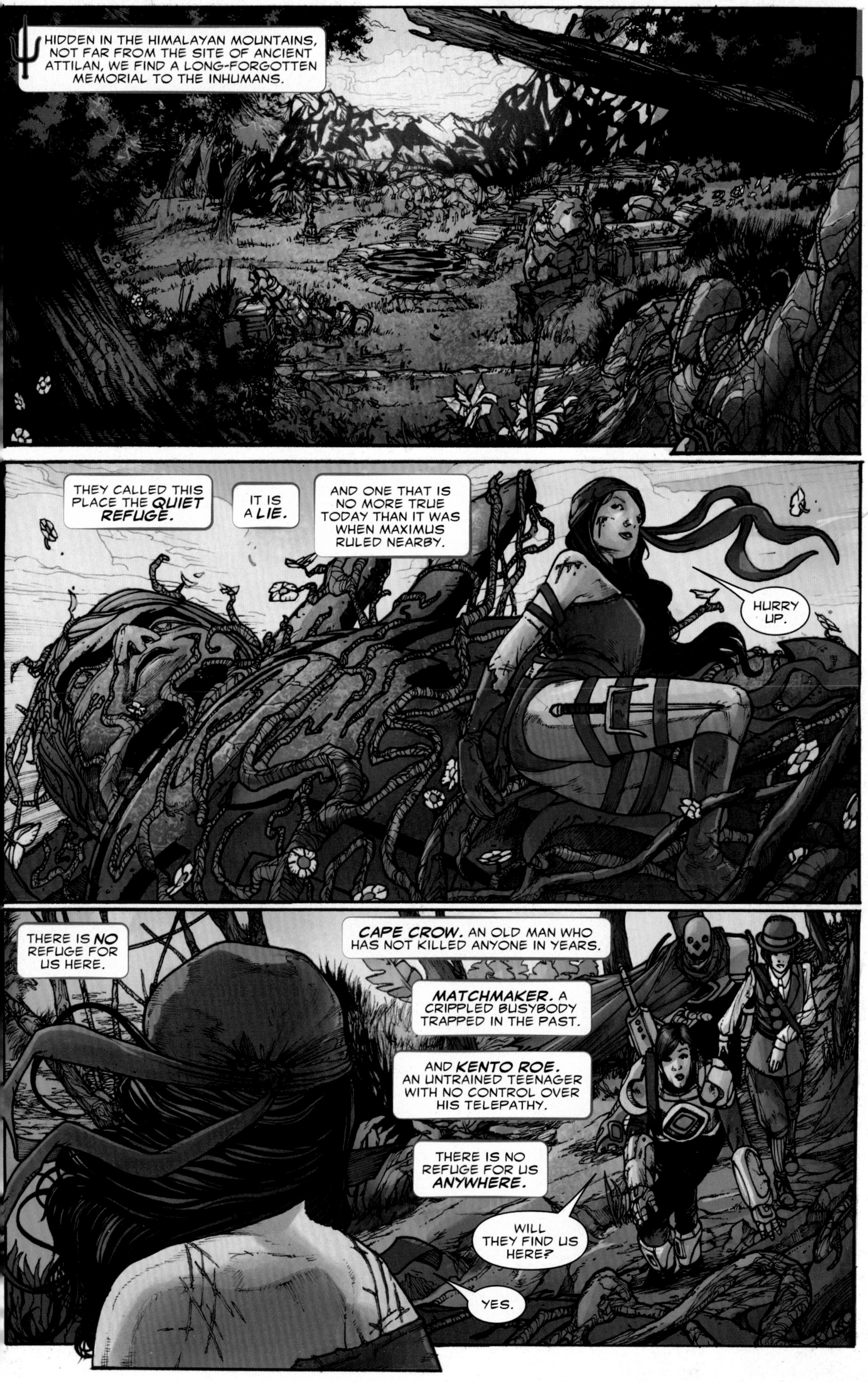
HIDDEN IN THE HIMALAYAN MOUNTAINS, NOT FAR FROM THE SITE OF ANCIENT ATTILAN, WE FIND A LONG-FORGOTTEN MEMORIAL TO THE INHUMANS.
THEY CALLED THIS PLACE THE *QUIET REFUGE*.
IT IS A *LIE*.
AND ONE THAT IS NO MORE TRUE TODAY THAN IT WAS WHEN MAXIMUS RULED NEARBY.
HURRY UP.
THERE IS *NO* REFUGE FOR US HERE.
CAPE CROW. AN OLD MAN WHO HAS NOT KILLED ANYONE IN YEARS.
MATCHMAKER. A CRIPPLED BUSYBODY TRAPPED IN THE PAST.
AND *KENTO ROE*. AN UNTRAINED TEENAGER WITH NO CONTROL OVER HIS TELEPATHY.
THERE IS NO REFUGE FOR US *ANYWHERE*.
WILL THEY FIND US HERE?
YES.

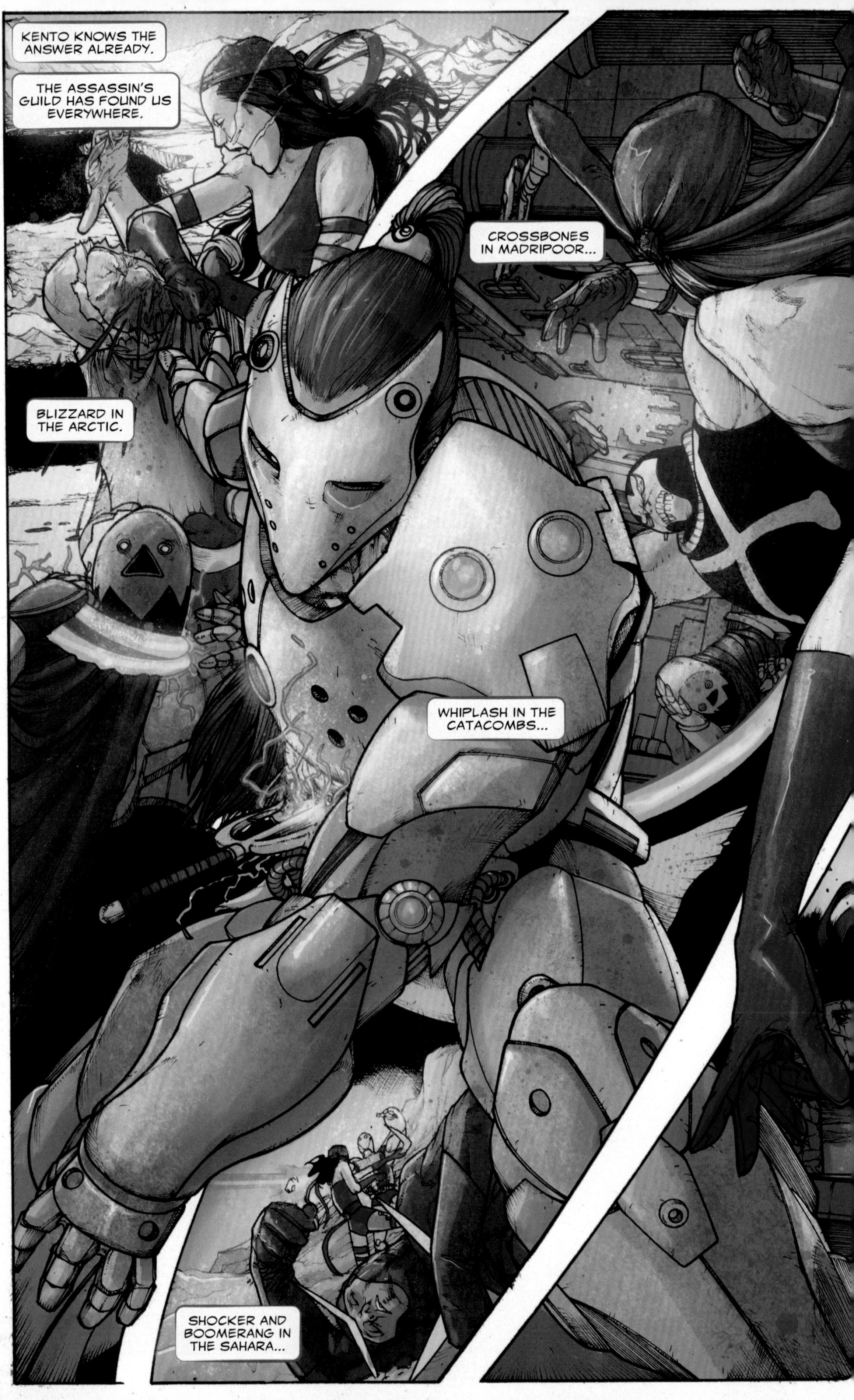
KENTO KNOWS THE ANSWER ALREADY.
THE ASSASSIN'S GUILD HAS FOUND US EVERYWHERE.
CROSSBONES IN MADRIPOOR...
BLIZZARD IN THE ARCTIC.
WHIPLASH IN THE CATACOMBS...
SHOCKER AND BOOMERANG IN THE SAHARA...

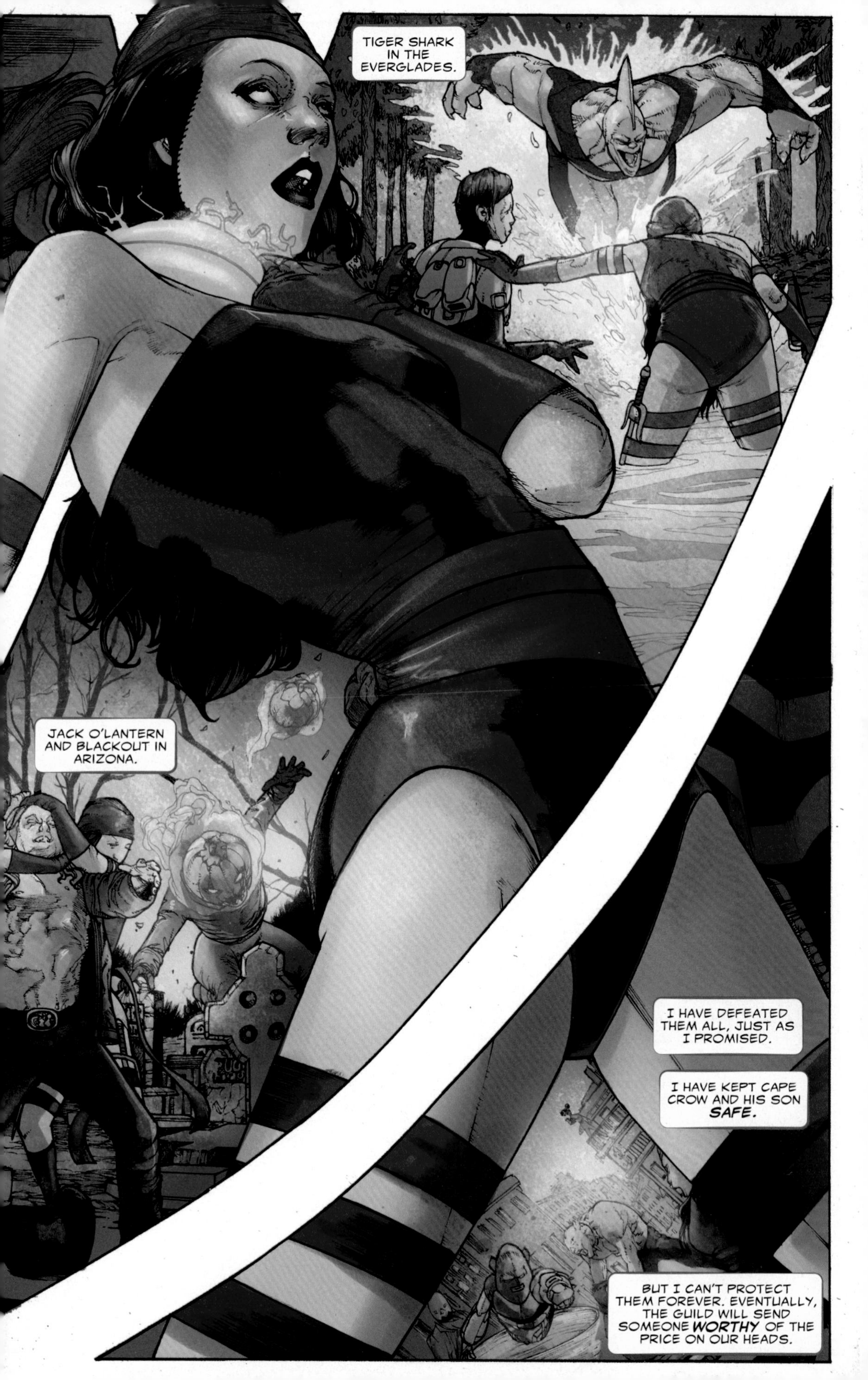
TIGER SHARK IN THE EVERGLADES.
JACK O'LANTERN AND BLACKOUT IN ARIZONA.
I HAVE DEFEATED THEM ALL, JUST AS I PROMISED.
I HAVE KEPT CAPE CROW AND HIS SON SAFE.
BUT I CAN'T PROTECT THEM FOREVER. EVENTUALLY, THE GUILD WILL SEND SOMEONE WORTHY OF THE PRICE ON OUR HEADS.

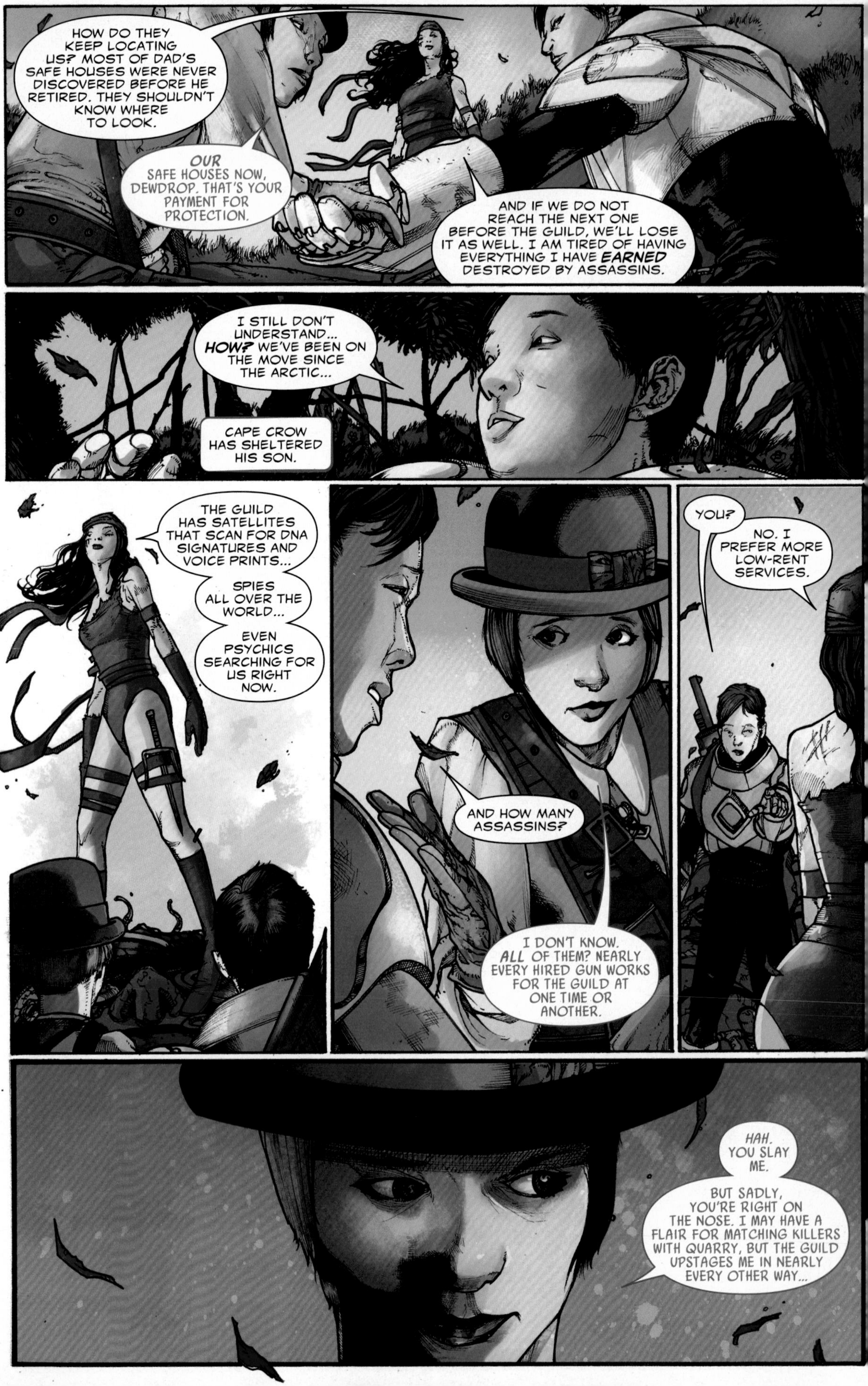
HOW DO THEY KEEP LOCATING US? MOST OF DAD'S SAFE HOUSES WERE NEVER DISCOVERED BEFORE HE RETIRED. THEY SHOULDN'T KNOW WHERE TO LOOK.
OUR SAFE HOUSES NOW, DEWDROP. THAT'S YOUR PAYMENT FOR PROTECTION.
AND IF WE DO NOT REACH THE NEXT ONE BEFORE THE GUILD, WE'LL LOSE IT AS WELL. I AM TIRED OF HAVING EVERYTHING I HAVE ***EARNED*** DESTROYED BY ASSASSINS.
I STILL DON'T UNDERSTAND... ***HOW?*** WE'VE BEEN ON THE MOVE SINCE THE ARCTIC...
CAPE CROW HAS SHELTERED HIS SON.
THE GUILD HAS SATELLITES THAT SCAN FOR DNA SIGNATURES AND VOICE PRINTS...
SPIES ALL OVER THE WORLD...
EVEN PSYCHICS SEARCHING FOR US RIGHT NOW.
AND HOW MANY ASSASSINS?
I DON'T KNOW. ***ALL*** OF THEM? NEARLY EVERY HIRED GUN WORKS FOR THE GUILD AT ONE TIME OR ANOTHER.
YOU?
NO. I PREFER MORE LOW-RENT SERVICES.
HAH. YOU SLAY ME.
BUT SADLY, YOU'RE RIGHT ON THE NOSE. I MAY HAVE A FLAIR FOR MATCHING KILLERS WITH QUARRY, BUT THE GUILD UPSTAGES ME IN NEARLY EVERY OTHER WAY...

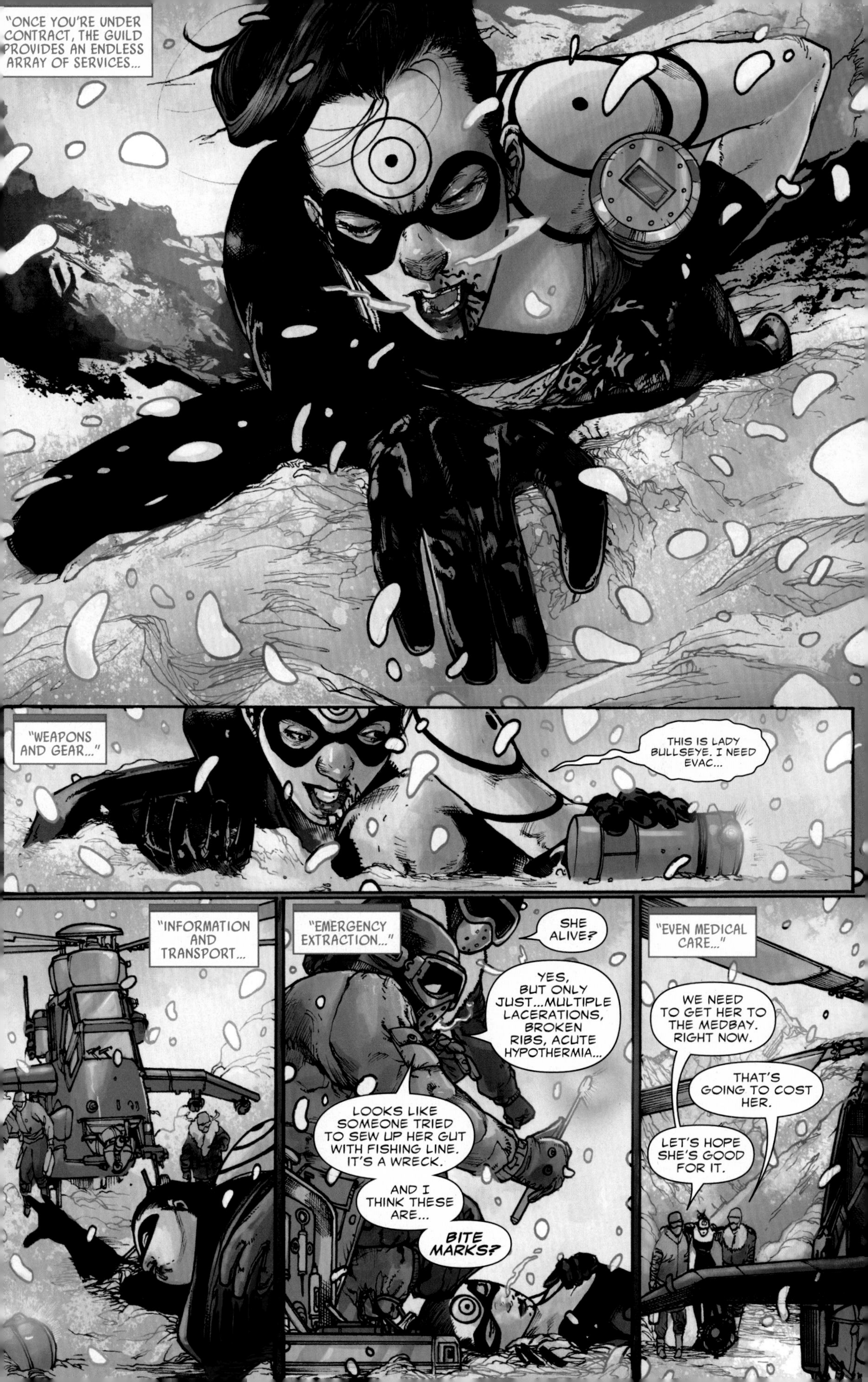
"ONCE YOU'RE UNDER CONTRACT, THE GUILD PROVIDES AN ENDLESS ARRAY OF SERVICES...
"WEAPONS AND GEAR..."
THIS IS LADY BULLSEYE. I NEED EVAC...
"INFORMATION AND TRANSPORT...
"EMERGENCY EXTRACTION..."
SHE ALIVE?
YES, BUT ONLY JUST...MULTIPLE LACERATIONS, BROKEN RIBS, ACUTE HYPOTHERMIA...
LOOKS LIKE SOMEONE TRIED TO SEW UP HER GUT WITH FISHING LINE. IT'S A WRECK.
AND I THINK THESE ARE...
BITE MARKS?
"EVEN MEDICAL CARE..."
WE NEED TO GET HER TO THE MEDBAY. RIGHT NOW.
THAT'S GOING TO COST HER.
LET'S HOPE SHE'S GOOD FOR IT.

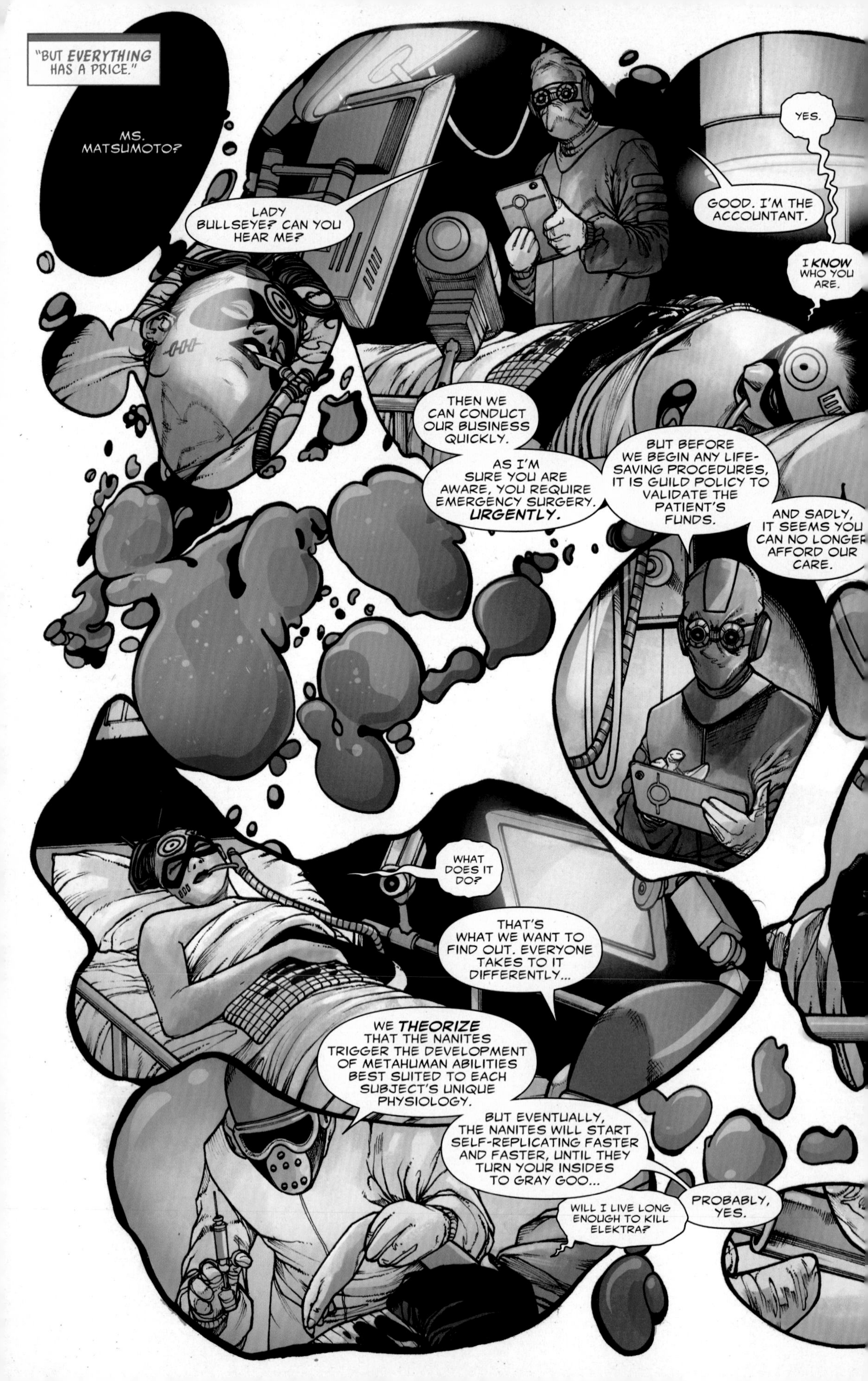
"BUT EVERYTHING HAS A PRICE."
MS. MATSUMOTO?
LADY BULLSEYE? CAN YOU HEAR ME?
YES.
GOOD. I'M THE ACCOUNTANT.
I KNOW WHO YOU ARE.
THEN WE CAN CONDUCT OUR BUSINESS QUICKLY.
AS I'M SURE YOU ARE AWARE, YOU REQUIRE EMERGENCY SURGERY. URGENTLY.
BUT BEFORE WE BEGIN ANY LIFE-SAVING PROCEDURES, IT IS GUILD POLICY TO VALIDATE THE PATIENT'S FUNDS.
AND SADLY, IT SEEMS YOU CAN NO LONGER AFFORD OUR CARE.
WHAT DOES IT DO?
THAT'S WHAT WE WANT TO FIND OUT. EVERYONE TAKES TO IT DIFFERENTLY...
WE THEORIZE THAT THE NANITES TRIGGER THE DEVELOPMENT OF METAHUMAN ABILITIES BEST SUITED TO EACH SUBJECT'S UNIQUE PHYSIOLOGY.
BUT EVENTUALLY, THE NANITES WILL START SELF-REPLICATING FASTER AND FASTER, UNTIL THEY TURN YOUR INSIDES TO GRAY GOO...
WILL I LIVE LONG ENOUGH TO KILL ELEKTRA?
PROBABLY, YES.

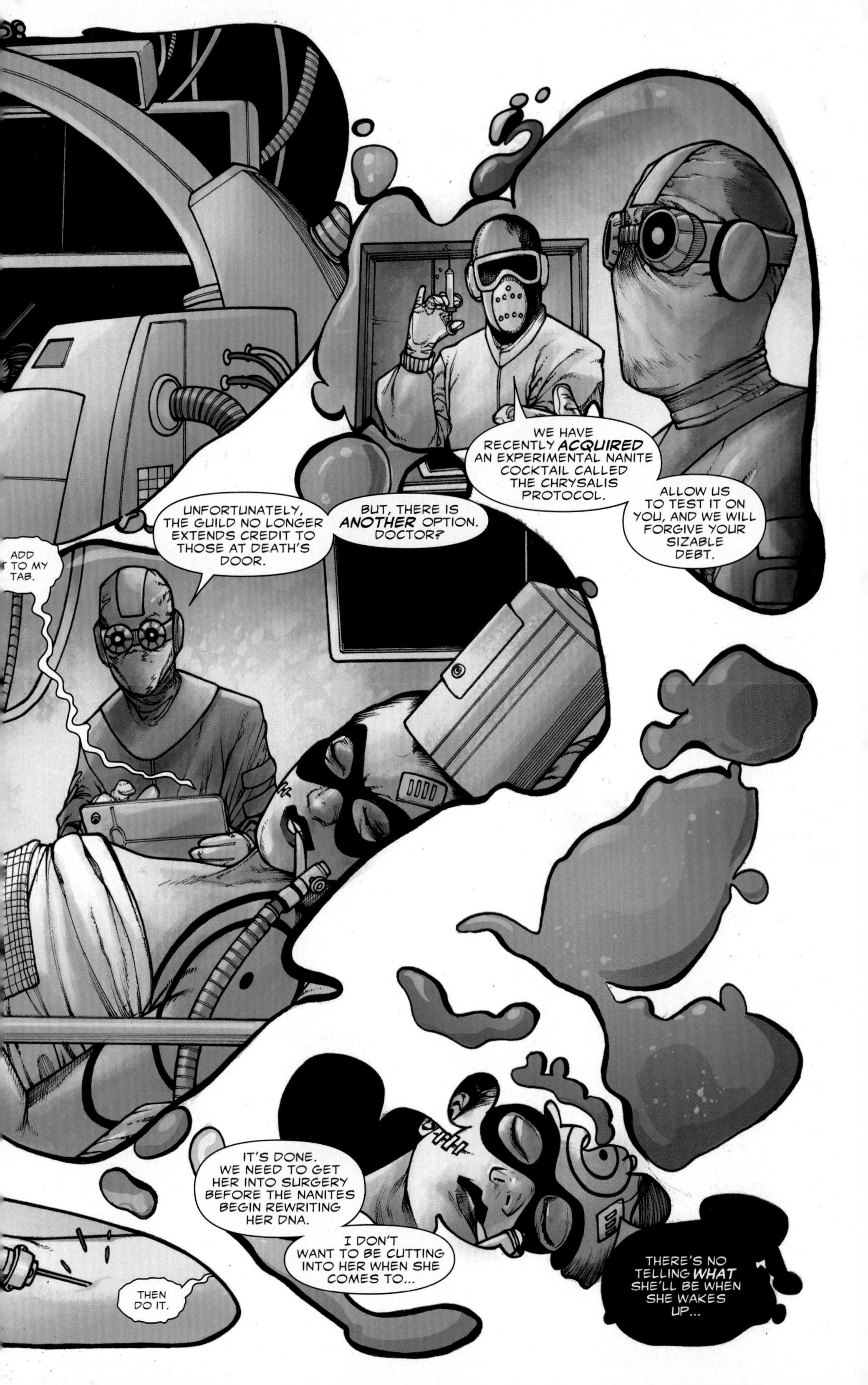
WE HAVE RECENTLY ACQUIRED AN EXPERIMENTAL NANITE COCKTAIL CALLED THE CHRYSALIS PROTOCOL.
ALLOW US TO TEST IT ON YOU, AND WE WILL FORGIVE YOUR SIZABLE DEBT.
UNFORTUNATELY, THE GUILD NO LONGER EXTENDS CREDIT TO THOSE AT DEATH'S DOOR.
BUT, THERE IS ANOTHER OPTION. DOCTOR?
ADD TO MY TAB.
IT'S DONE. WE NEED TO GET HER INTO SURGERY BEFORE THE NANITES BEGIN REWRITING HER DNA.
I DON'T WANT TO BE CUTTING INTO HER WHEN SHE COMES TO...
THEN DO IT.
THERE'S NO TELLING WHAT SHE'LL BE WHEN SHE WAKES UP...

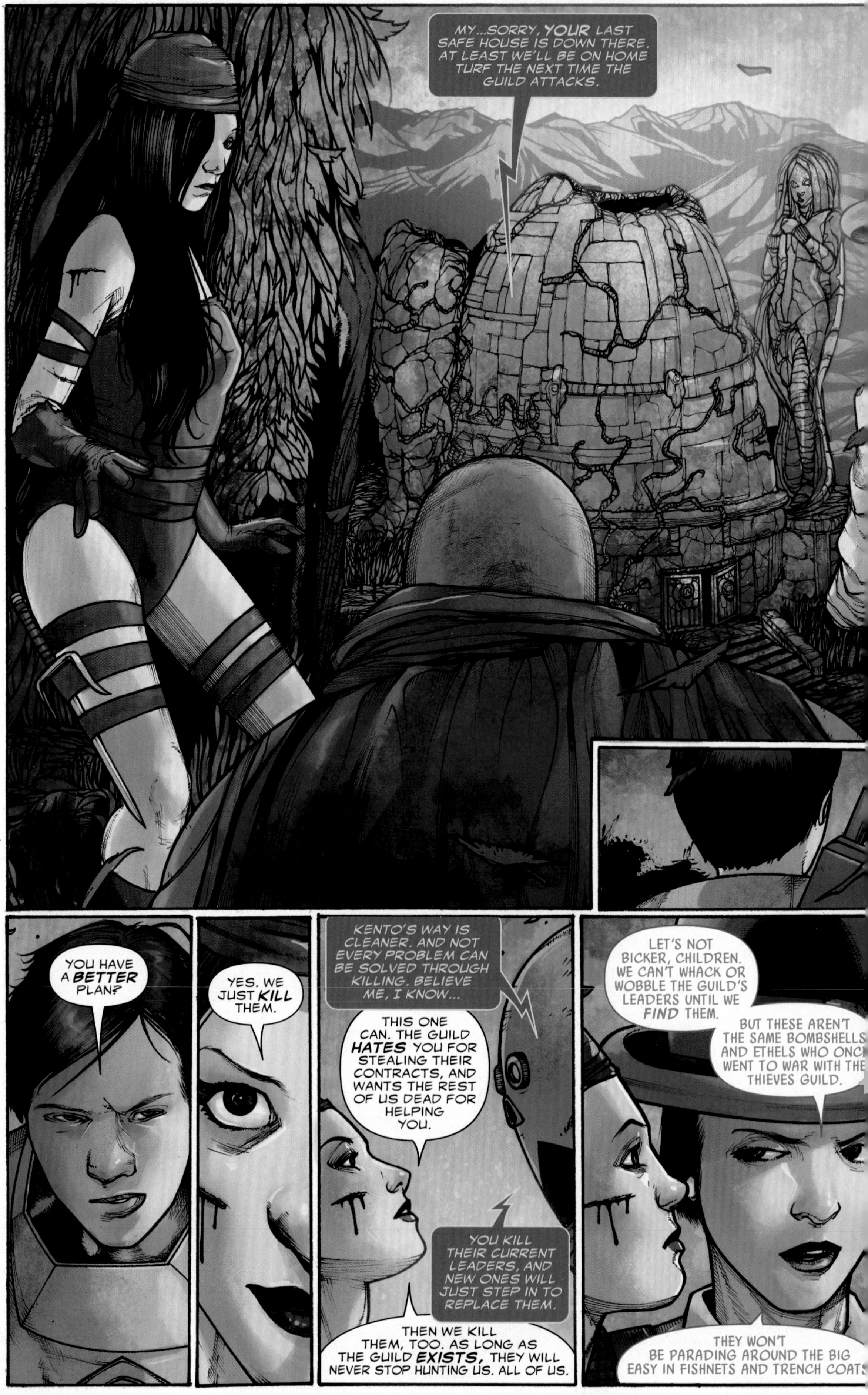
MY...SORRY, YOUR LAST SAFE HOUSE IS DOWN THERE. AT LEAST WE'LL BE ON HOME TURF THE NEXT TIME THE GUILD ATTACKS.
YOU HAVE A BETTER PLAN?
YES. WE JUST KILL THEM.
KENTO'S WAY IS CLEANER. AND NOT EVERY PROBLEM CAN BE SOLVED THROUGH KILLING. BELIEVE ME, I KNOW...
THIS ONE CAN. THE GUILD HATES YOU FOR STEALING THEIR CONTRACTS, AND WANTS THE REST OF US DEAD FOR HELPING YOU.
YOU KILL THEIR CURRENT LEADERS, AND NEW ONES WILL JUST STEP IN TO REPLACE THEM.
THEN WE KILL THEM, TOO. AS LONG AS THE GUILD EXISTS, THEY WILL NEVER STOP HUNTING US. ALL OF US.
LET'S NOT BICKER, CHILDREN. WE CAN'T WHACK OR WOBBLE THE GUILD'S LEADERS UNTIL WE FIND THEM.
BUT THESE AREN'T THE SAME BOMBSHELLS AND ETHELS WHO ONC WENT TO WAR WITH THE THIEVES GUILD.
THEY WON'T BE PARADING AROUND THE BIG EASY IN FISHNETS AND TRENCH COATS

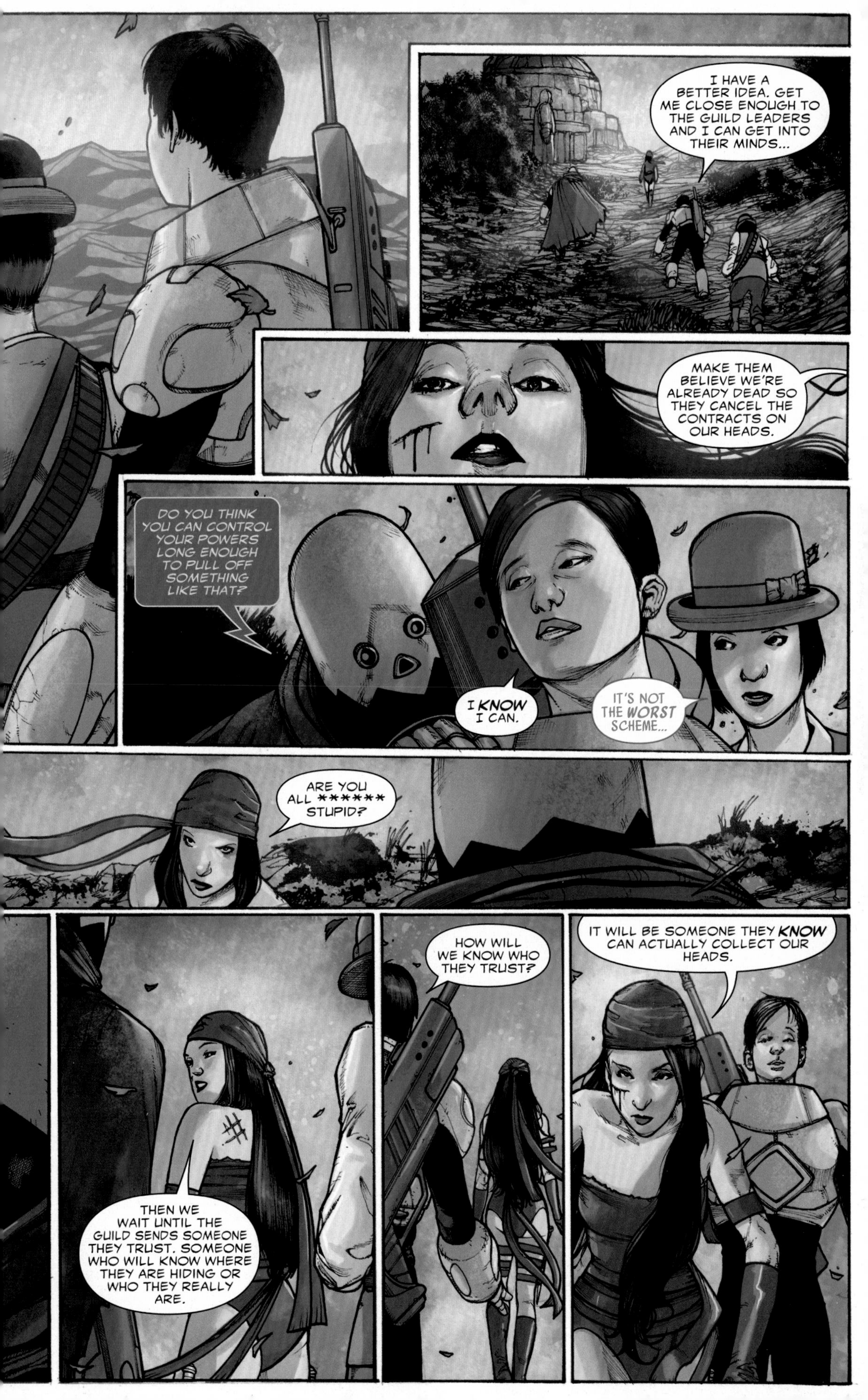
I HAVE A BETTER IDEA. GET ME CLOSE ENOUGH TO THE GUILD LEADERS AND I CAN GET INTO THEIR MINDS...
MAKE THEM BELIEVE WE'RE ALREADY DEAD SO THEY CANCEL THE CONTRACTS ON OUR HEADS.
DO YOU THINK YOU CAN CONTROL YOUR POWERS LONG ENOUGH TO PULL OFF SOMETHING LIKE THAT?
I KNOW I CAN.
IT'S NOT THE WORST SCHEME...
ARE YOU ALL ****** STUPID?
THEN WE WAIT UNTIL THE GUILD SENDS SOMEONE THEY TRUST. SOMEONE WHO WILL KNOW WHERE THEY ARE HIDING OR WHO THEY REALLY ARE.
HOW WILL WE KNOW WHO THEY TRUST?
IT WILL BE SOMEONE THEY KNOW CAN ACTUALLY COLLECT OUR HEADS.

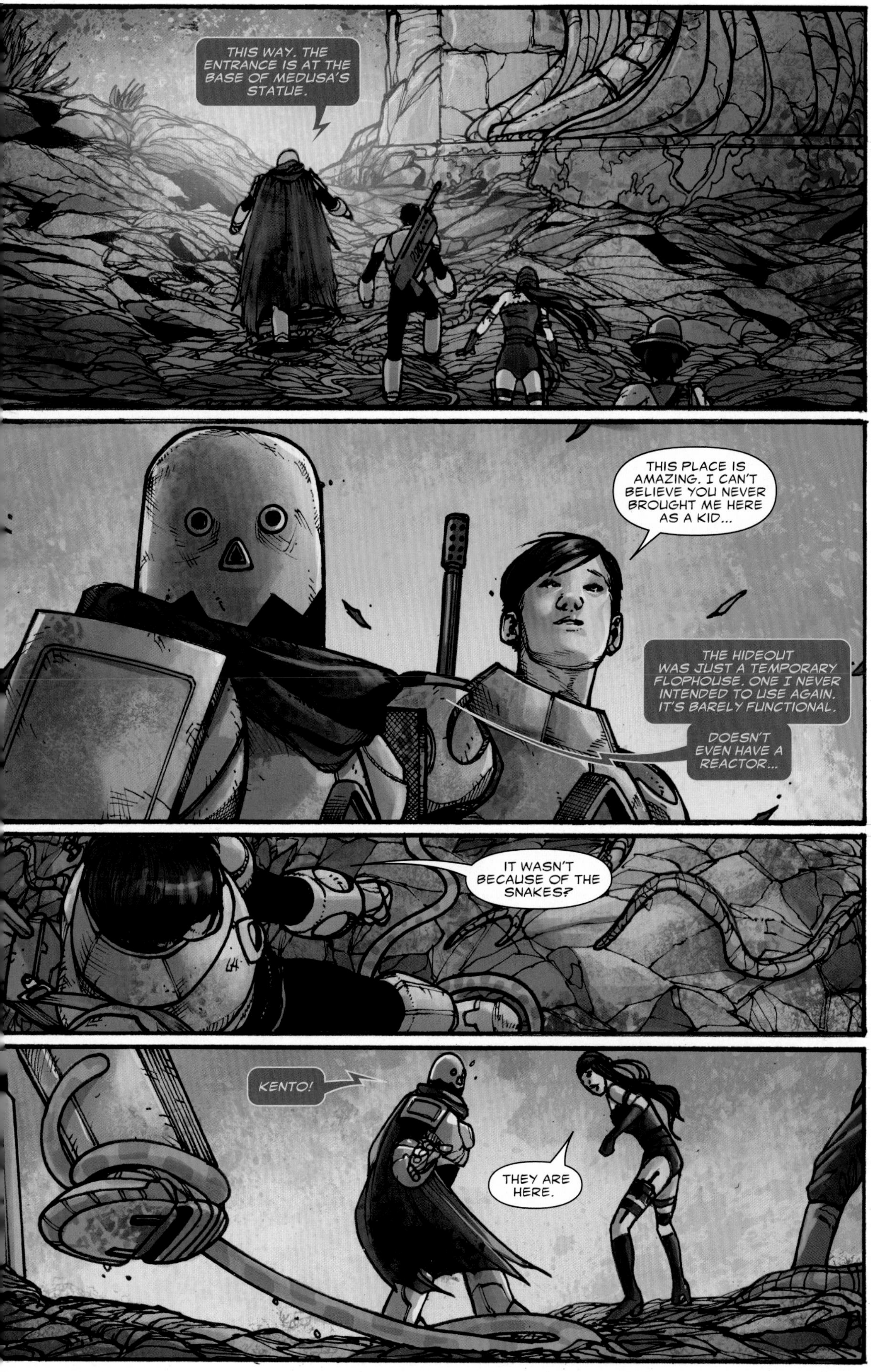
THIS WAY. THE ENTRANCE IS AT THE BASE OF MEDUSA'S STATUE.
THIS PLACE IS AMAZING. I CAN'T BELIEVE YOU NEVER BROUGHT ME HERE AS A KID...
THE HIDEOUT WAS JUST A TEMPORARY FLOPHOUSE. ONE I NEVER INTENDED TO USE AGAIN. IT'S BARELY FUNCTIONAL.
DOESN'T EVEN HAVE A REACTOR...
IT WASN'T BECAUSE OF THE SNAKES?
KENTO!
THEY ARE HERE.

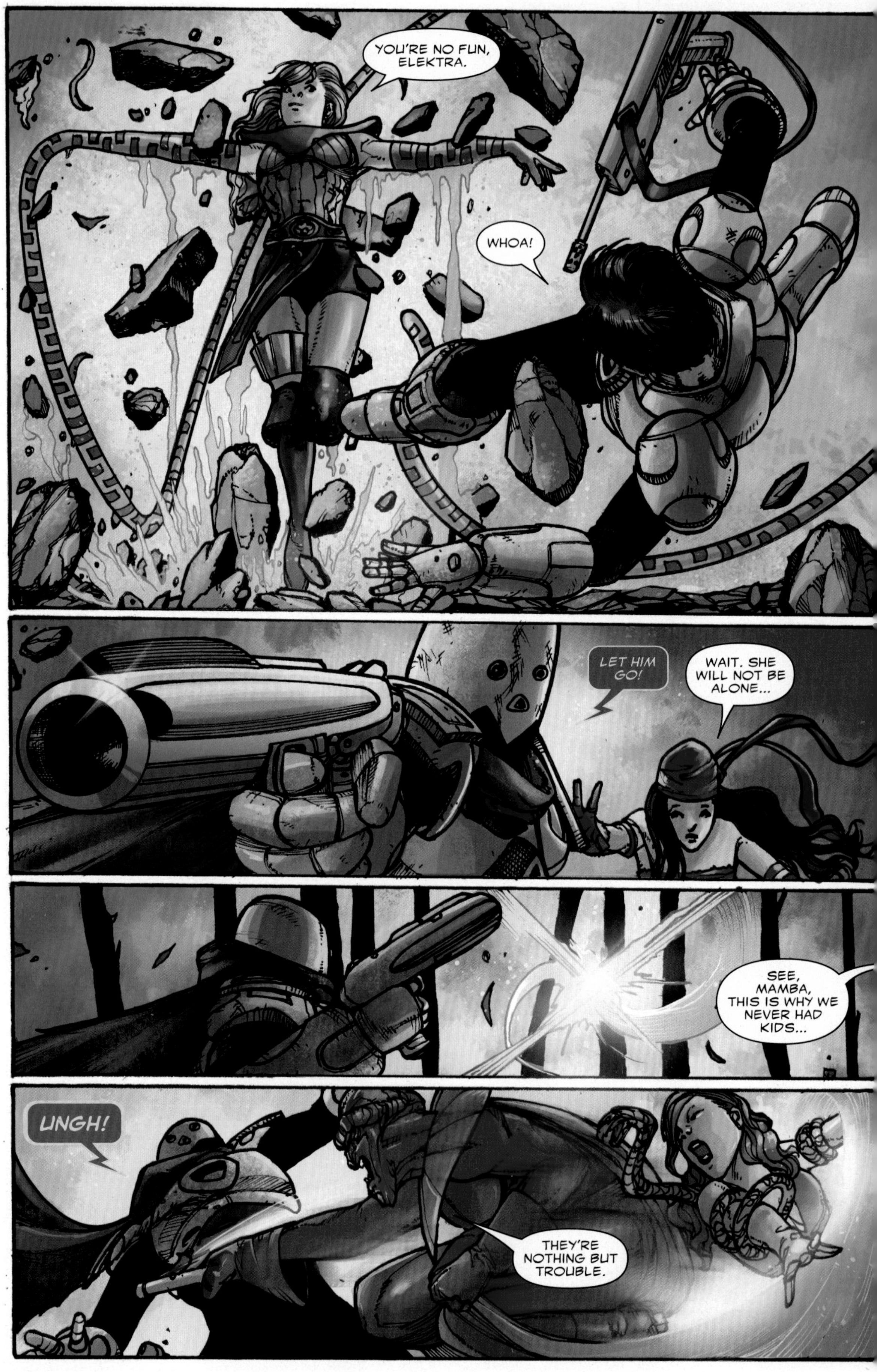
YOU'RE NO FUN, ELEKTRA.
WHOA!
LET HIM GO!
WAIT. SHE WILL NOT BE ALONE...
SEE, MAMBA, THIS IS WHY WE NEVER HAD KIDS...
UNGH!
THEY'RE NOTHING BUT TROUBLE.

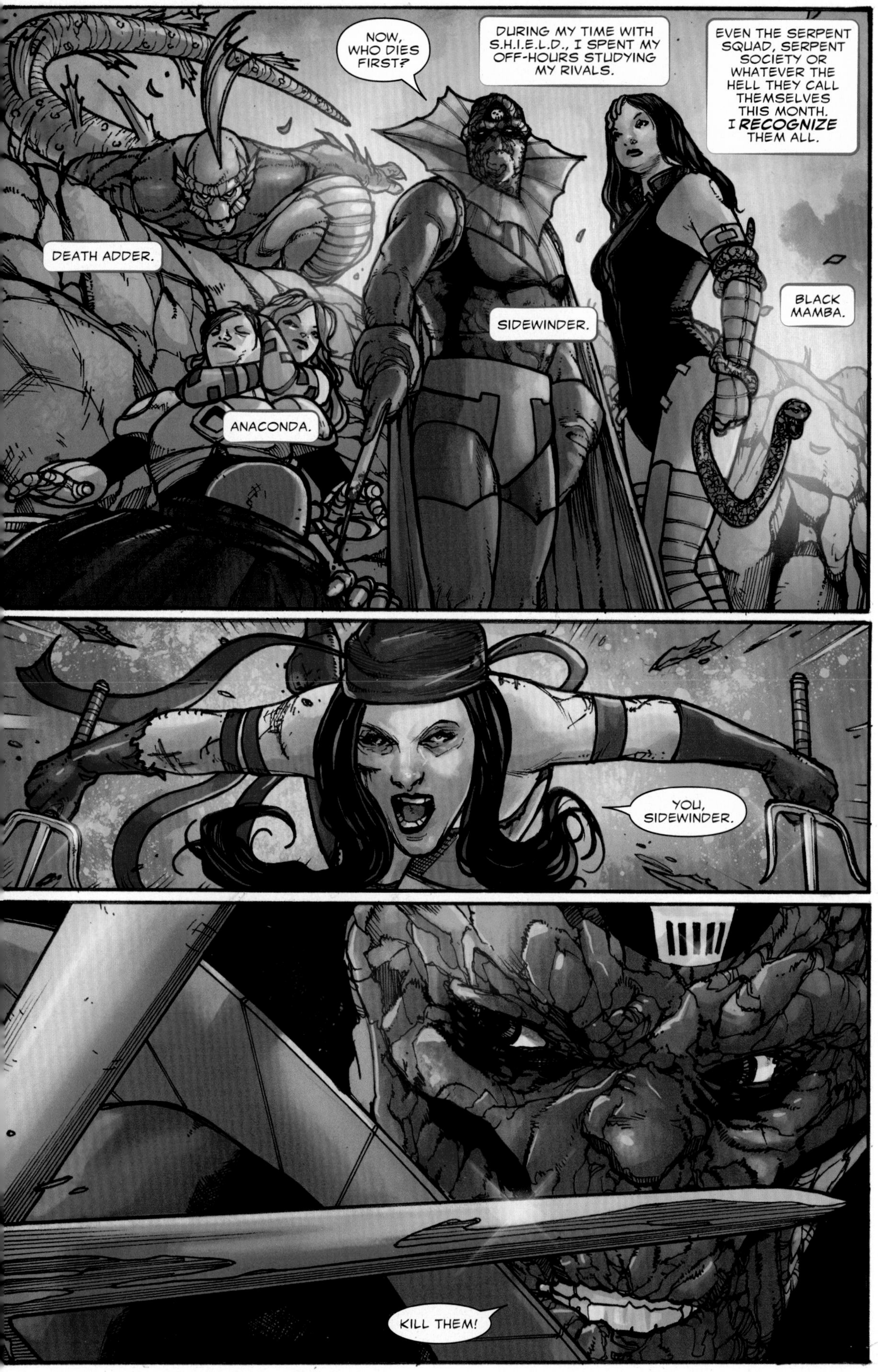
NOW, WHO DIES FIRST?
DURING MY TIME WITH S.H.I.E.L.D., I SPENT MY OFF-HOURS STUDYING MY RIVALS.
EVEN THE SERPENT SQUAD, SERPENT SOCIETY OR WHATEVER THE HELL THEY CALL THEMSELVES THIS MONTH. I RECOGNIZE THEM ALL.
DEATH ADDER.
SIDEWINDER.
BLACK MAMBA.
ANACONDA.
YOU, SIDEWINDER.
KILL THEM!

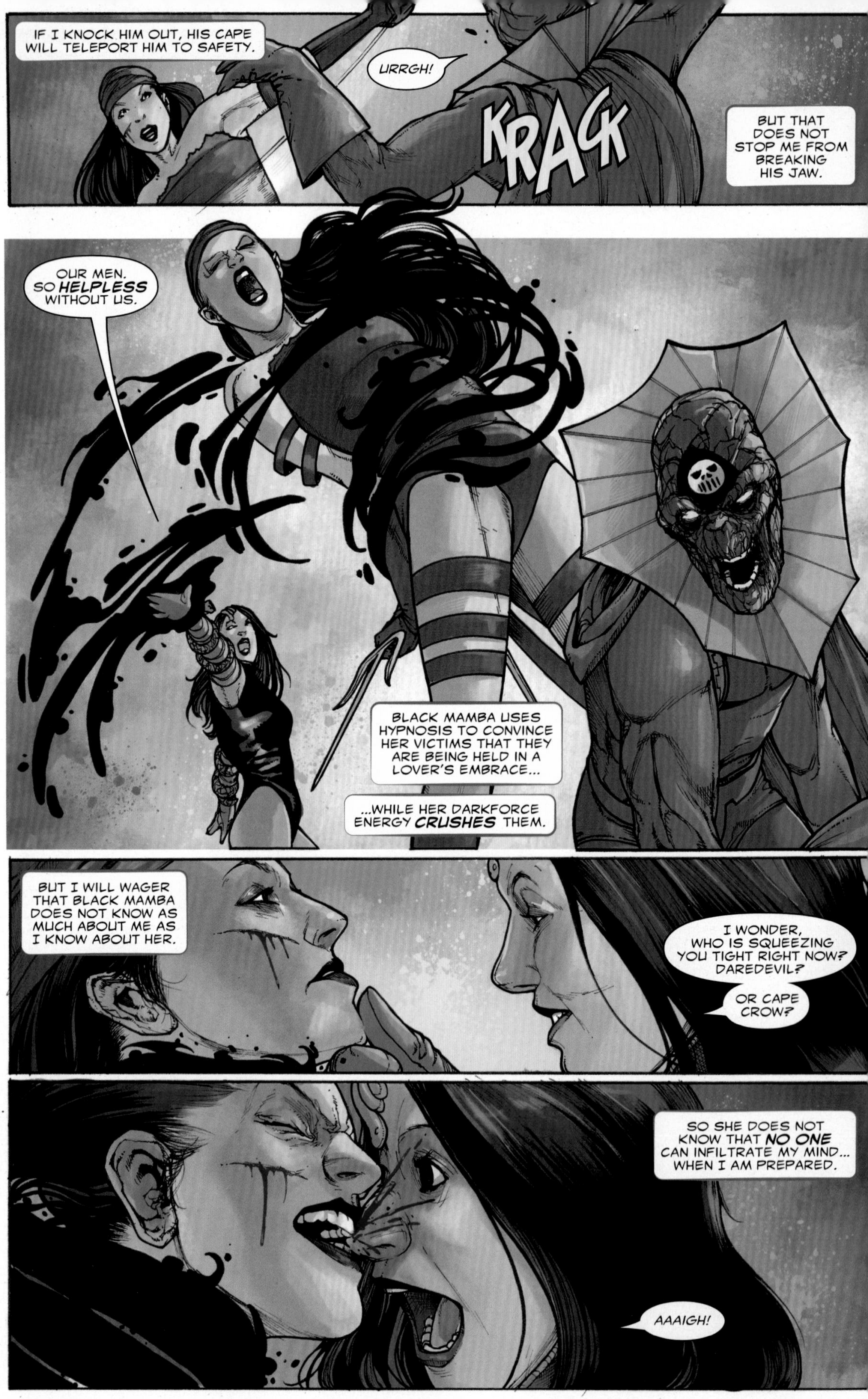
IF I KNOCK HIM OUT, HIS CAPE WILL TELEPORT HIM TO SAFETY.
URRGH!
KRACK
BUT THAT DOES NOT STOP ME FROM BREAKING HIS JAW.
OUR MEN. SO HELPLESS WITHOUT US.
BLACK MAMBA USES HYPNOSIS TO CONVINCE HER VICTIMS THAT THEY ARE BEING HELD IN A LOVER'S EMBRACE...
...WHILE HER DARKFORCE ENERGY CRUSHES THEM.
BUT I WILL WAGER THAT BLACK MAMBA DOES NOT KNOW AS MUCH ABOUT ME AS I KNOW ABOUT HER.
I WONDER, WHO IS SQUEEZING YOU TIGHT RIGHT NOW? DAREDEVIL?
OR CAPE CROW?
SO SHE DOES NOT KNOW THAT NO ONE CAN INFILTRATE MY MIND... WHEN I AM PREPARED.
AAAIGH!

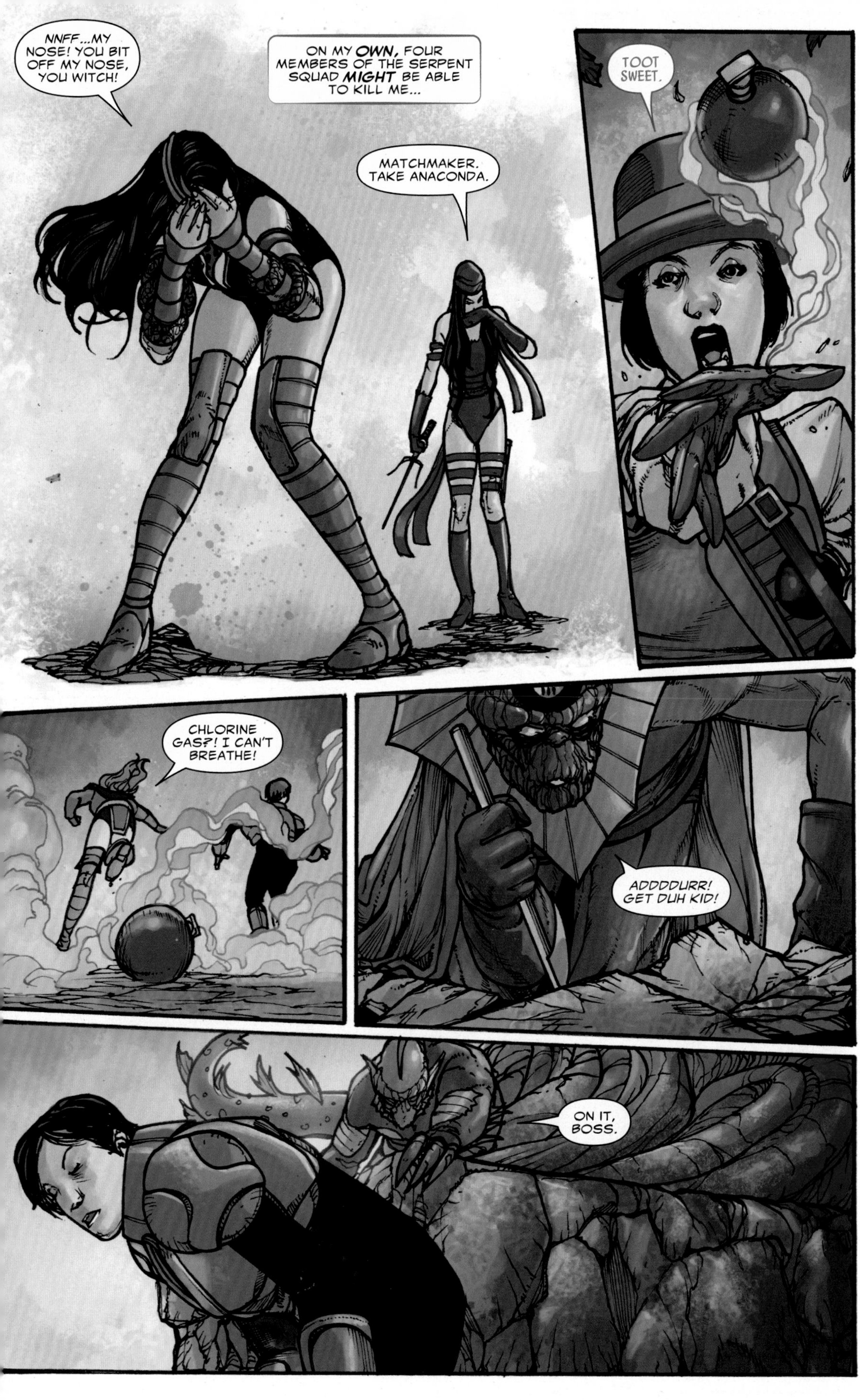
NNFF...MY NOSE! YOU BIT OFF MY NOSE, YOU WITCH!
ON MY OWN, FOUR MEMBERS OF THE SERPENT SQUAD MIGHT BE ABLE TO KILL ME...
MATCHMAKER. TAKE ANACONDA.
TOOT SWEET.
CHLORINE GAS?! I CAN'T BREATHE!
ADDDDURR! GET DUH KID!
ON IT, BOSS.

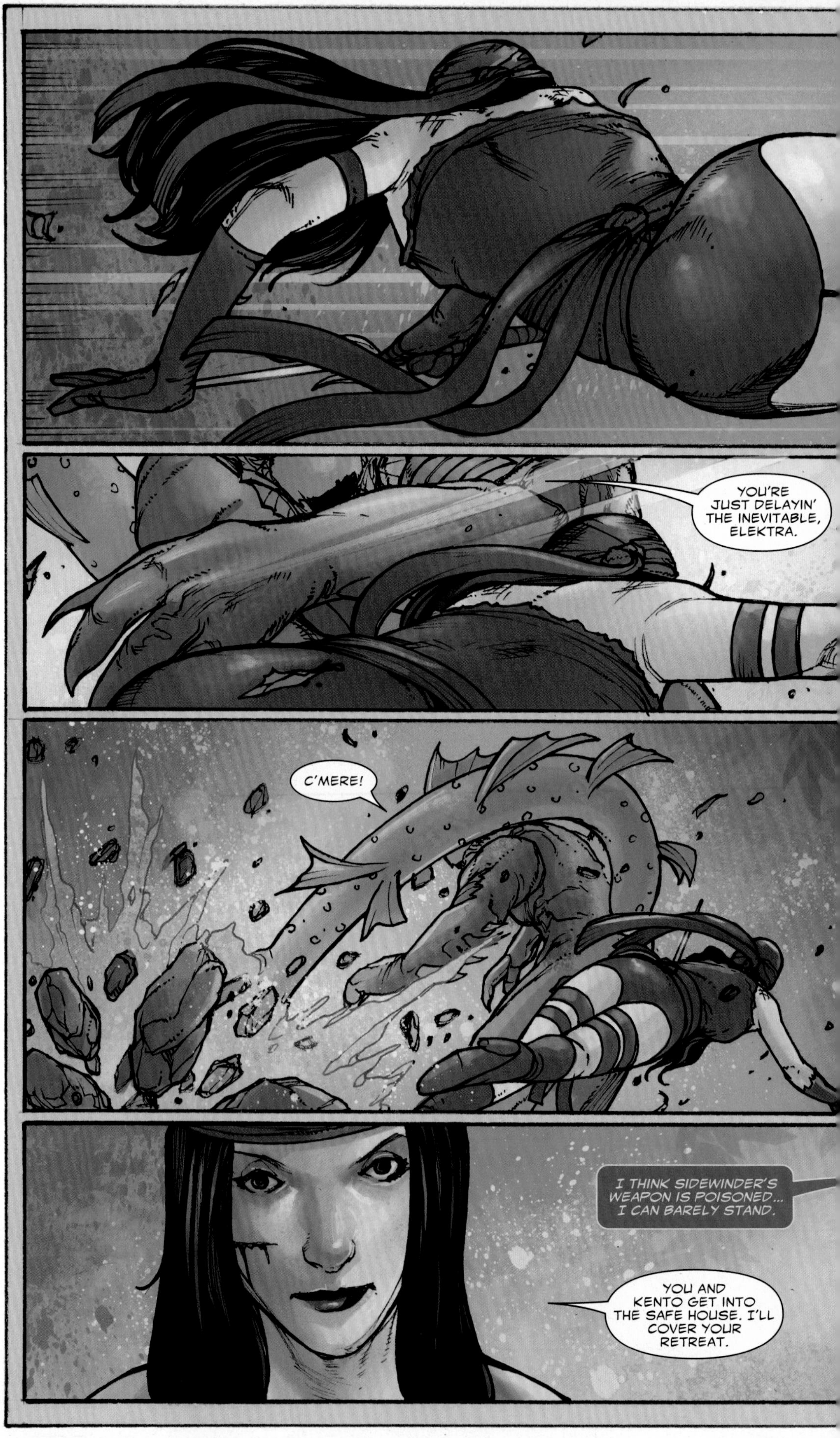
YOU'RE JUST DELAYIN' THE INEVITABLE, ELEKTRA.
C'MERE!
I THINK SIDEWINDER'S WEAPON IS POISONED... I CAN BARELY STAND.
YOU AND KENTO GET INTO THE SAFE HOUSE. I'LL COVER YOUR RETREAT.

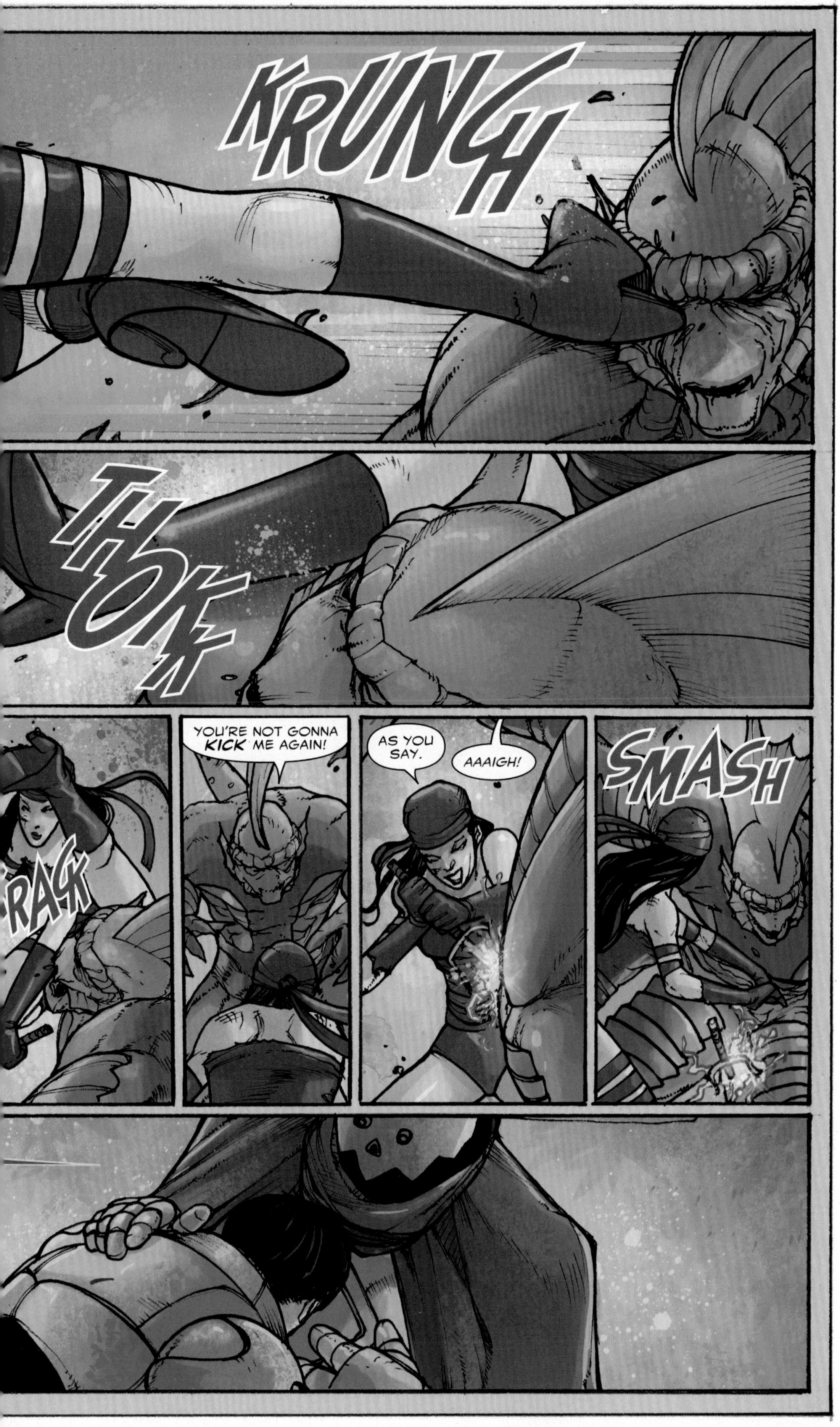

KRUNCH
THOOK
KRACK
YOU'RE NOT GONNA KICK ME AGAIN!
AS YOU SAY.
AAAIGH!
SMASH

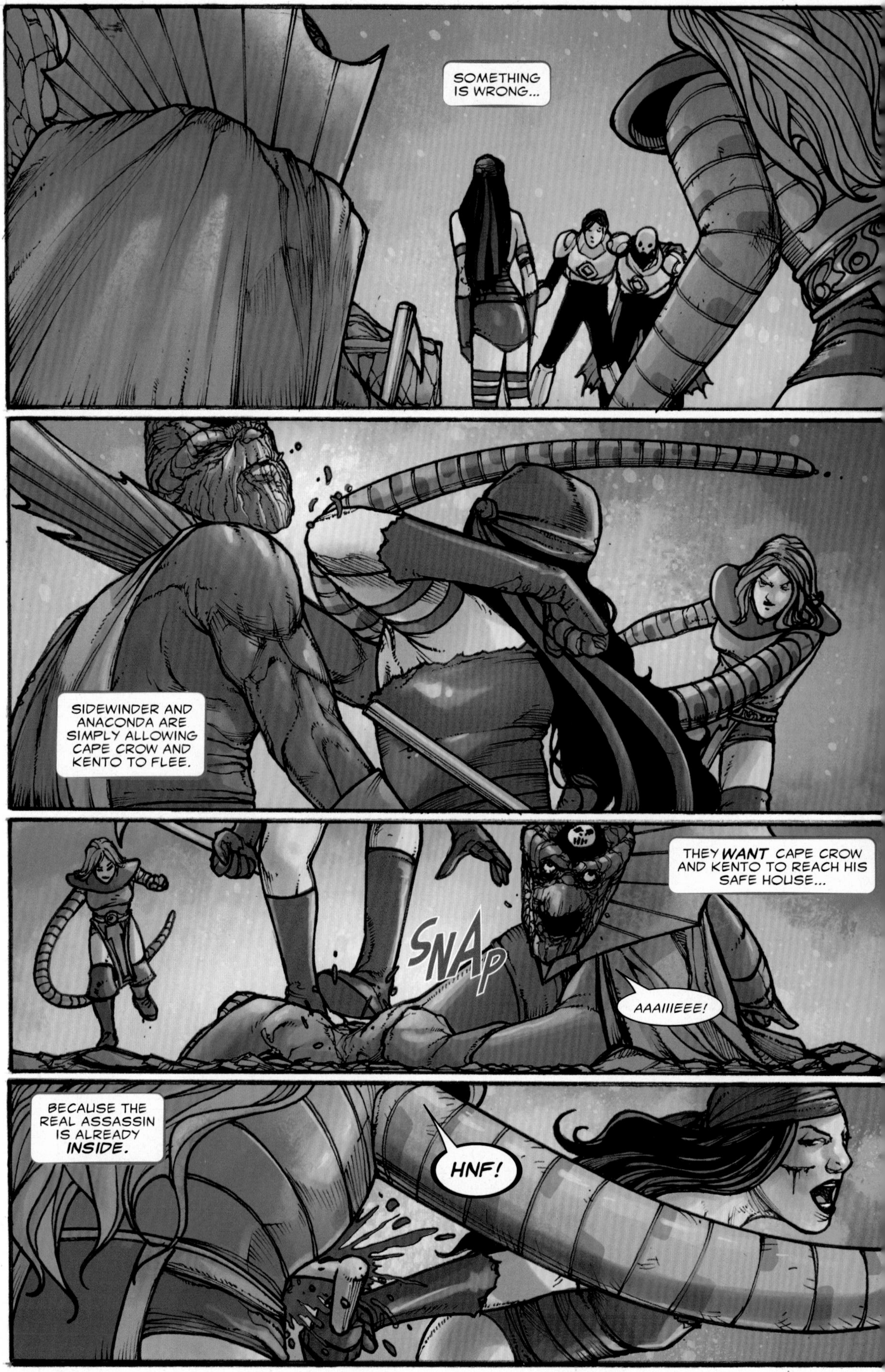
SOMETHING IS WRONG...
SIDEWINDER AND ANACONDA ARE SIMPLY ALLOWING CAPE CROW AND KENTO TO FLEE.
THEY WANT CAPE CROW AND KENTO TO REACH HIS SAFE HOUSE...
SNAP
AAAIIIEEE!
BECAUSE THE REAL ASSASSIN IS ALREADY INSIDE.
HNF!

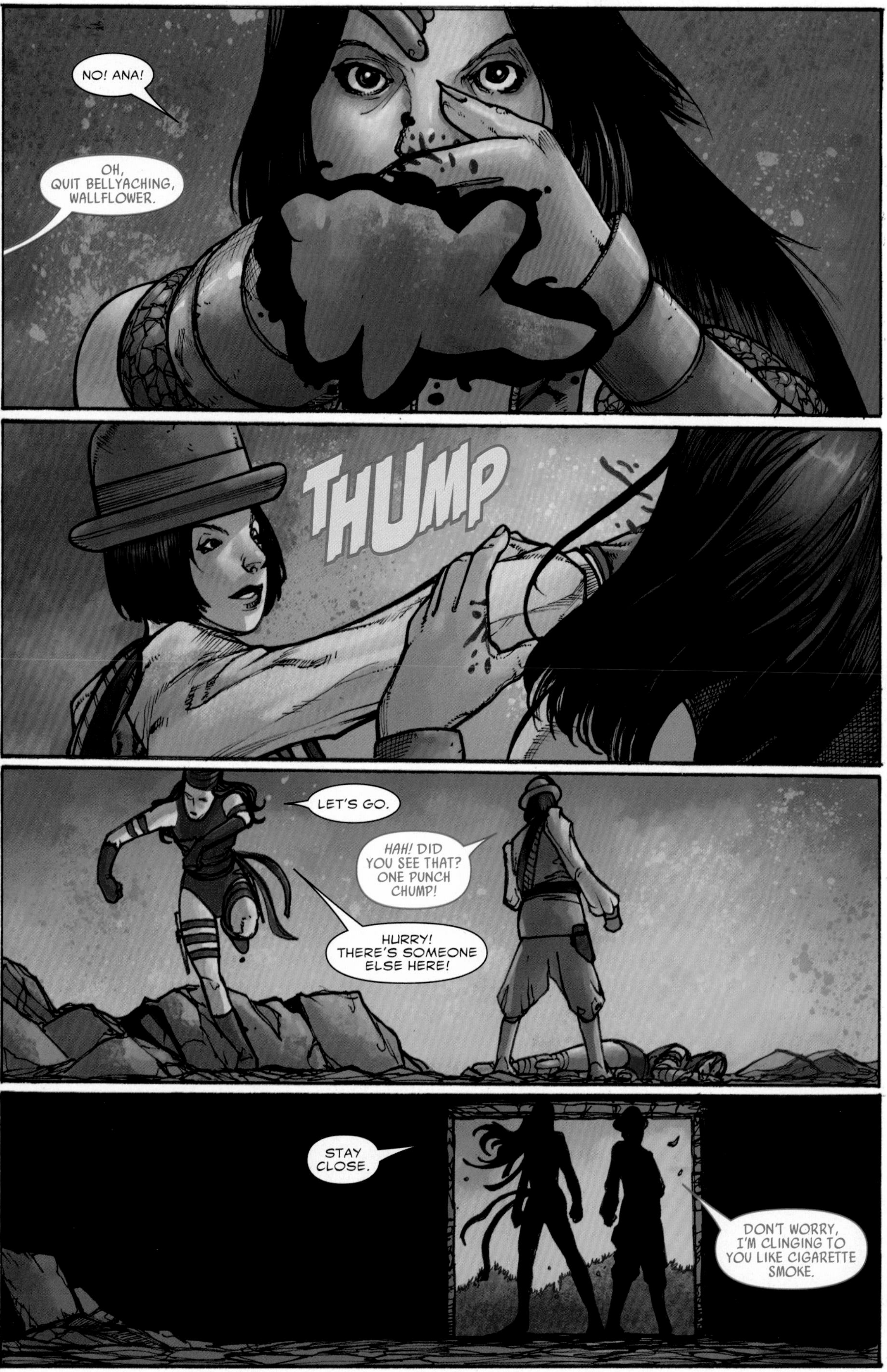
NO! ANA!
OH, QUIT BELLYACHING, WALLFLOWER.
THUMP
LET'S GO.
HAH! DID YOU SEE THAT? ONE PUNCH CHUMP!
HURRY! THERE'S SOMEONE ELSE HERE!
STAY CLOSE.
DON'T WORRY, I'M CLINGING TO YOU LIKE CIGARETTE SMOKE.

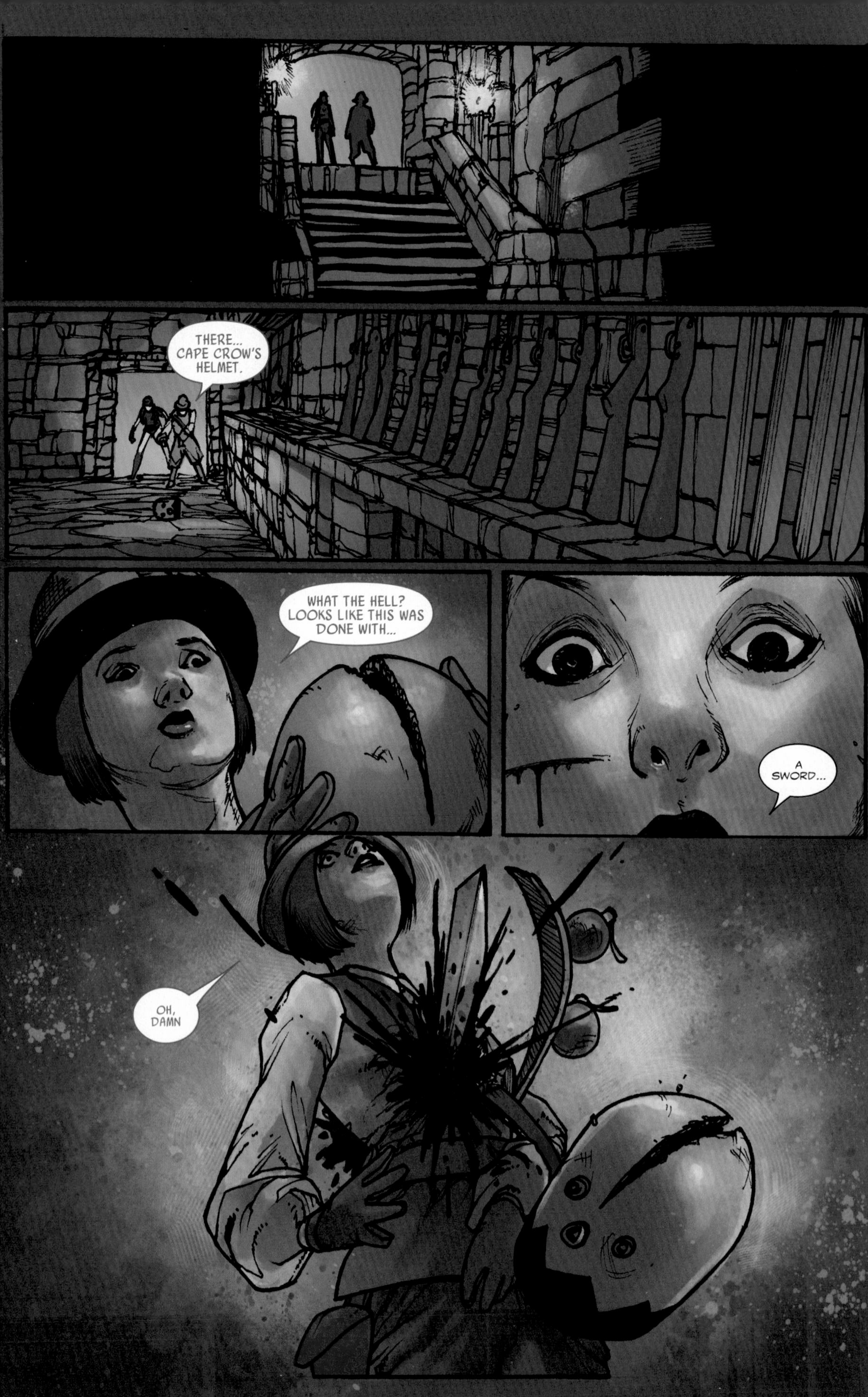
THERE... CAPE CROW'S HELMET.
WHAT THE HELL? LOOKS LIKE THIS WAS DONE WITH...
A SWORD...
OH, DAMN

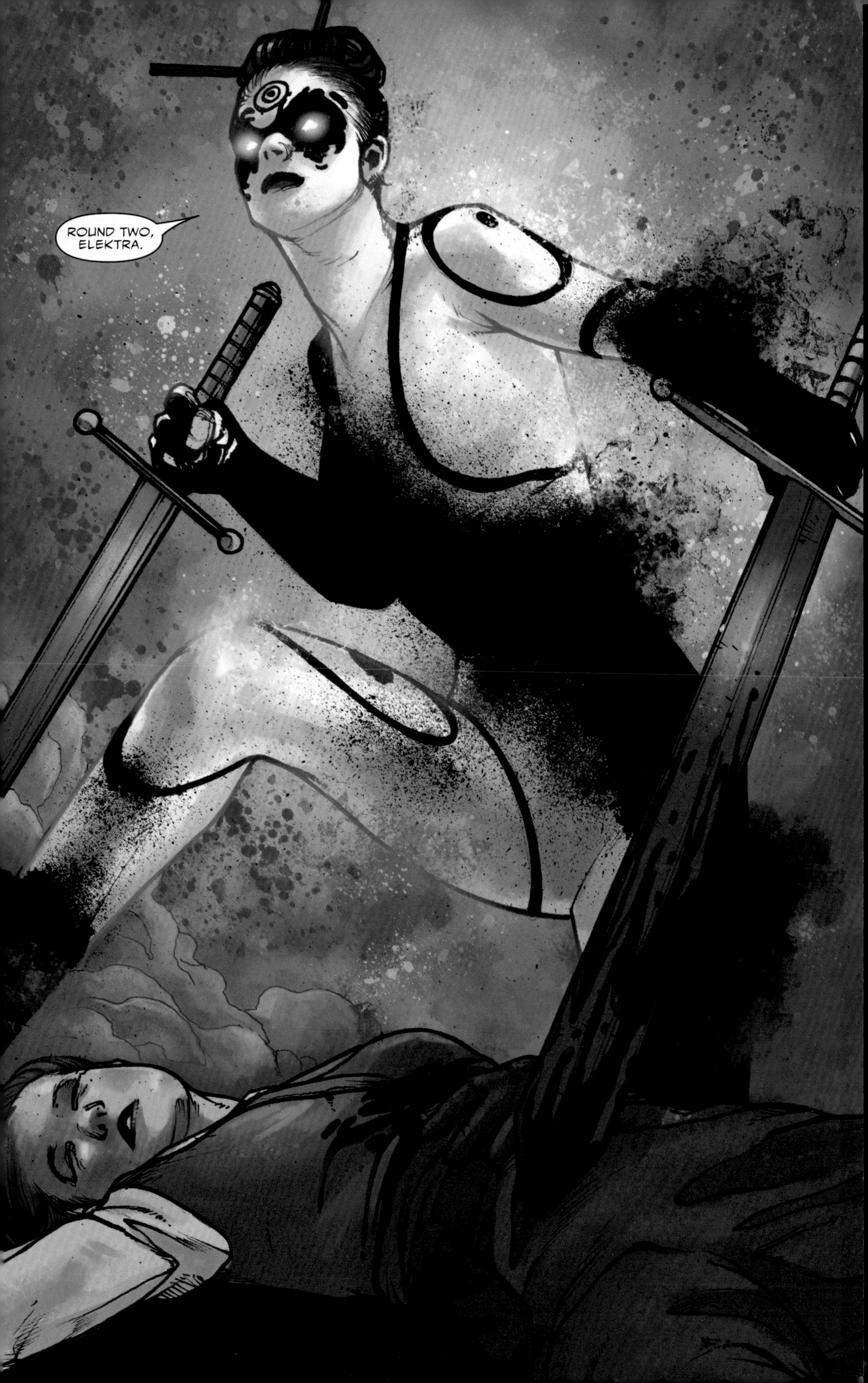
ROUND TWO, ELEKTRA.

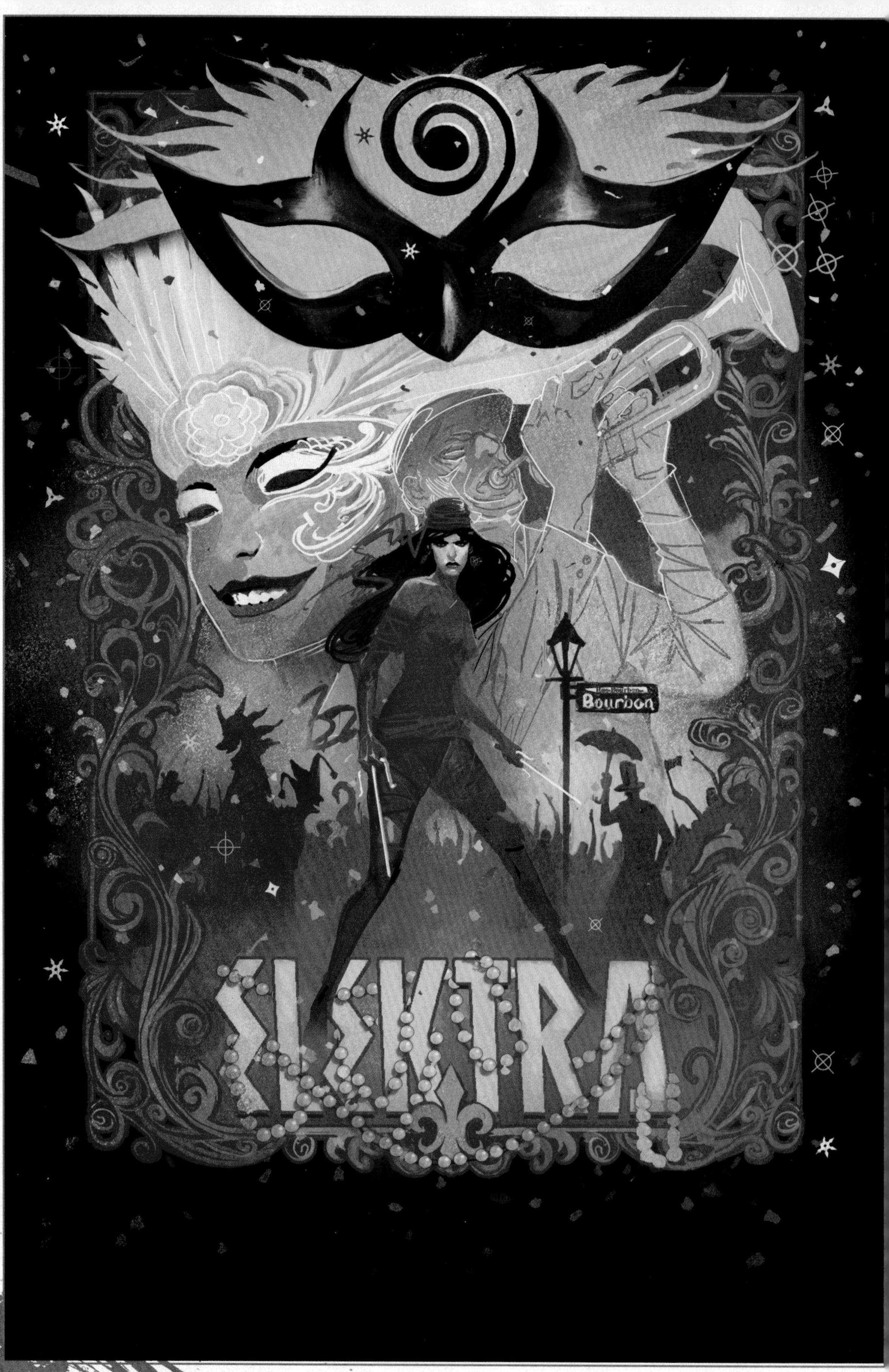
Bourbon
ELEKTRA

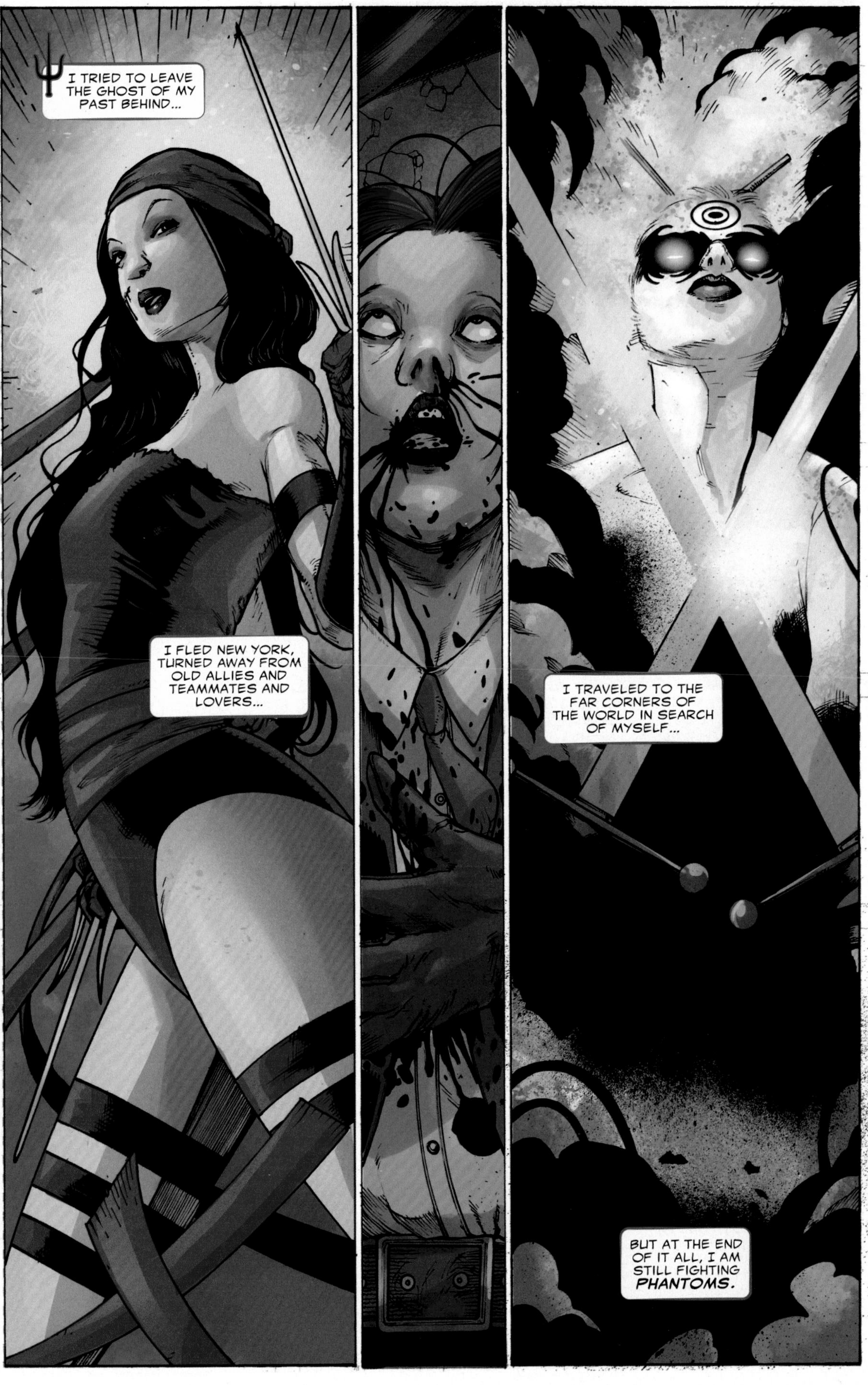
I TRIED TO LEAVE THE GHOST OF MY PAST BEHIND...
I FLED NEW YORK, TURNED AWAY FROM OLD ALLIES AND TEAMMATES AND LOVERS...
I TRAVELED TO THE FAR CORNERS OF THE WORLD IN SEARCH OF MYSELF...
BUT AT THE END OF IT ALL, I AM STILL FIGHTING *PHANTOMS.*

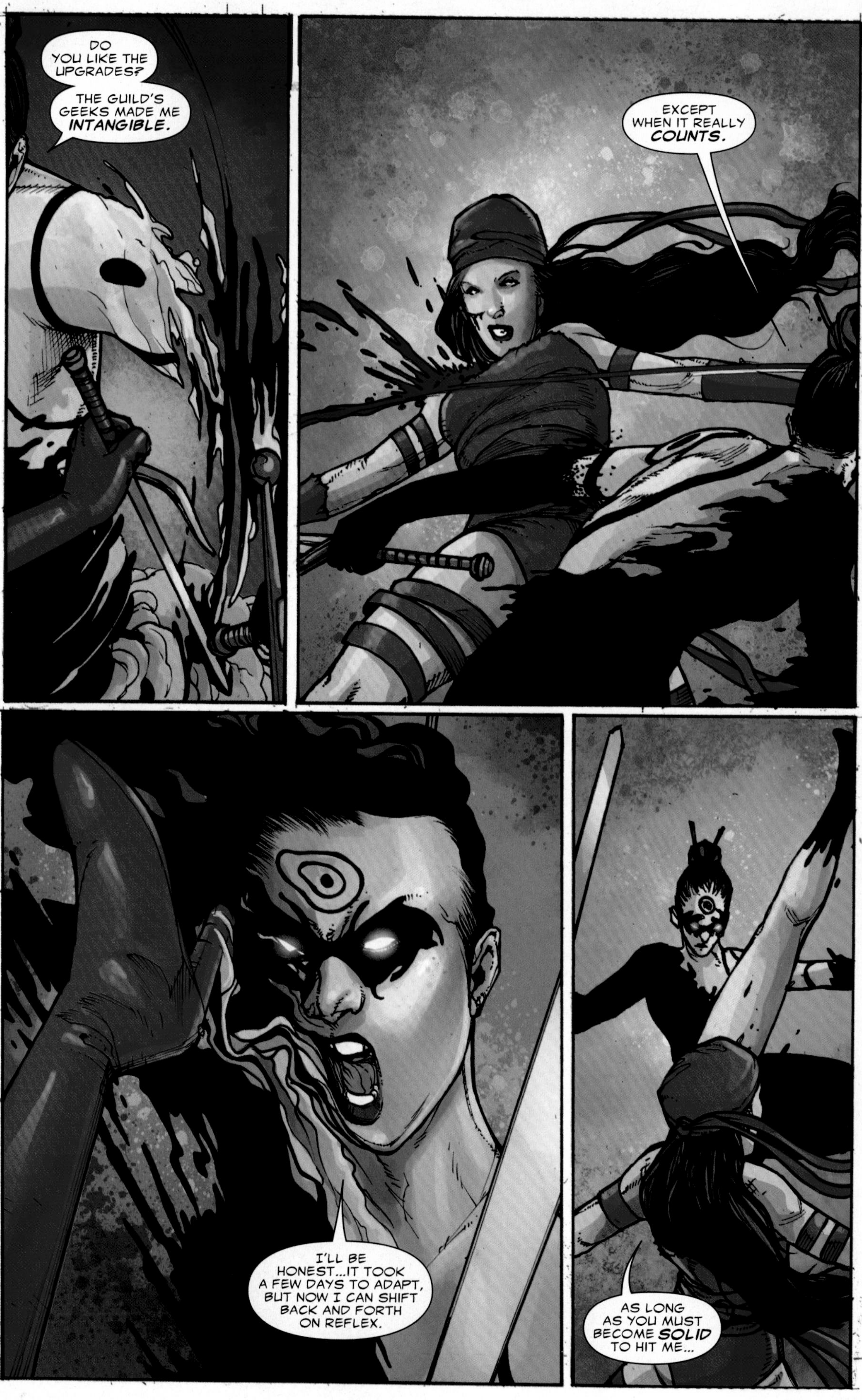
DO YOU LIKE THE UPGRADES?
THE GUILD'S GEEKS MADE ME INTANGIBLE.
EXCEPT WHEN IT REALLY COUNTS.
I'LL BE HONEST...IT TOOK A FEW DAYS TO ADAPT, BUT NOW I CAN SHIFT BACK AND FORTH ON REFLEX.
AS LONG AS YOU MUST BECOME SOLID TO HIT ME...

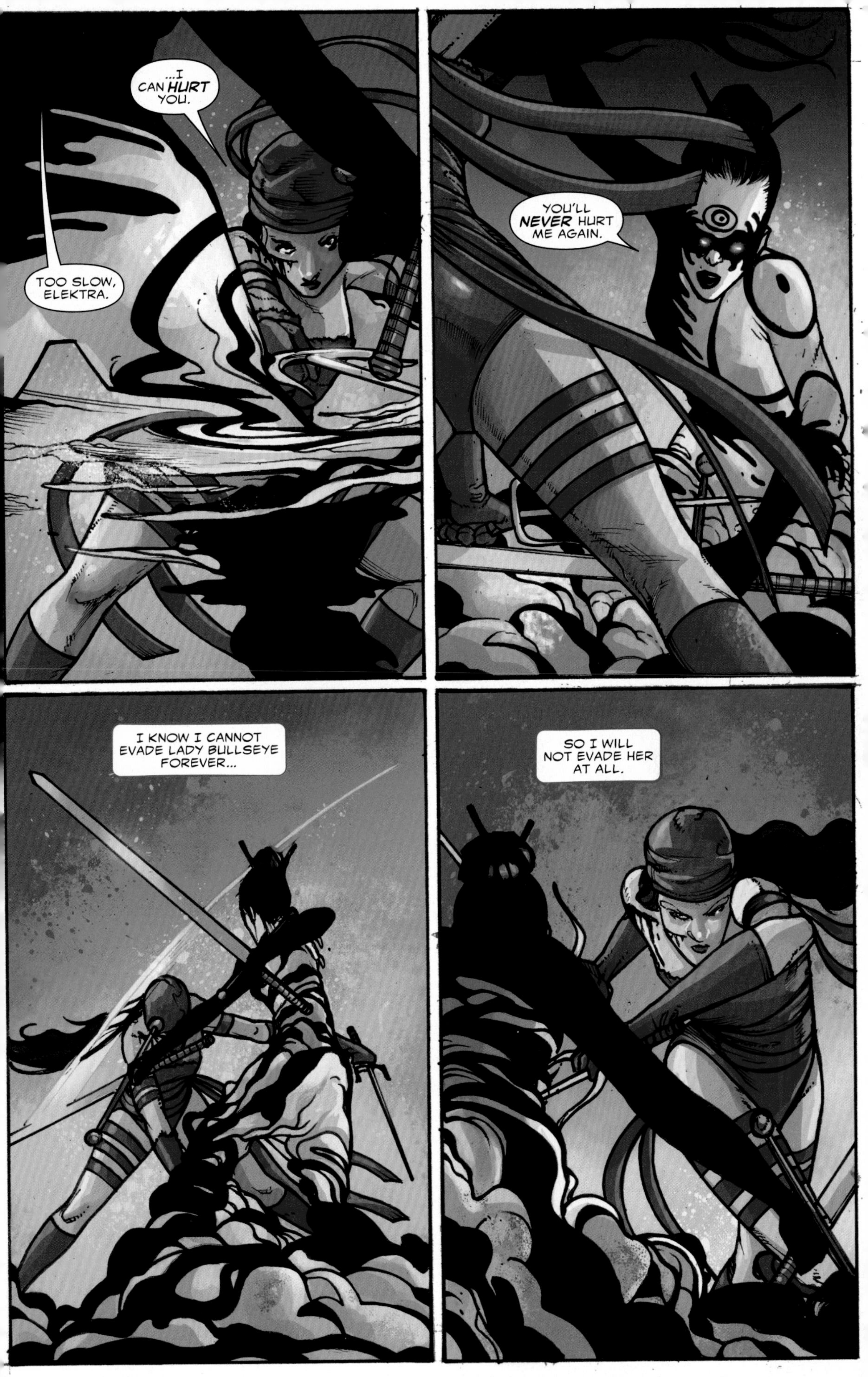

...I CAN HURT YOU.
TOO SLOW, ELEKTRA.
YOU'LL NEVER HURT ME AGAIN.
I KNOW I CANNOT EVADE LADY BULLSEYE FOREVER...
SO I WILL NOT EVADE HER AT ALL.

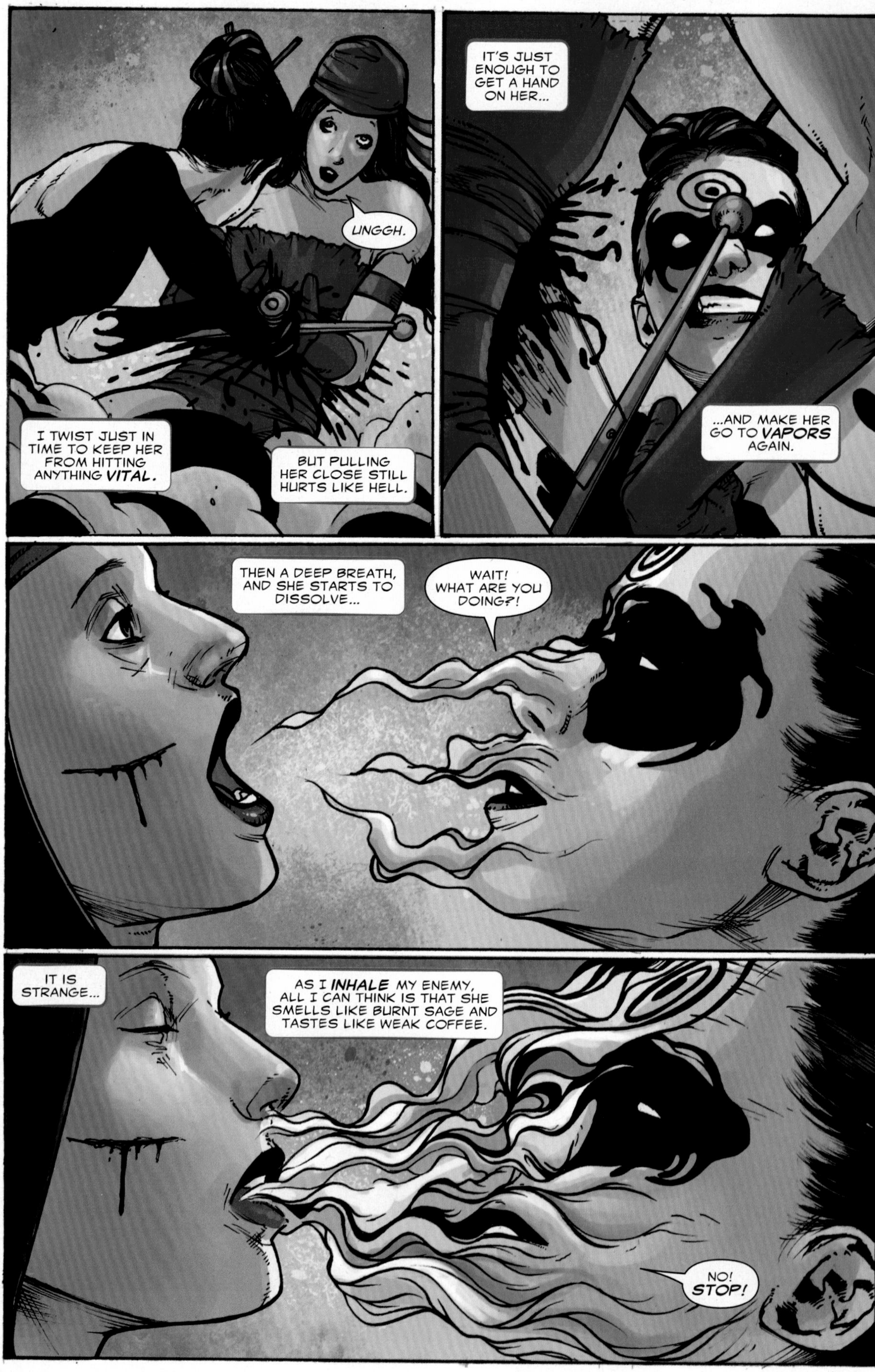
UNGGH.
I TWIST JUST IN TIME TO KEEP HER FROM HITTING ANYTHING VITAL.
BUT PULLING HER CLOSE STILL HURTS LIKE HELL.
IT'S JUST ENOUGH TO GET A HAND ON HER...
...AND MAKE HER GO TO VAPORS AGAIN.
THEN A DEEP BREATH, AND SHE STARTS TO DISSOLVE...
WAIT! WHAT ARE YOU DOING?!
IT IS STRANGE...
AS I INHALE MY ENEMY, ALL I CAN THINK IS THAT SHE SMELLS LIKE BURNT SAGE AND TASTES LIKE WEAK COFFEE.
NO! STOP!

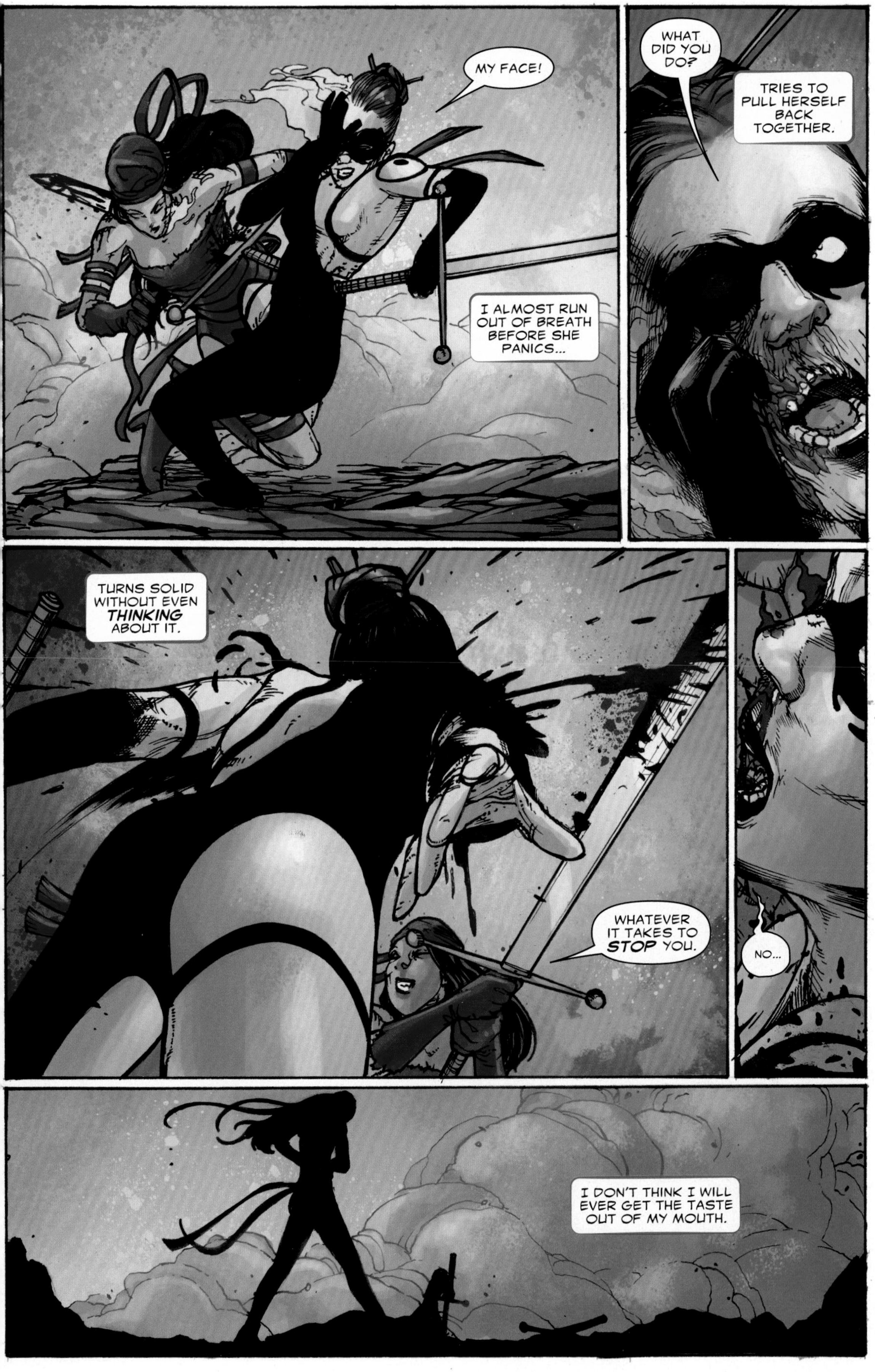
MY FACE!
I ALMOST RUN OUT OF BREATH BEFORE SHE PANICS...
WHAT DID YOU DO?
TRIES TO PULL HERSELF BACK TOGETHER.
TURNS SOLID WITHOUT EVEN THINKING ABOUT IT.
WHATEVER IT TAKES TO STOP YOU.
NO...
I DON'T THINK I WILL EVER GET THE TASTE OUT OF MY MOUTH.

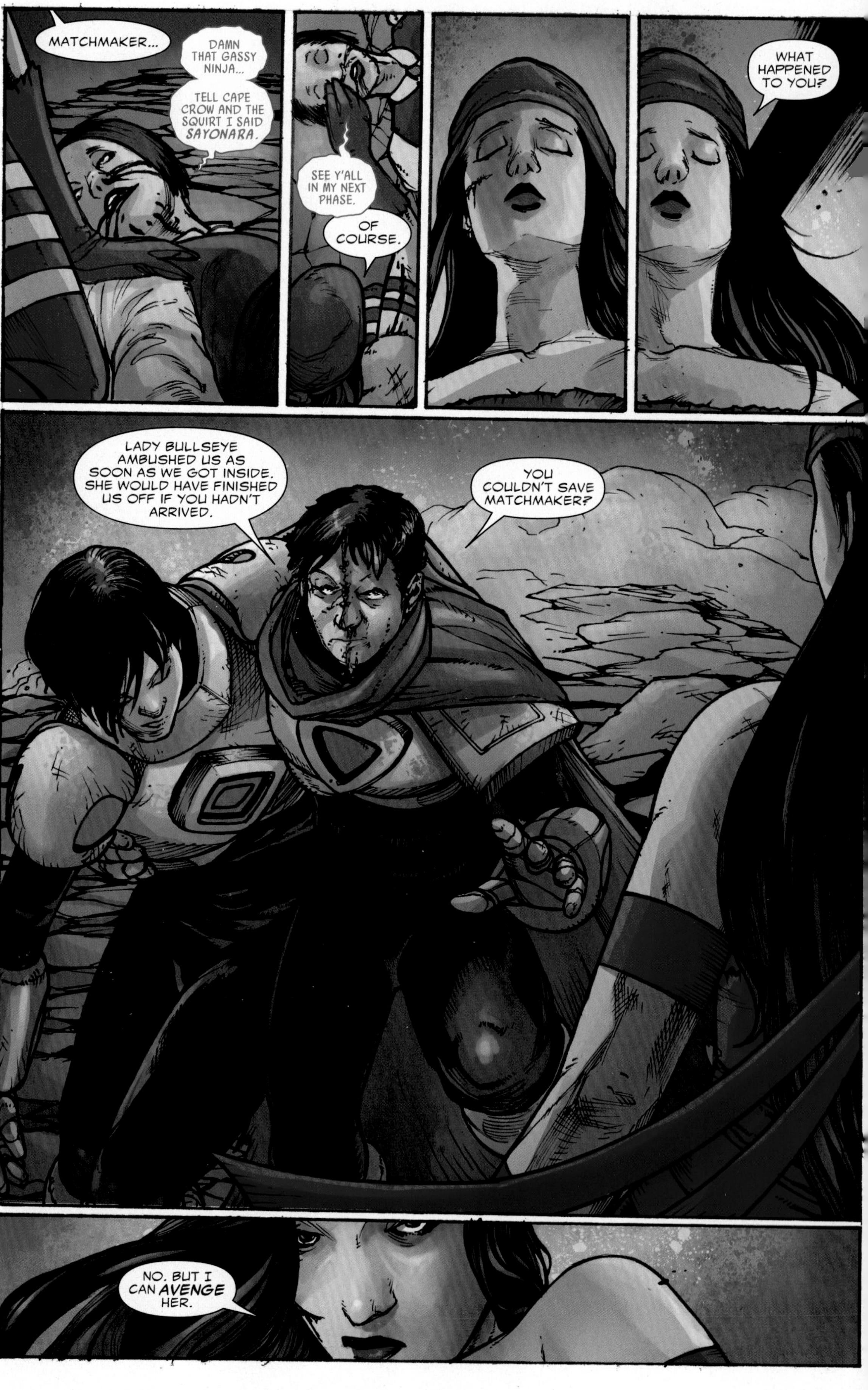
MATCHMAKER...
DAMN THAT GASSY NINJA...
TELL CAPE CROW AND THE SQUIRT I SAID SAYONARA.
SEE Y'ALL IN MY NEXT PHASE.
OF COURSE.
WHAT HAPPENED TO YOU?
LADY BULLSEYE AMBUSHED US AS SOON AS WE GOT INSIDE. SHE WOULD HAVE FINISHED US OFF IF YOU HADN'T ARRIVED.
YOU COULDN'T SAVE MATCHMAKER?
NO. BUT I CAN AVENGE HER.

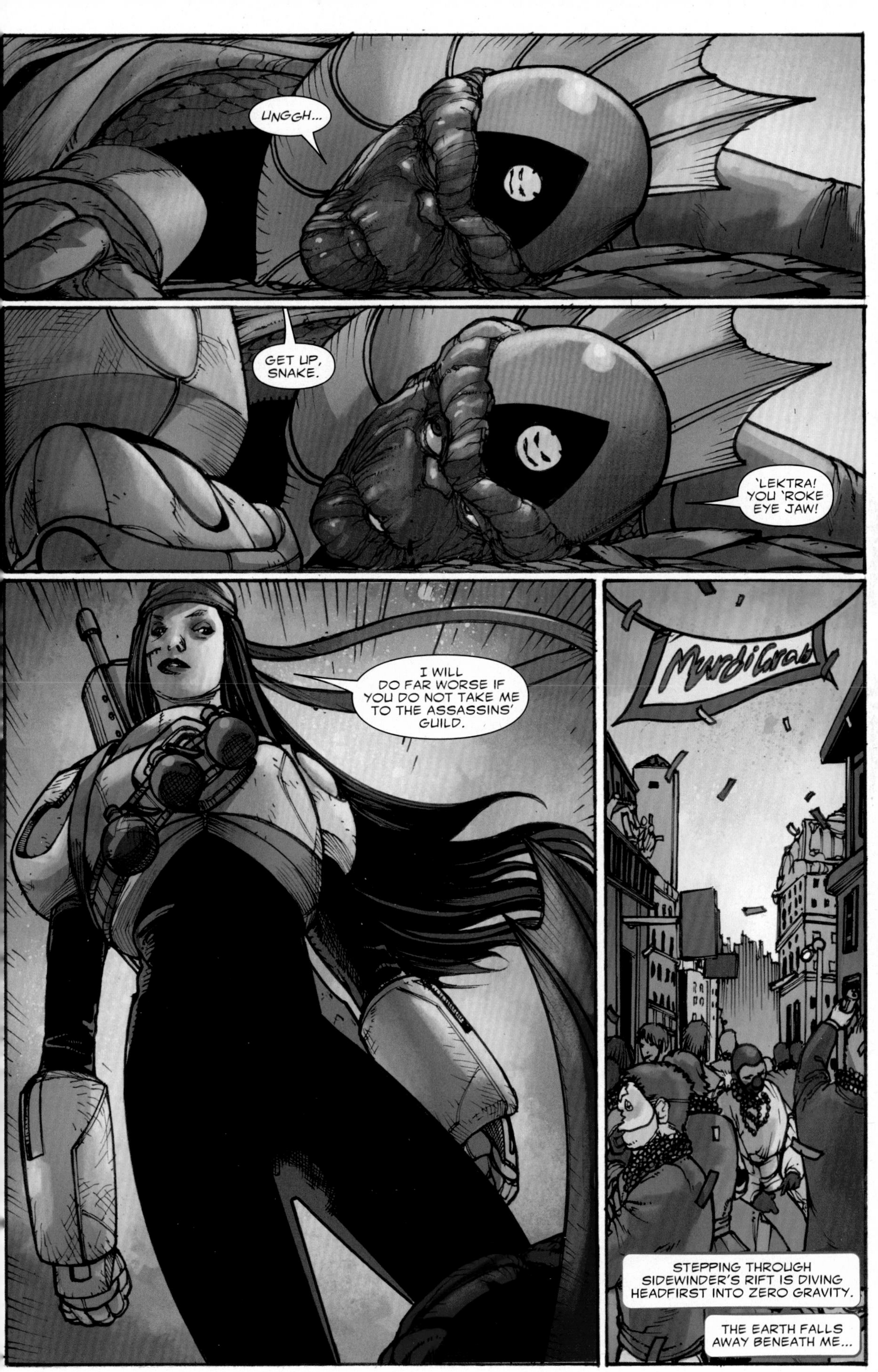
UNGGH...
GET UP, SNAKE.
'LEKTRA! YOU 'ROKE EYE JAW!
I WILL DO FAR WORSE IF YOU DO NOT TAKE ME TO THE ASSASSINS' GUILD.
Murdi Gras
STEPPING THROUGH SIDEWINDER'S RIFT IS DIVING HEADFIRST INTO ZERO GRAVITY.
THE EARTH FALLS AWAY BENEATH ME...

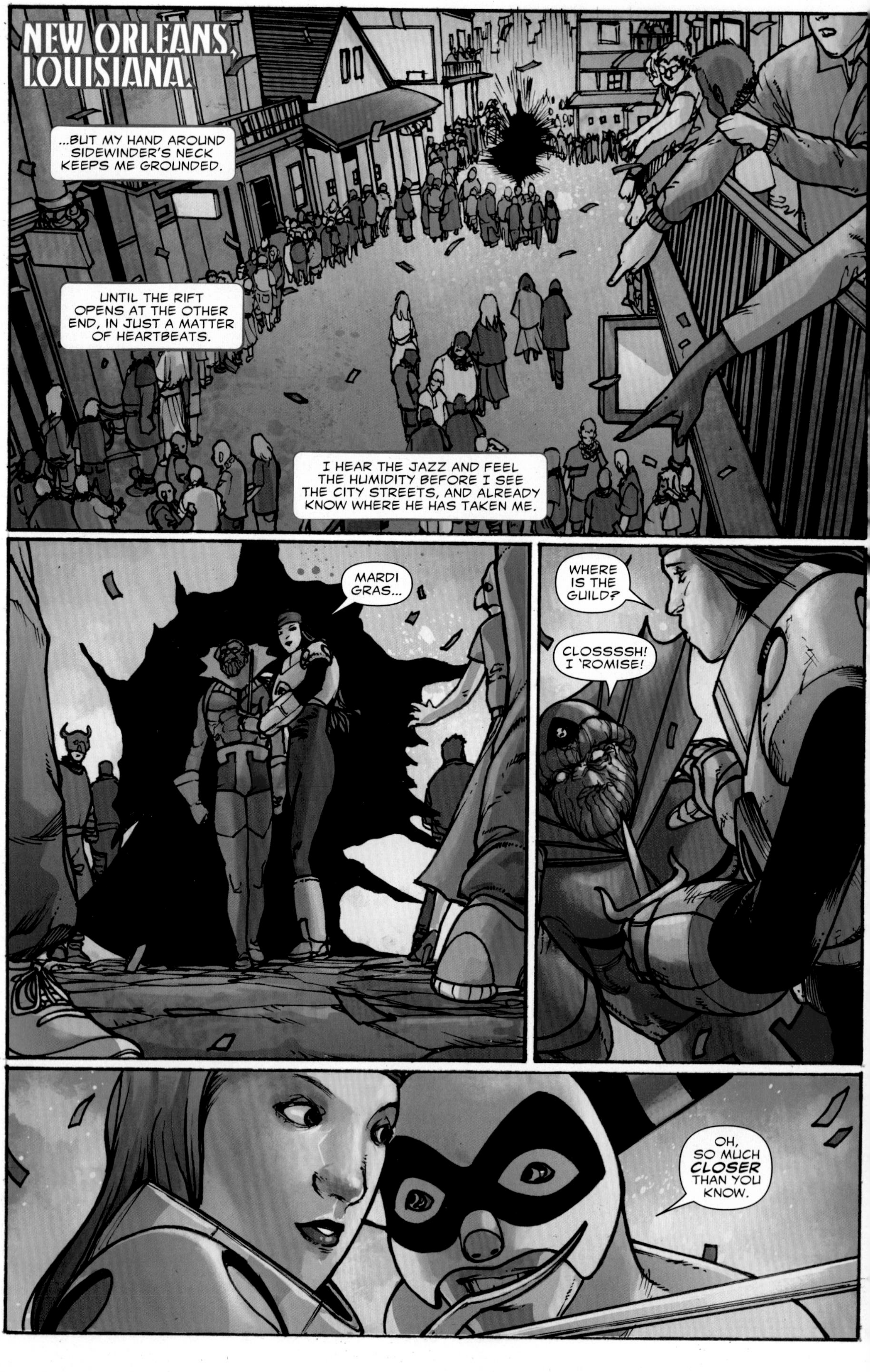

NEW ORLEANS, LOUISIANA.
...BUT MY HAND AROUND SIDEWINDER'S NECK KEEPS ME GROUNDED.
UNTIL THE RIFT OPENS AT THE OTHER END, IN JUST A MATTER OF HEARTBEATS.
I HEAR THE JAZZ AND FEEL THE HUMIDITY BEFORE I SEE THE CITY STREETS, AND ALREADY KNOW WHERE HE HAS TAKEN ME.
MARDI GRAS...
WHERE IS THE GUILD?
CLOSSSSH! I 'ROMISE!
OH, SO MUCH CLOSER THAN YOU KNOW.

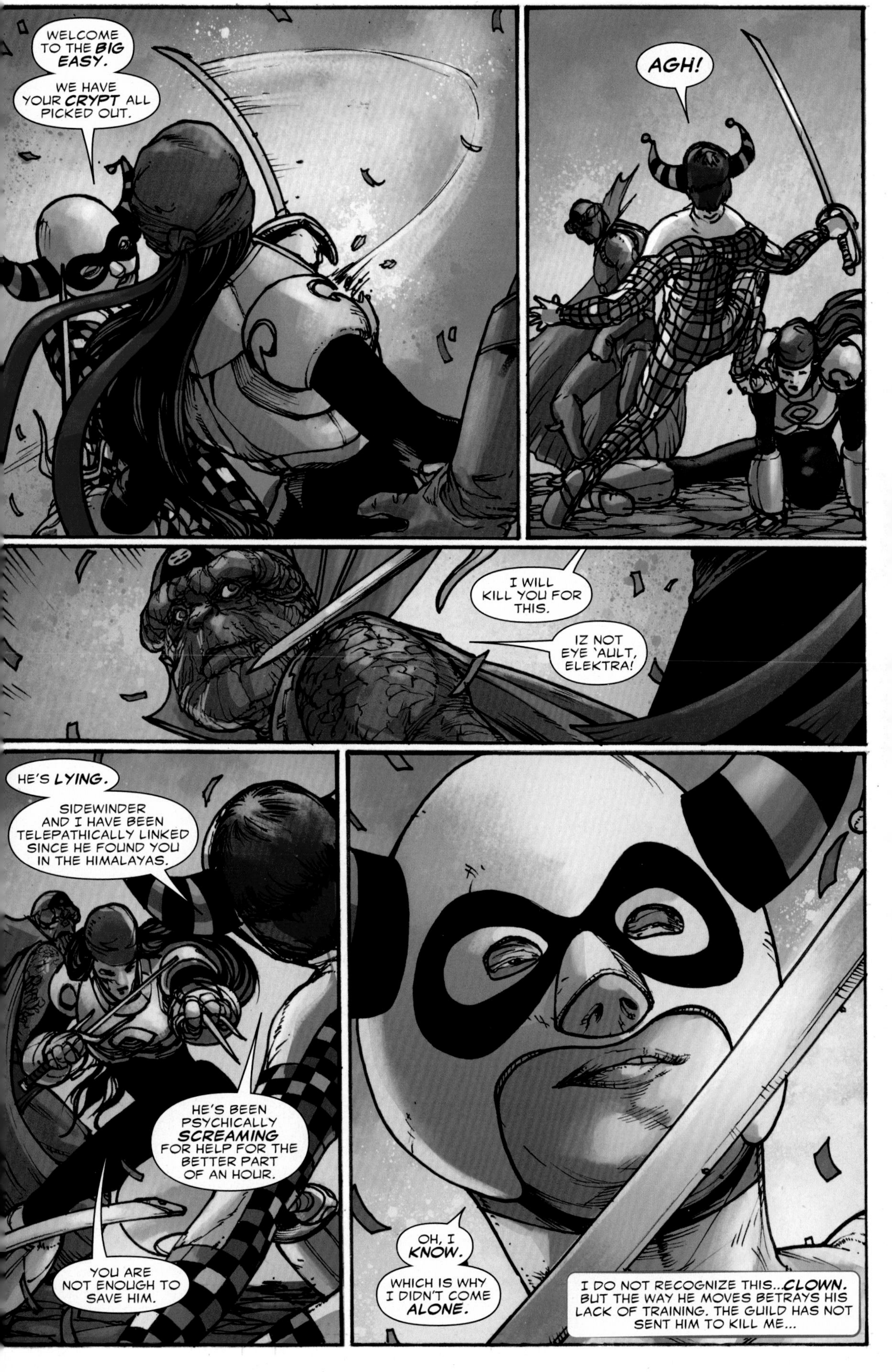
WELCOME TO THE BIG EASY.
WE HAVE YOUR CRYPT ALL PICKED OUT.
AGH!
I WILL KILL YOU FOR THIS.
IZ NOT EYE 'AULT, ELEKTRA!
HE'S LYING.
SIDEWINDER AND I HAVE BEEN TELEPATHICALLY LINKED SINCE HE FOUND YOU IN THE HIMALAYAS.
HE'S BEEN PSYCHICALLY SCREAMING FOR HELP FOR THE BETTER PART OF AN HOUR.
YOU ARE NOT ENOUGH TO SAVE HIM.
OH, I KNOW.
WHICH IS WHY I DIDN'T COME ALONE.
I DO NOT RECOGNIZE THIS...CLOWN. BUT THE WAY HE MOVES BETRAYS HIS LACK OF TRAINING. THE GUILD HAS NOT SENT HIM TO KILL ME...

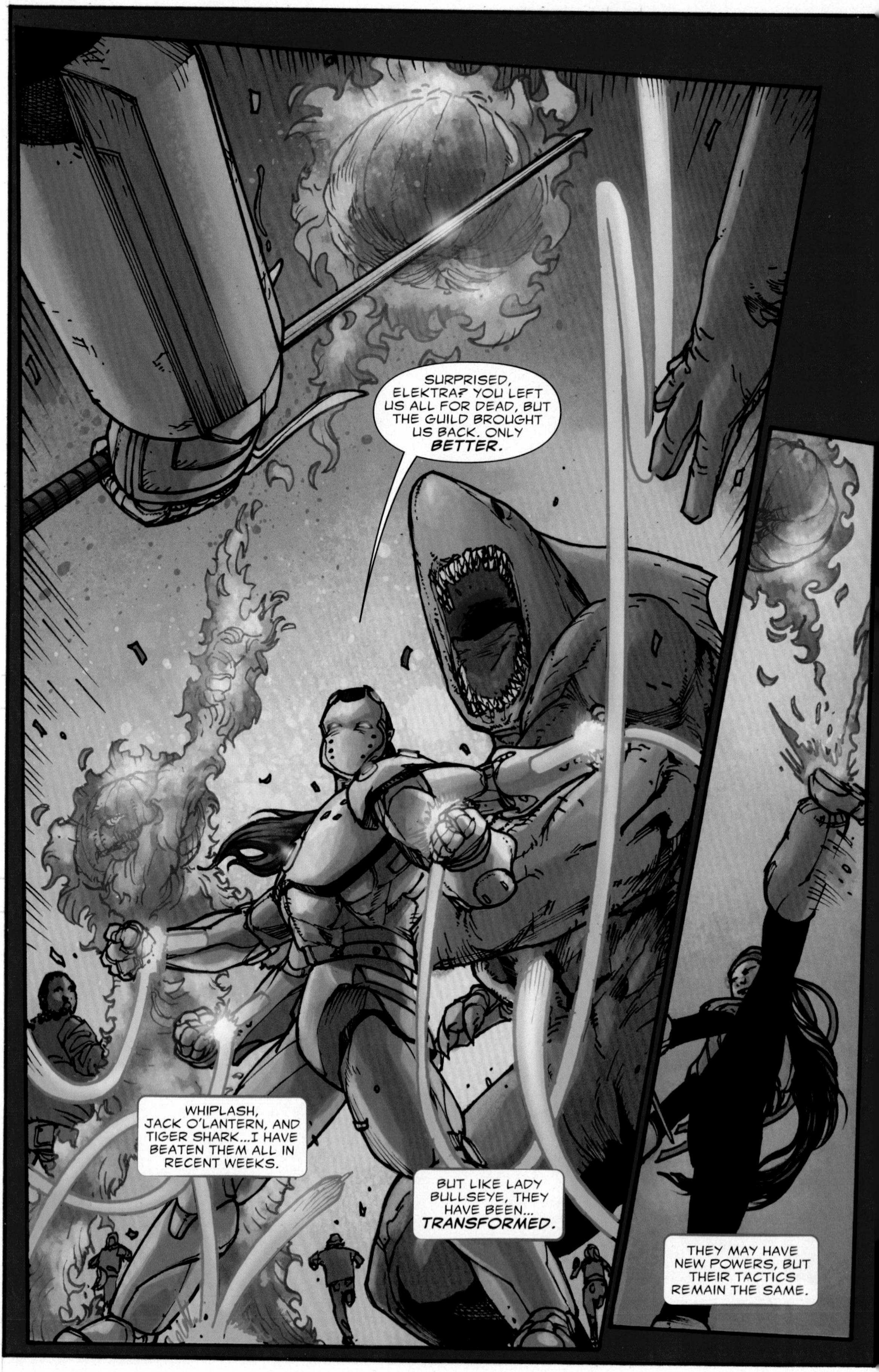
SURPRISED, ELEKTRA? YOU LEFT US ALL FOR DEAD, BUT THE GUILD BROUGHT US BACK. ONLY BETTER.
WHIPLASH, JACK O'LANTERN, AND TIGER SHARK...I HAVE BEATEN THEM ALL IN RECENT WEEKS.
BUT LIKE LADY BULLSEYE, THEY HAVE BEEN... TRANSFORMED.
THEY MAY HAVE NEW POWERS, BUT THEIR TACTICS REMAIN THE SAME.

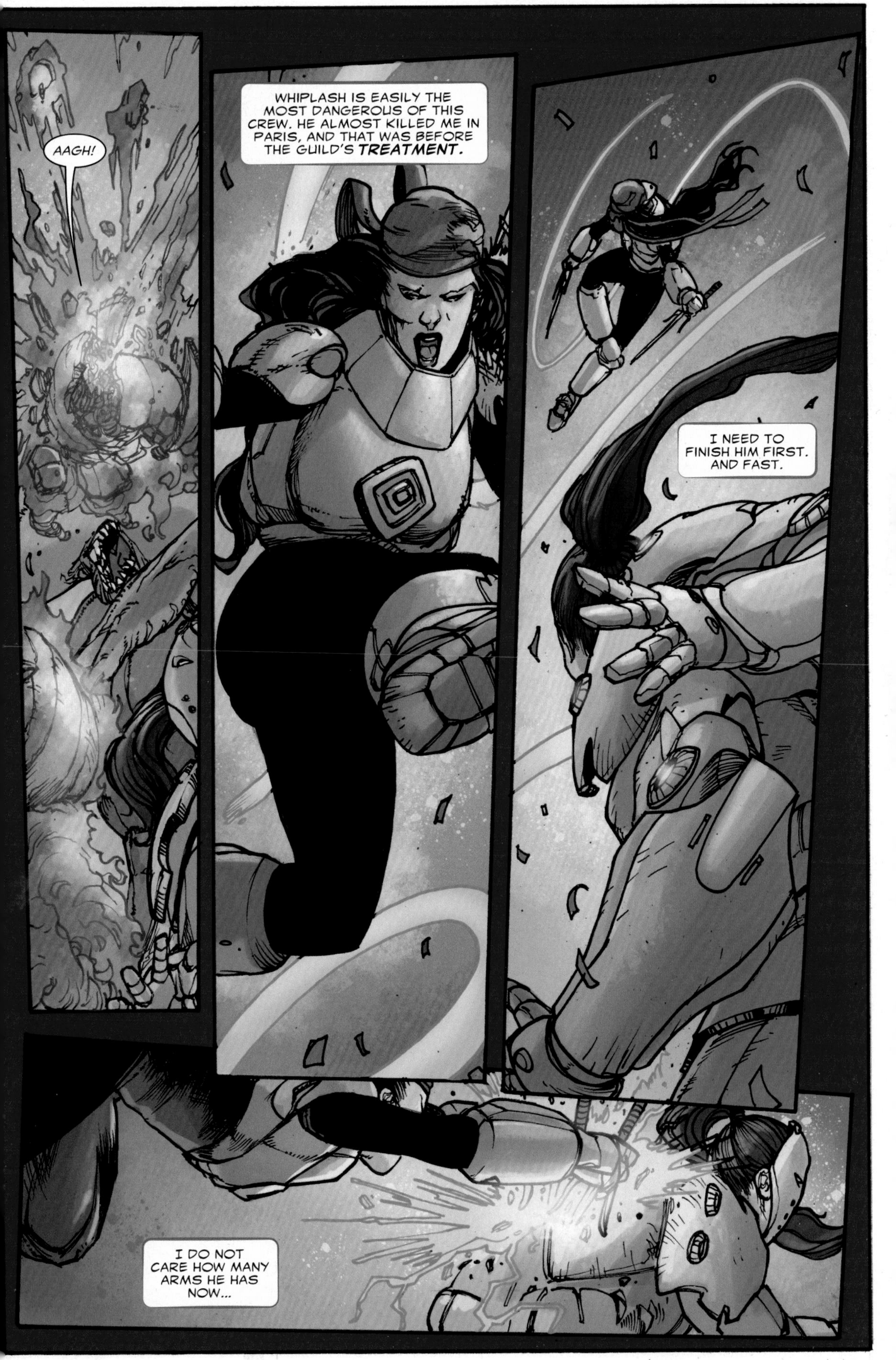
AAGH!
WHIPLASH IS EASILY THE MOST DANGEROUS OF THIS CREW. HE ALMOST KILLED ME IN PARIS, AND THAT WAS BEFORE THE GUILD'S TREATMENT.
I NEED TO FINISH HIM FIRST. AND FAST.
I DO NOT CARE HOW MANY ARMS HE HAS NOW...

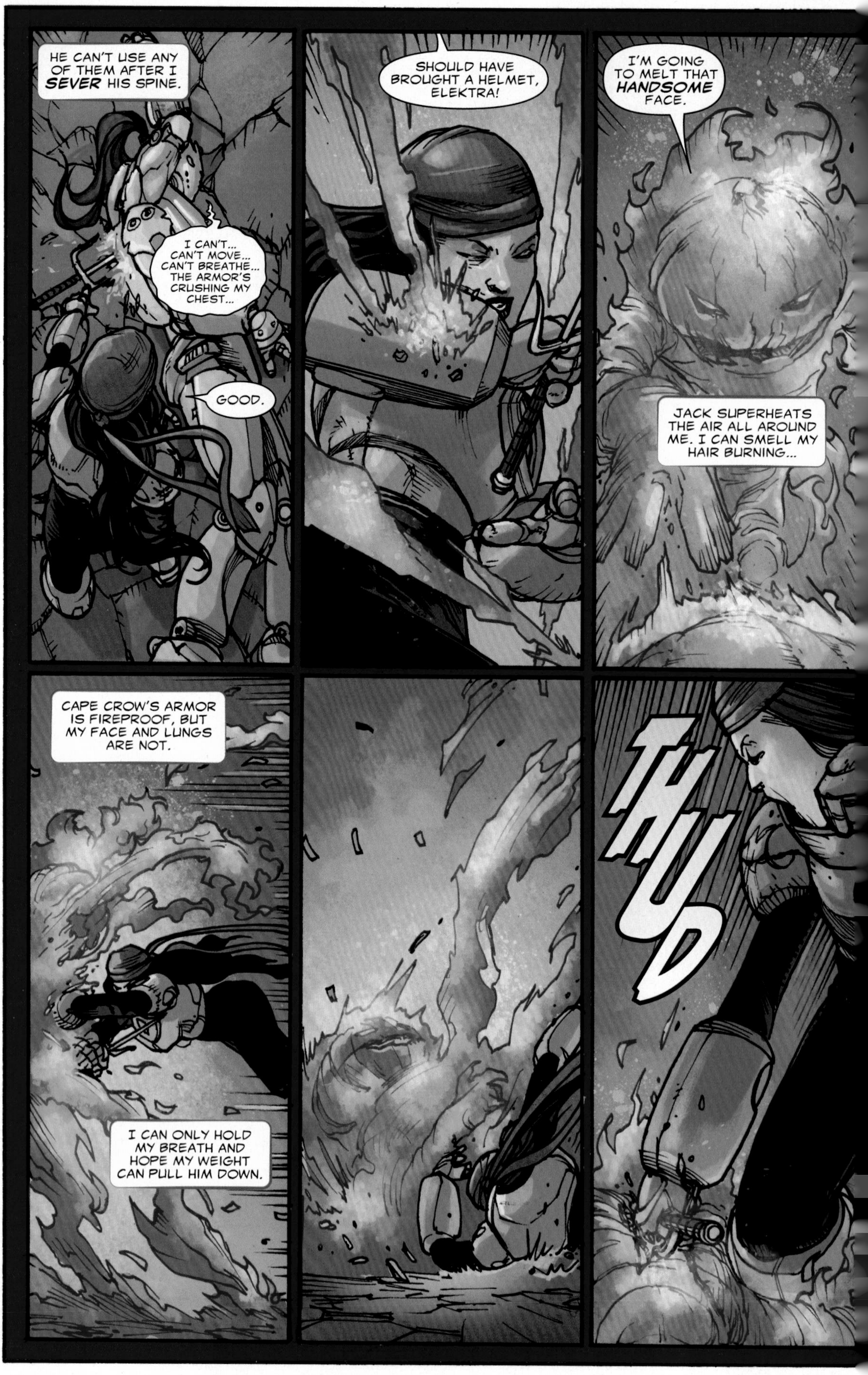
HE CAN'T USE ANY OF THEM AFTER I SEVER HIS SPINE.
I CAN'T... CAN'T MOVE... CAN'T BREATHE... THE ARMOR'S CRUSHING MY CHEST...
GOOD.
SHOULD HAVE BROUGHT A HELMET, ELEKTRA!
I'M GOING TO MELT THAT HANDSOME FACE.
JACK SUPERHEATS THE AIR ALL AROUND ME. I CAN SMELL MY HAIR BURNING...
CAPE CROW'S ARMOR IS FIREPROOF, BUT MY FACE AND LUNGS ARE NOT.
I CAN ONLY HOLD MY BREATH AND HOPE MY WEIGHT CAN PULL HIM DOWN.
THUD

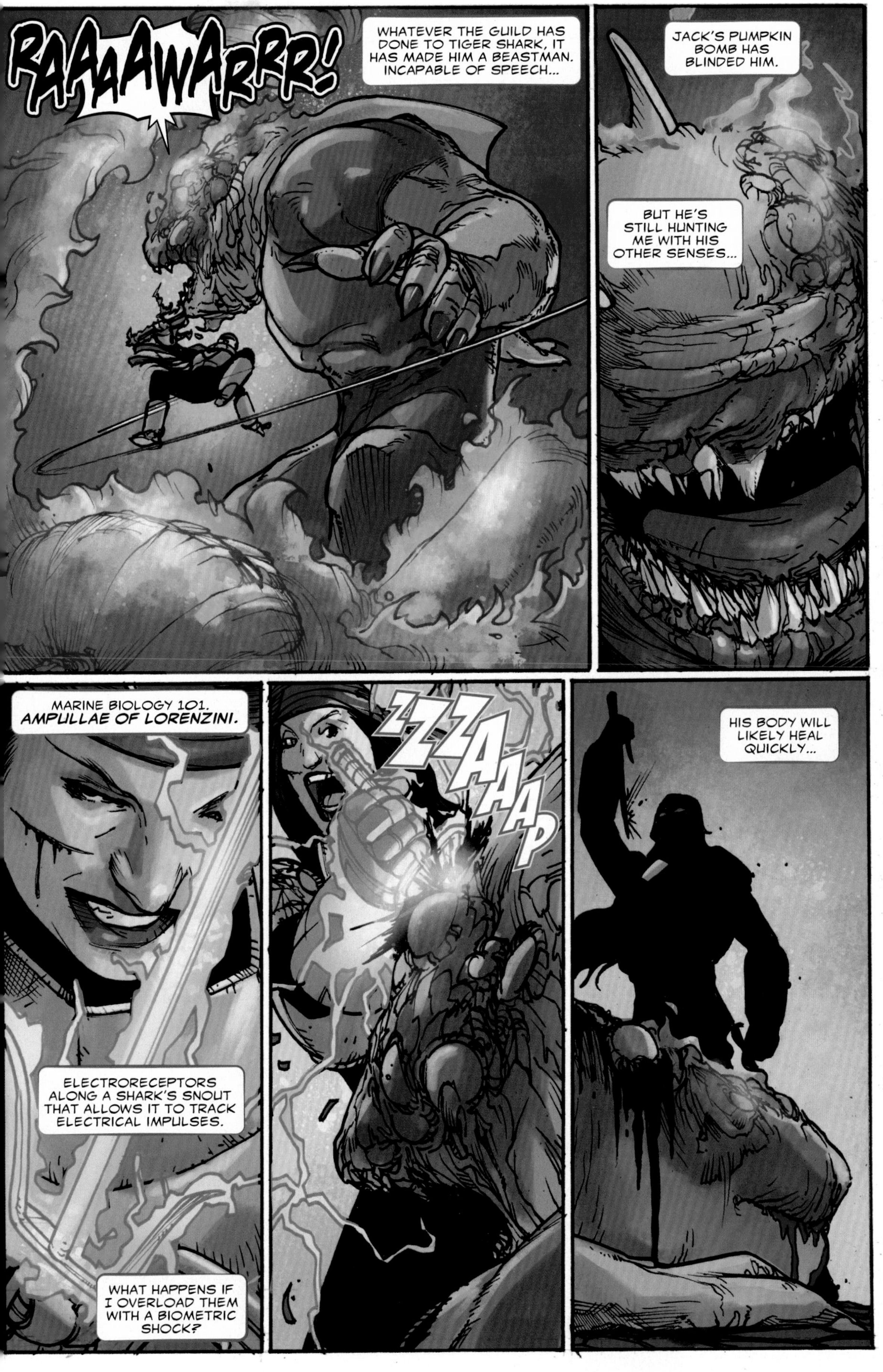
RAAAAAWARRR!
WHATEVER THE GUILD HAS DONE TO TIGER SHARK, IT HAS MADE HIM A BEASTMAN. INCAPABLE OF SPEECH...
JACK'S PUMPKIN BOMB HAS BLINDED HIM.
BUT HE'S STILL HUNTING ME WITH HIS OTHER SENSES...
MARINE BIOLOGY 101. *AMPULLAE OF LORENZINI.*
ELECTRORECEPTORS ALONG A SHARK'S SNOUT THAT ALLOWS IT TO TRACK ELECTRICAL IMPULSES.
WHAT HAPPENS IF I OVERLOAD THEM WITH A BIOMETRIC SHOCK?
ZZZAAAAP
HIS BODY WILL LIKELY HEAL QUICKLY...

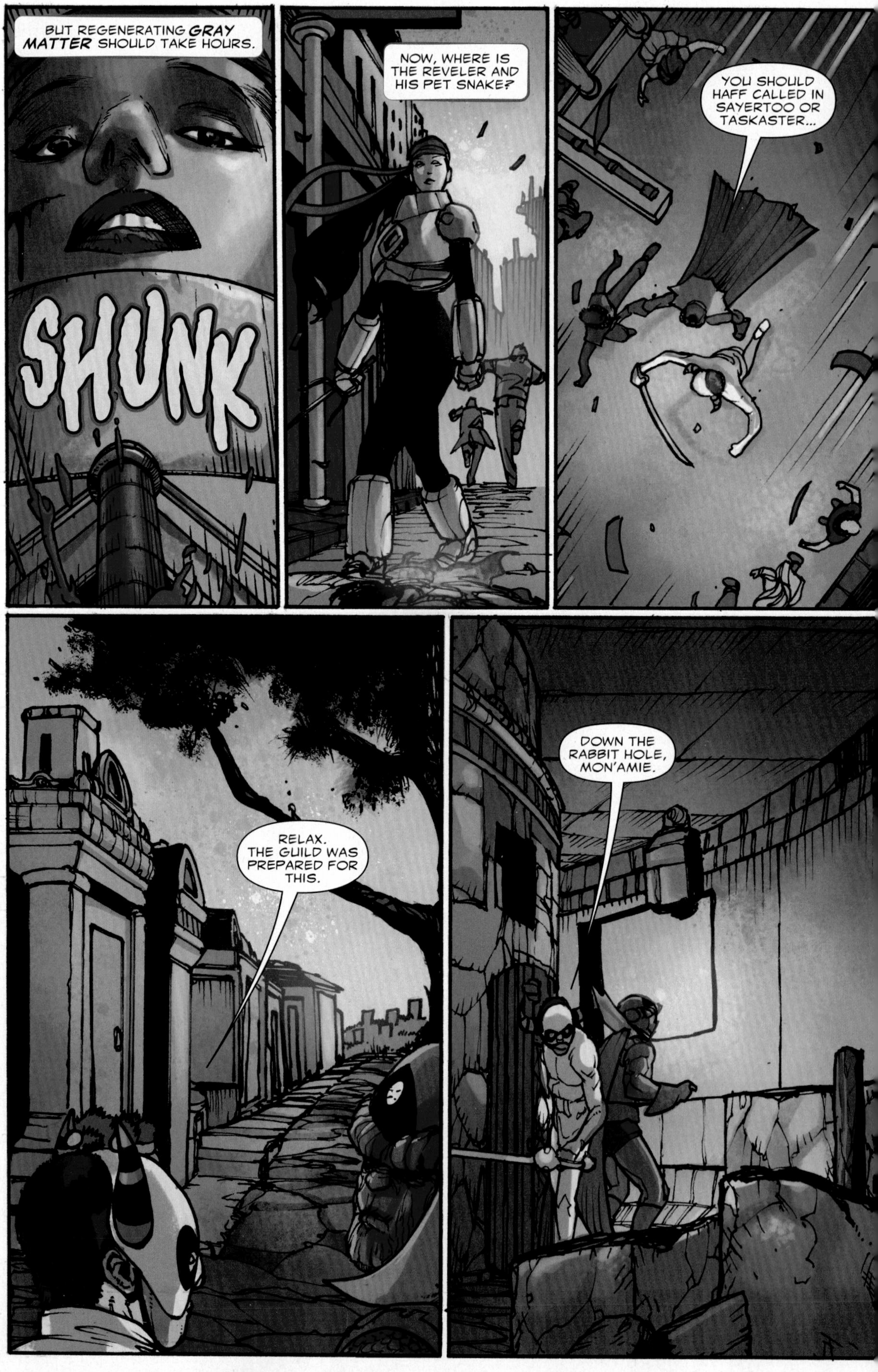
BUT REGENERATING GRAY MATTER SHOULD TAKE HOURS.
SHUNK
NOW, WHERE IS THE REVELER AND HIS PET SNAKE?
YOU SHOULD HAFF CALLED IN SAYERTOO OR TASKASTER...
RELAX. THE GUILD WAS PREPARED FOR THIS.
DOWN THE RABBIT HOLE, MON'AMIE.

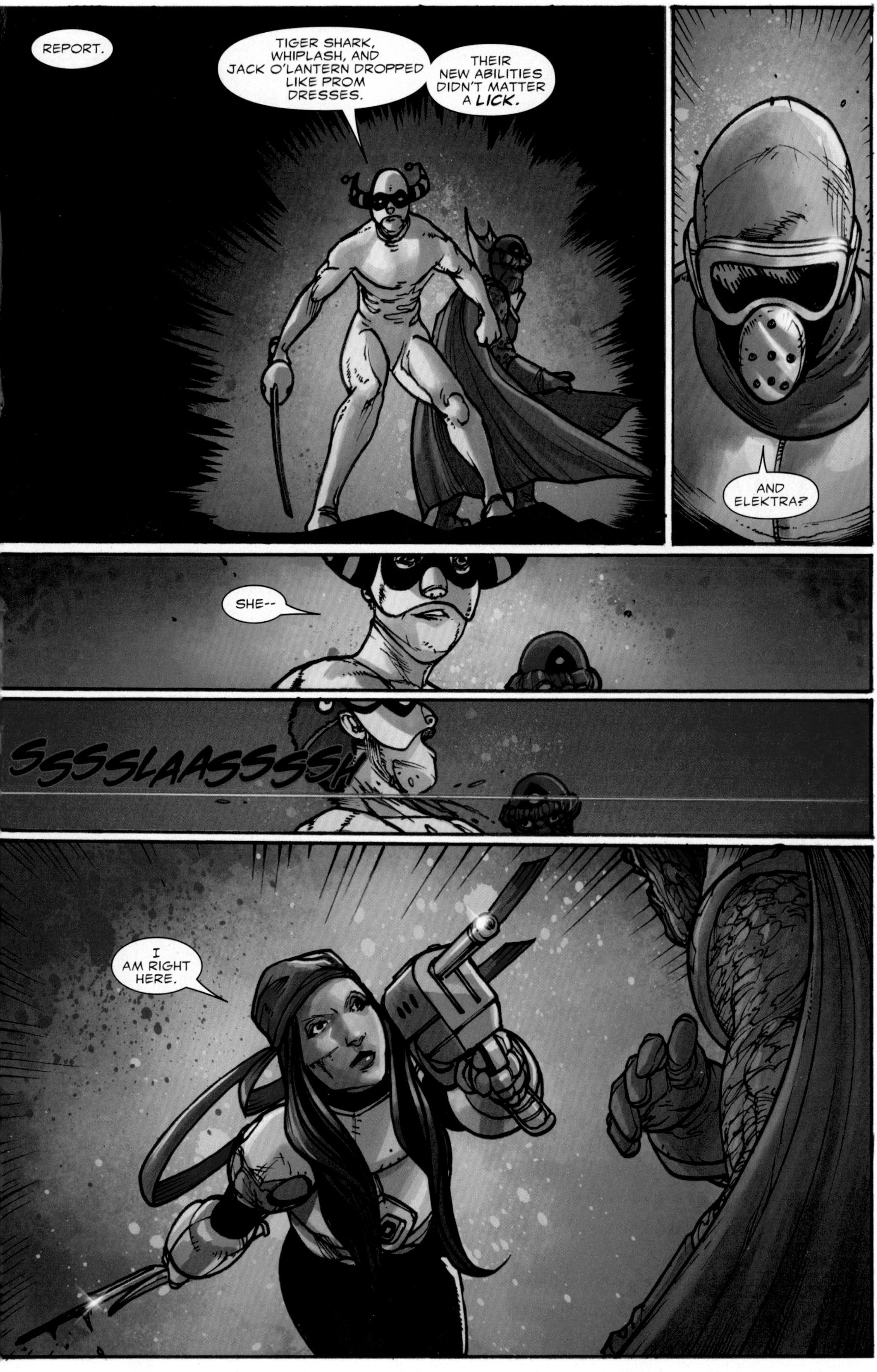
REPORT.
TIGER SHARK, WHIPLASH, AND JACK O'LANTERN DROPPED LIKE PROM DRESSES.
THEIR NEW ABILITIES DIDN'T MATTER A LICK.
AND ELEKTRA?
SHE--
SSSSLAASSSSSH
I AM RIGHT HERE.

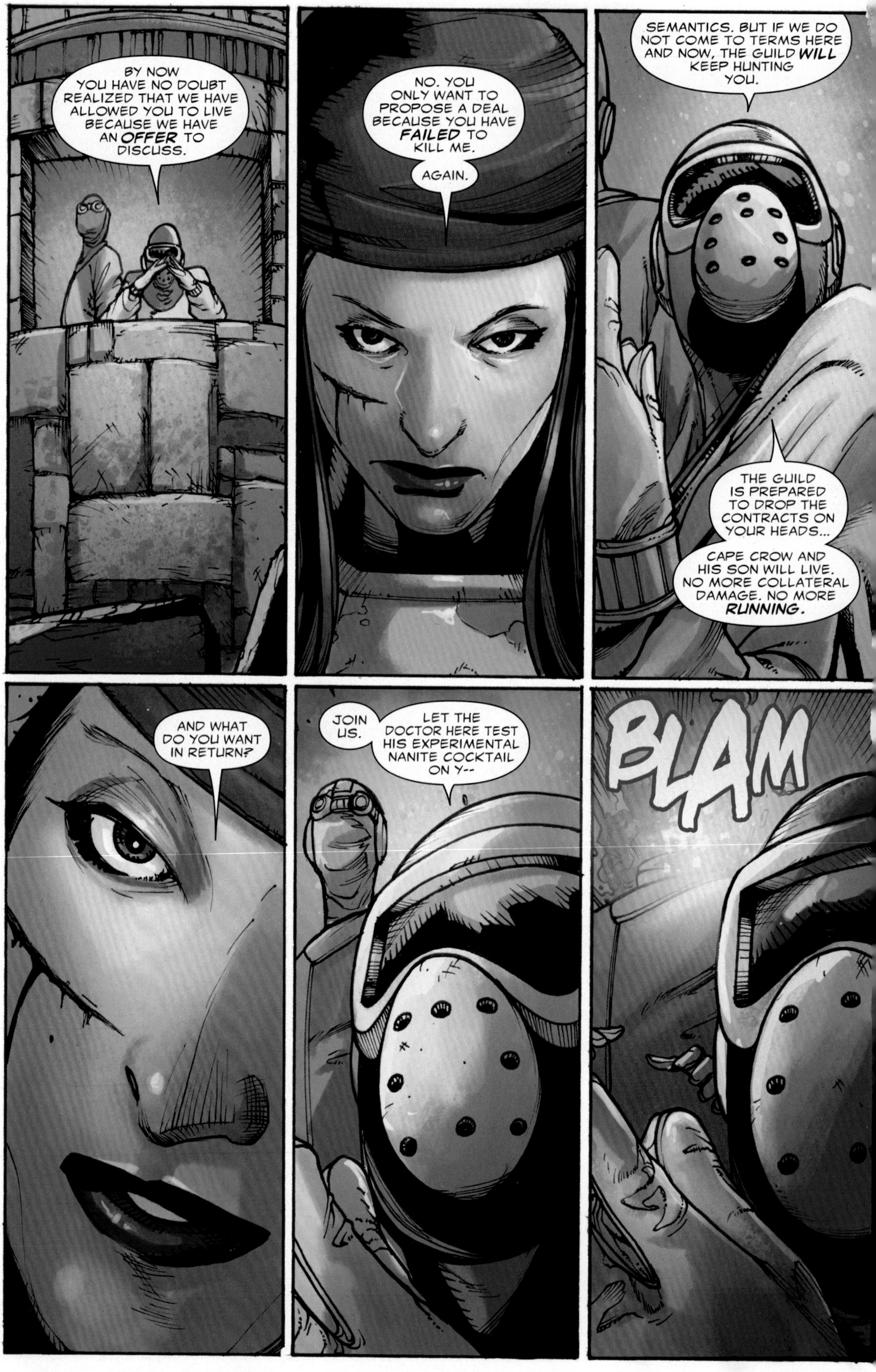
BY NOW YOU HAVE NO DOUBT REALIZED THAT WE HAVE ALLOWED YOU TO LIVE BECAUSE WE HAVE AN OFFER TO DISCUSS.
NO. YOU ONLY WANT TO PROPOSE A DEAL BECAUSE YOU HAVE FAILED TO KILL ME.
AGAIN.
SEMANTICS. BUT IF WE DO NOT COME TO TERMS HERE AND NOW, THE GUILD WILL KEEP HUNTING YOU.
THE GUILD IS PREPARED TO DROP THE CONTRACTS ON YOUR HEADS...
CAPE CROW AND HIS SON WILL LIVE. NO MORE COLLATERAL DAMAGE. NO MORE RUNNING.
AND WHAT DO YOU WANT IN RETURN?
JOIN US.
LET THE DOCTOR HERE TEST HIS EXPERIMENTAL NANITE COCKTAIL ON Y--
BLAM

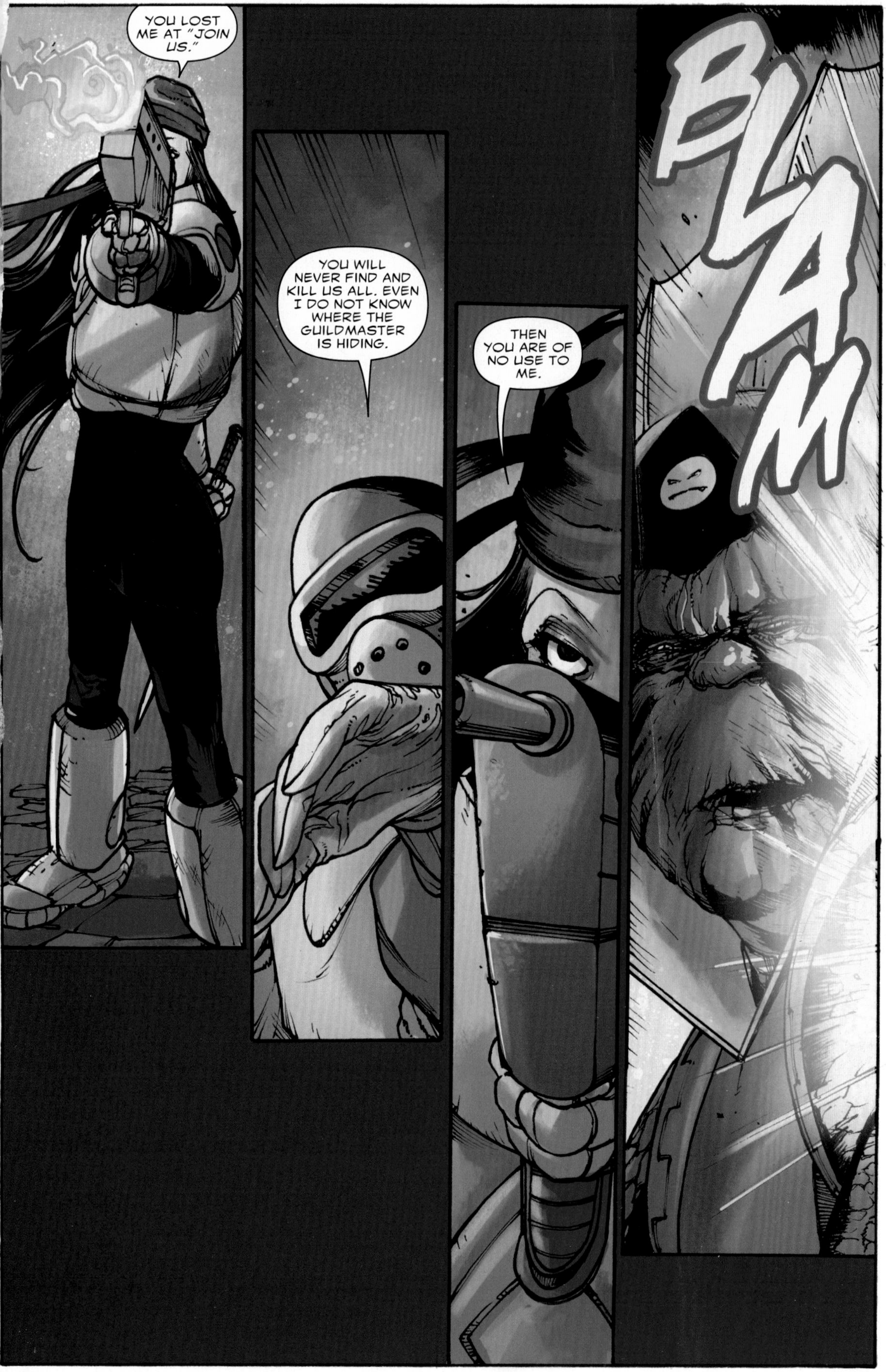
YOU LOST ME AT "JOIN US."
YOU WILL NEVER FIND AND KILL US ALL. EVEN I DO NOT KNOW WHERE THE GUILDMASTER IS HIDING.
THEN YOU ARE OF NO USE TO ME.
BLAM

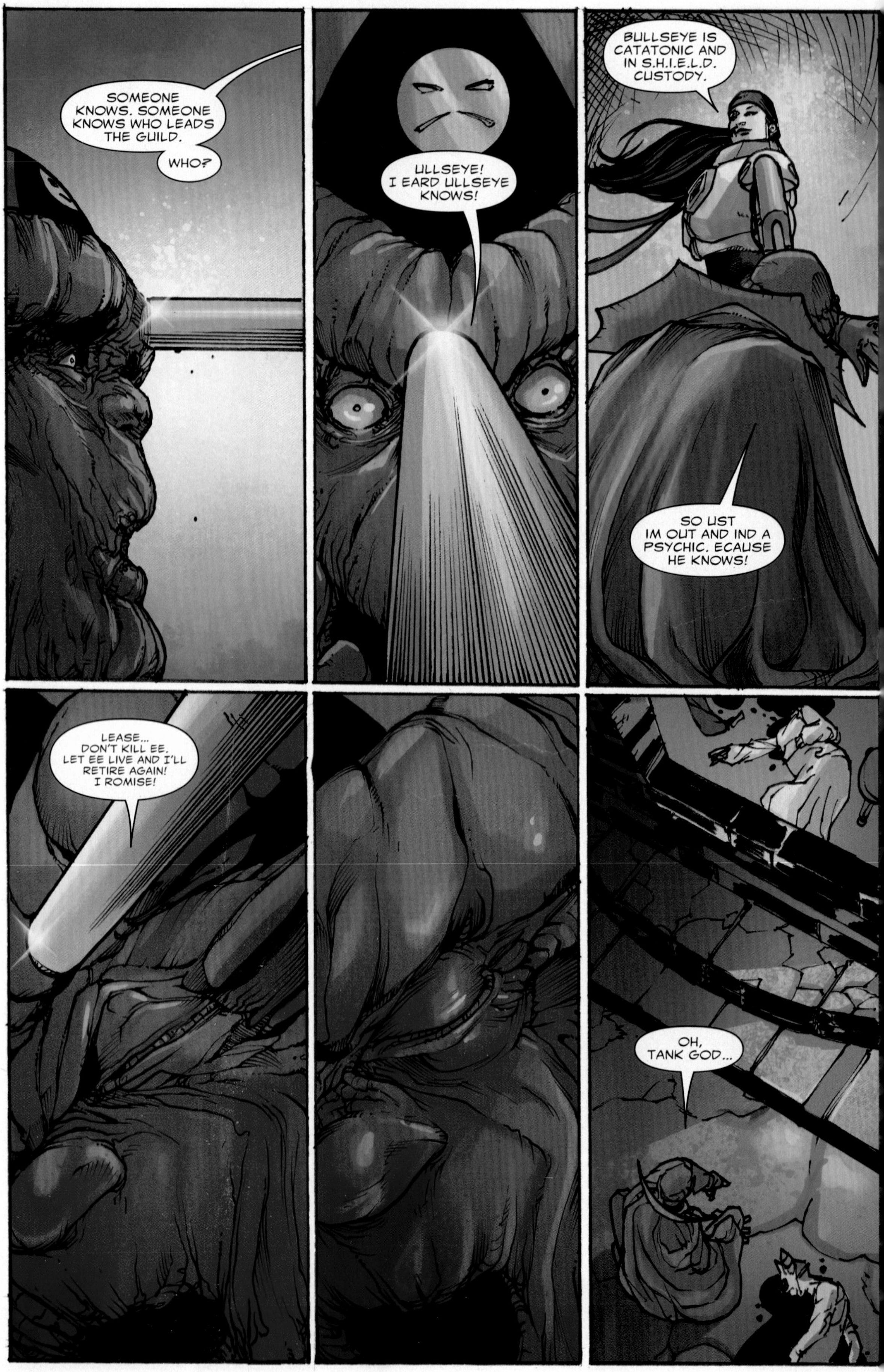
SOMEONE KNOWS. SOMEONE KNOWS WHO LEADS THE GUILD.
WHO?
ULLSEYE! I EARD ULLSEYE KNOWS!
BULLSEYE IS CATATONIC AND IN S.H.I.E.L.D. CUSTODY.
SO UST IM OUT AND IND A PSYCHIC. ECAUSE HE KNOWS!
LEASE... DON'T KILL EE. LET EE LIVE AND I'LL RETIRE AGAIN! I ROMISE!
OH, TANK GOD...

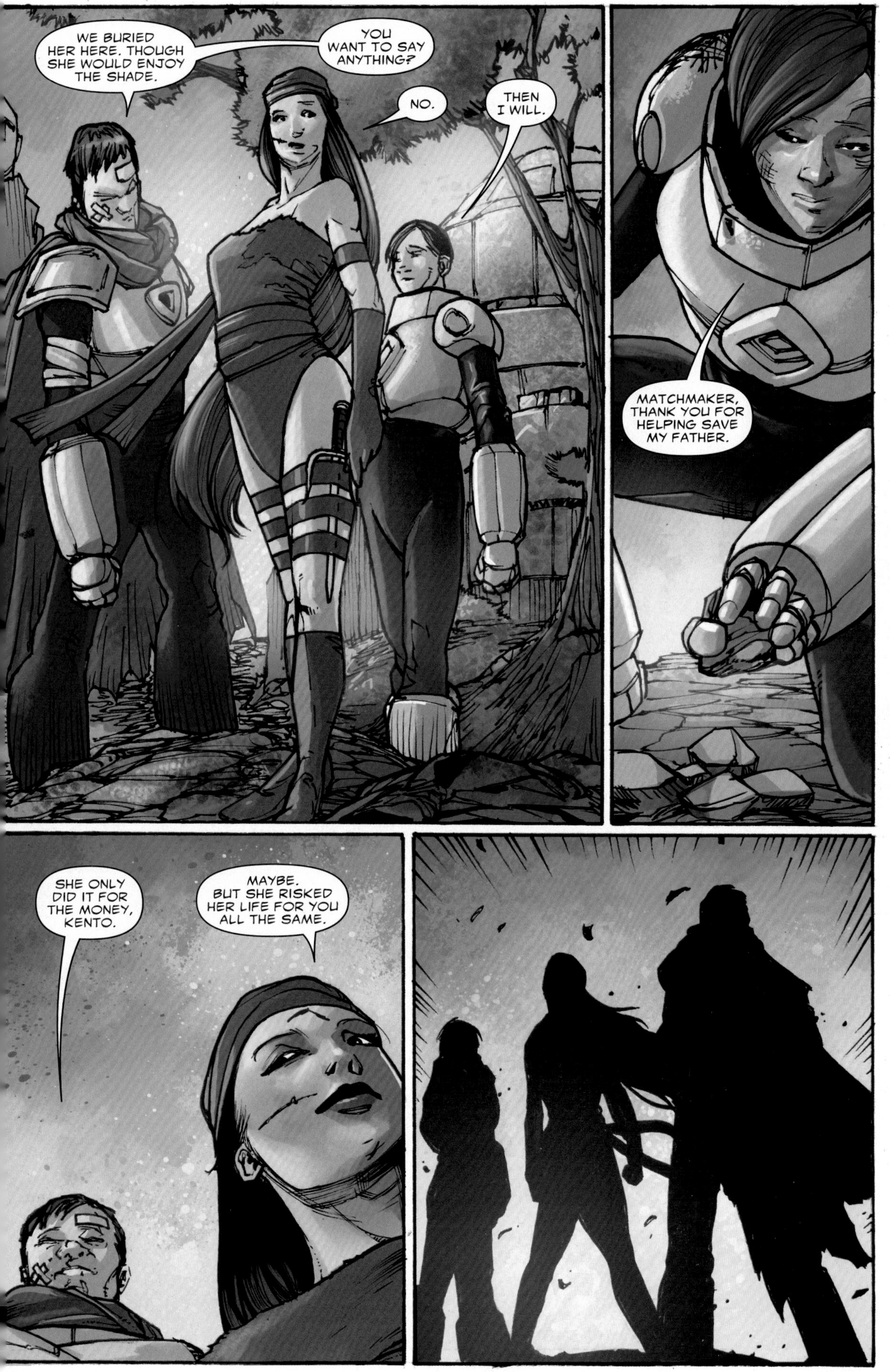
WE BURIED HER HERE. THOUGH SHE WOULD ENJOY THE SHADE.
YOU WANT TO SAY ANYTHING?
NO.
THEN I WILL.
MATCHMAKER, THANK YOU FOR HELPING SAVE MY FATHER.
SHE ONLY DID IT FOR THE MONEY, KENTO.
MAYBE. BUT SHE RISKED HER LIFE FOR YOU ALL THE SAME.

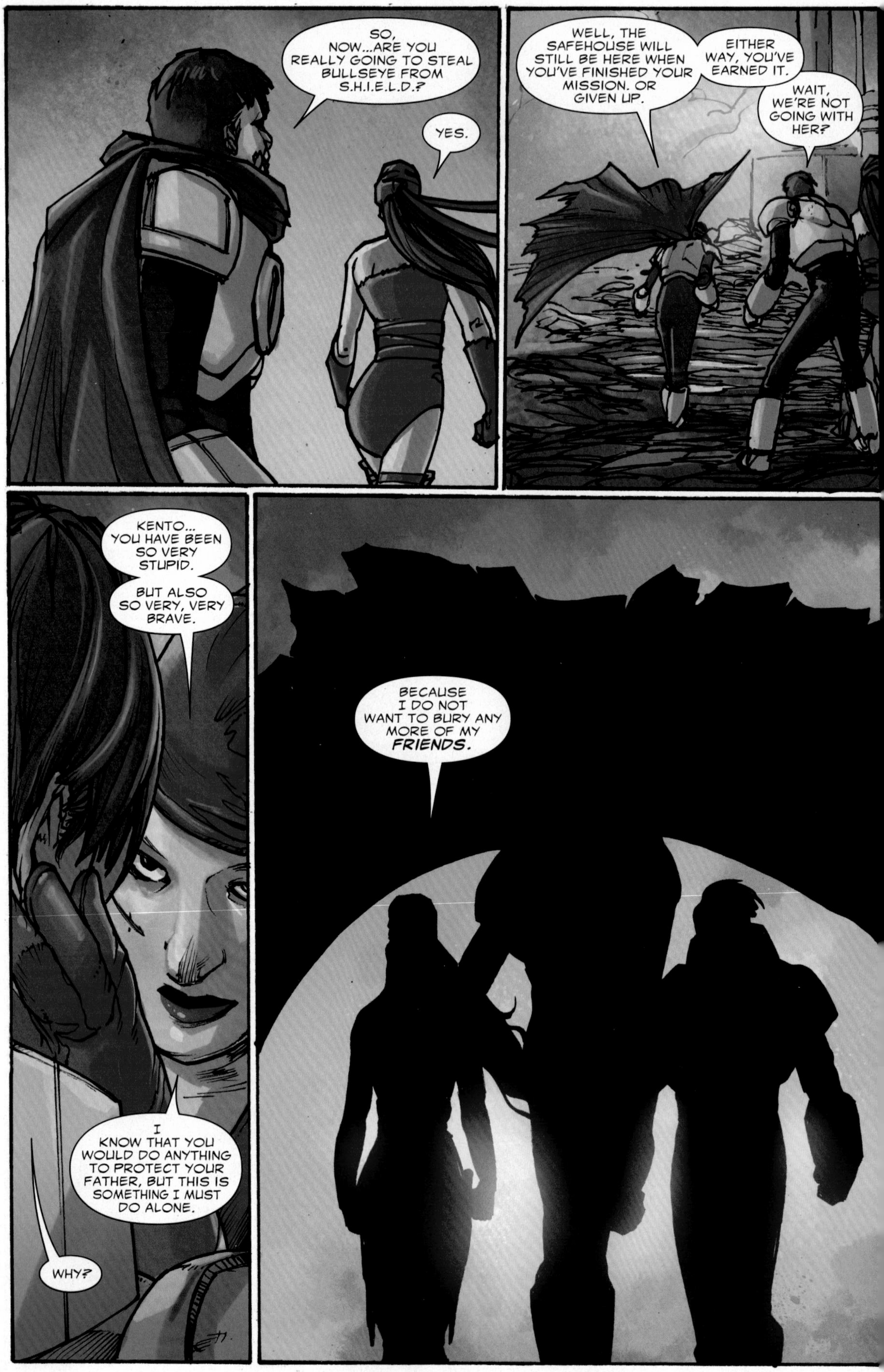

SO, NOW...ARE YOU REALLY GOING TO STEAL BULLSEYE FROM S.H.I.E.L.D.?
YES.
WELL, THE SAFEHOUSE WILL STILL BE HERE WHEN YOU'VE FINISHED YOUR MISSION. OR GIVEN UP.
EITHER WAY, YOU'VE EARNED IT.
WAIT, WE'RE NOT GOING WITH HER?
KENTO... YOU HAVE BEEN SO VERY STUPID.
BUT ALSO SO VERY, VERY BRAVE.
I KNOW THAT YOU WOULD DO ANYTHING TO PROTECT YOUR FATHER, BUT THIS IS SOMETHING I MUST DO ALONE.
WHY?
BECAUSE I DO NOT WANT TO BURY ANY MORE OF MY FRIENDS.

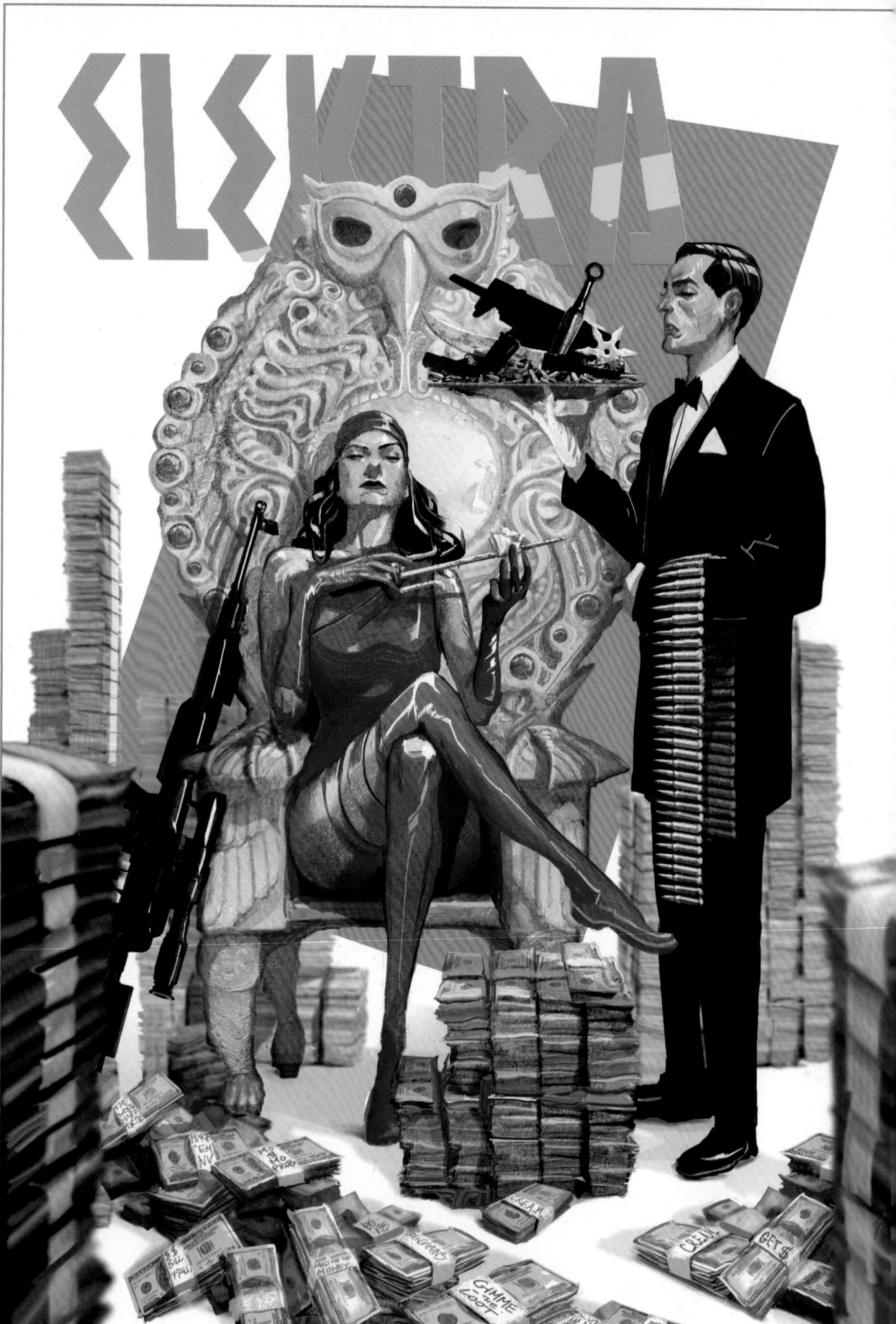

ELEKTRA
C.R.E.A.M.
GIMME THE LOOT
GET $

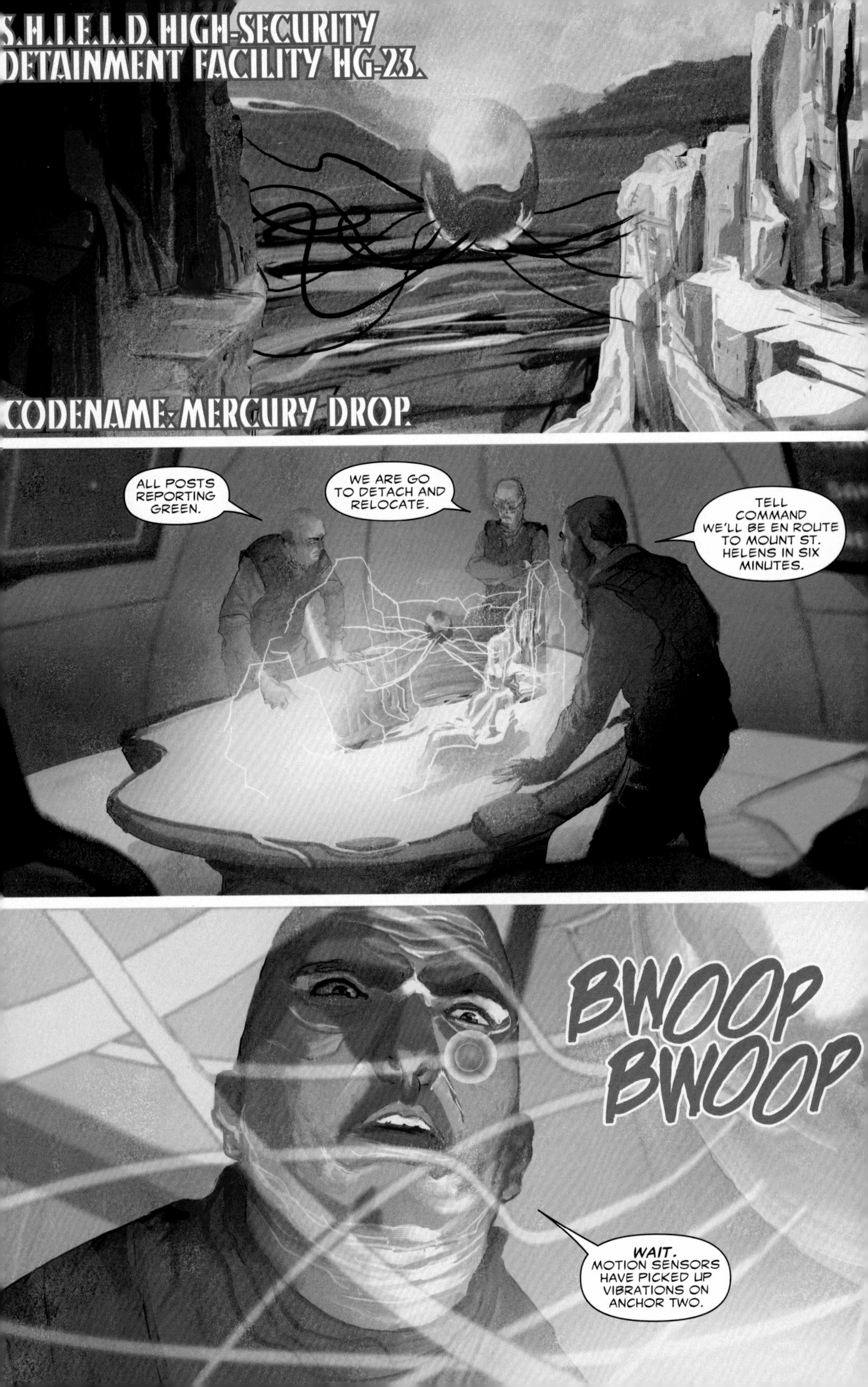
S.H.I.E.L.D. HIGH-SECURITY DETAINMENT FACILITY HG-23.
CODENAME: MERCURY DROP.
ALL POSTS REPORTING GREEN.
WE ARE GO TO DETACH AND RELOCATE.
TELL COMMAND WE'LL BE EN ROUTE TO MOUNT ST. HELENS IN SIX MINUTES.
BWOOP BWOOP
WAIT. MOTION SENSORS HAVE PICKED UP VIBRATIONS ON ANCHOR TWO.

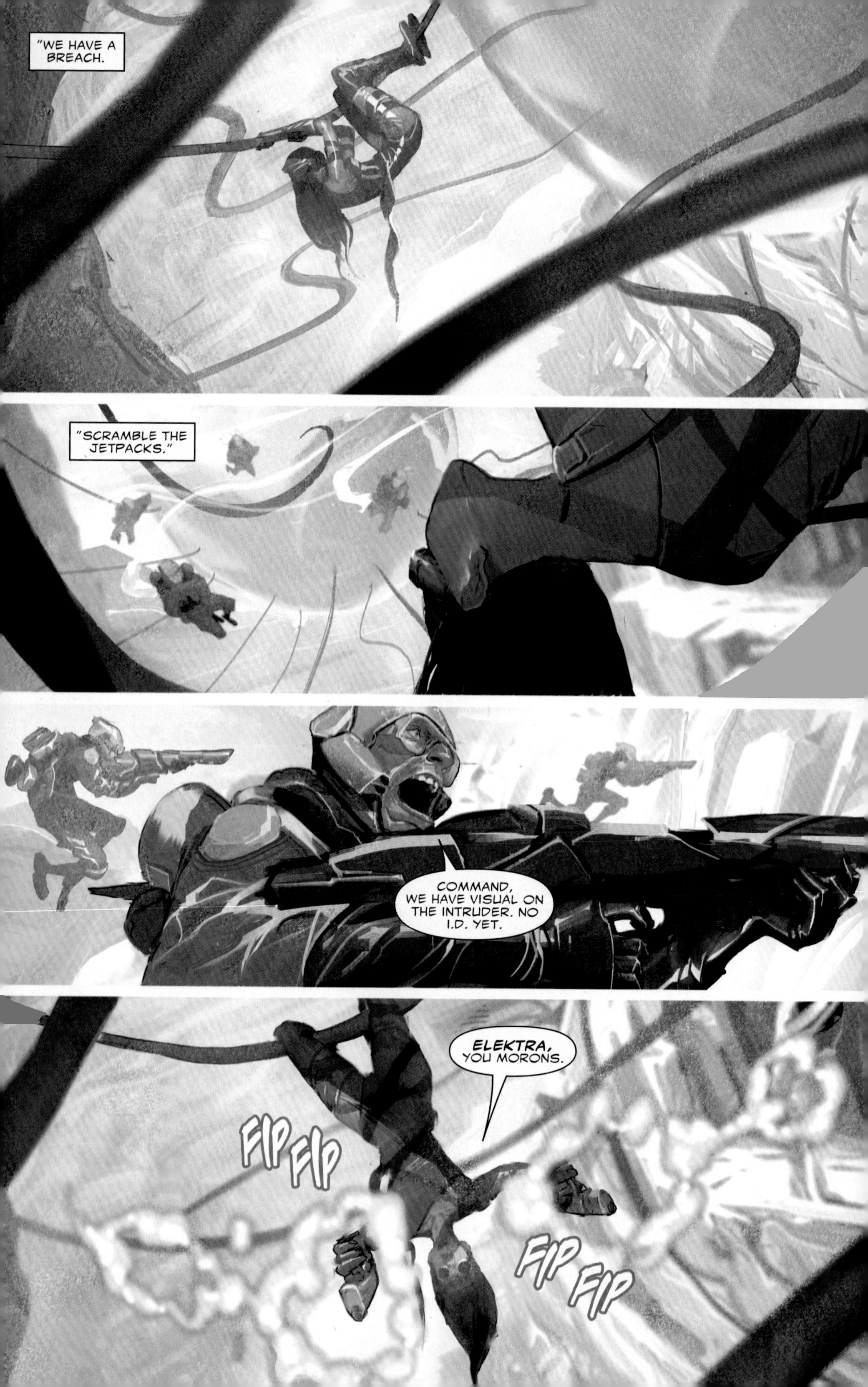
"WE HAVE A BREACH.
"SCRAMBLE THE JETPACKS."
COMMAND, WE HAVE VISUAL ON THE INTRUDER. NO I.D. YET.
ELEKTRA, YOU MORONS.
FIP FIP
FIP FIP

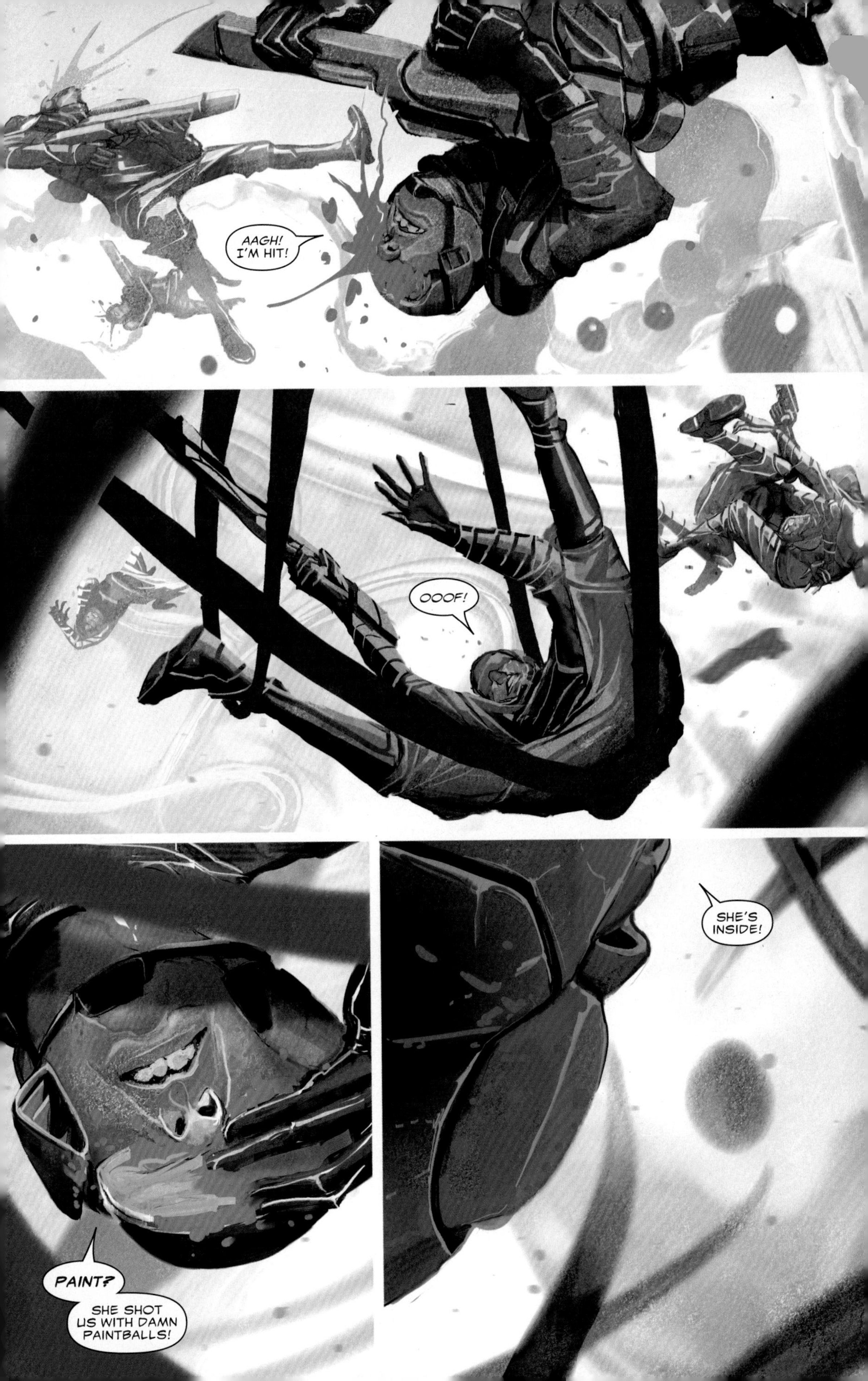
AAGH! I'M HIT!
OOOF!
PAINT?
SHE SHOT US WITH DAMN PAINTBALLS!
SHE'S INSIDE!

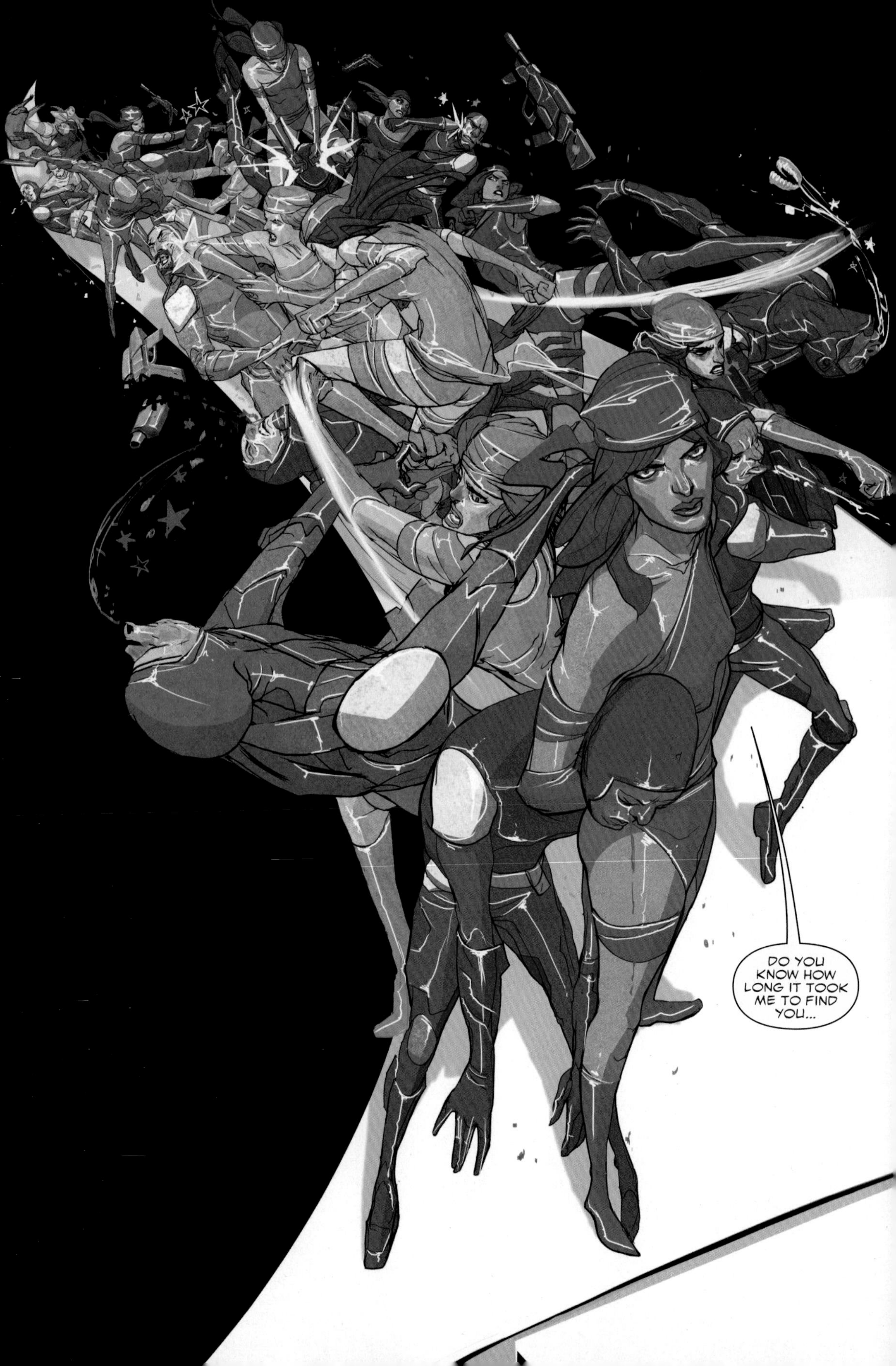
DO YOU KNOW HOW LONG IT TOOK ME TO FIND YOU...

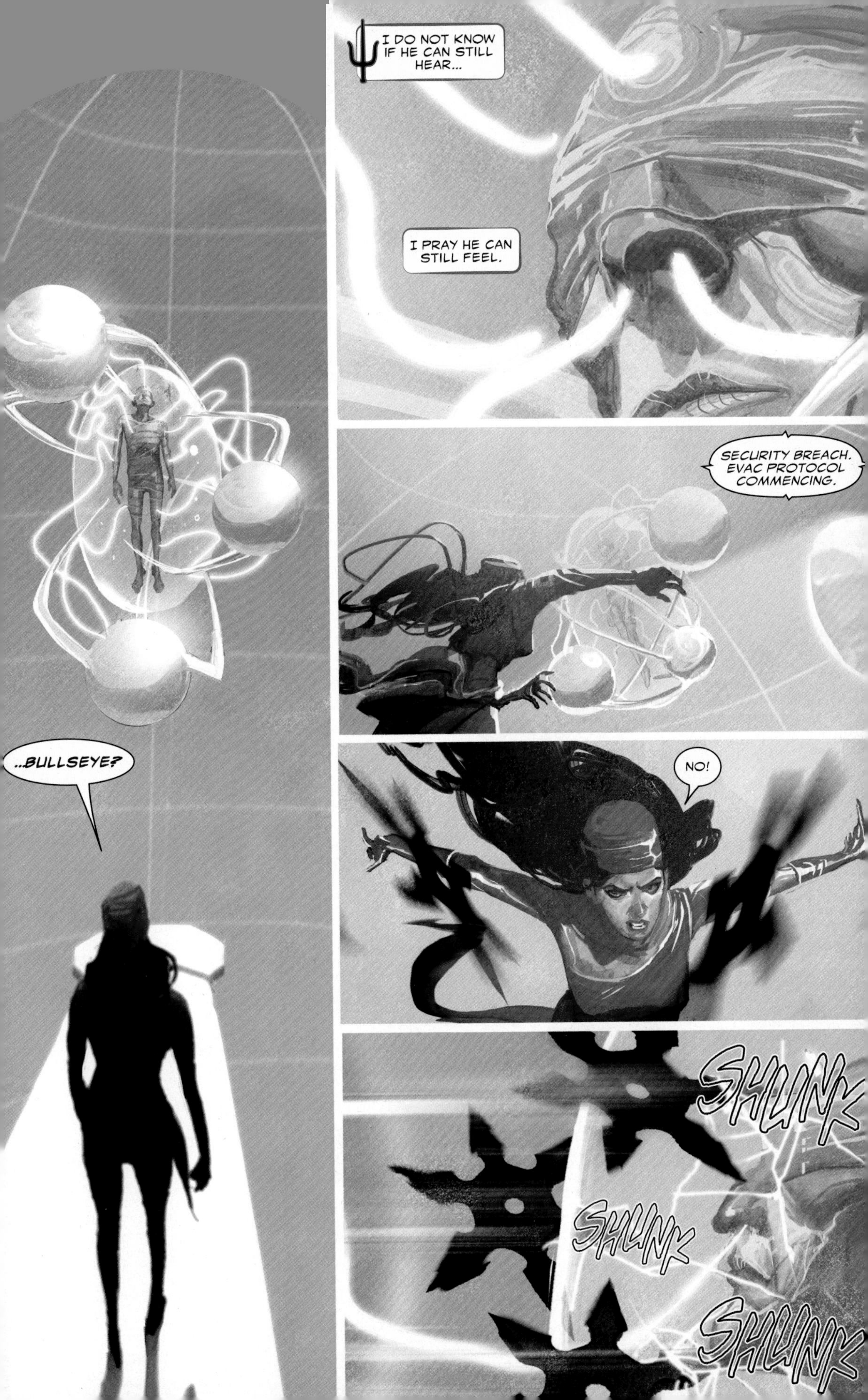

...BULLSEYE?
I DO NOT KNOW IF HE CAN STILL HEAR...
I PRAY HE CAN STILL FEEL.
SECURITY BREACH. EVAC PROTOCOL COMMENCING.
NO!
SHUNK
SHUNK
SHUNK

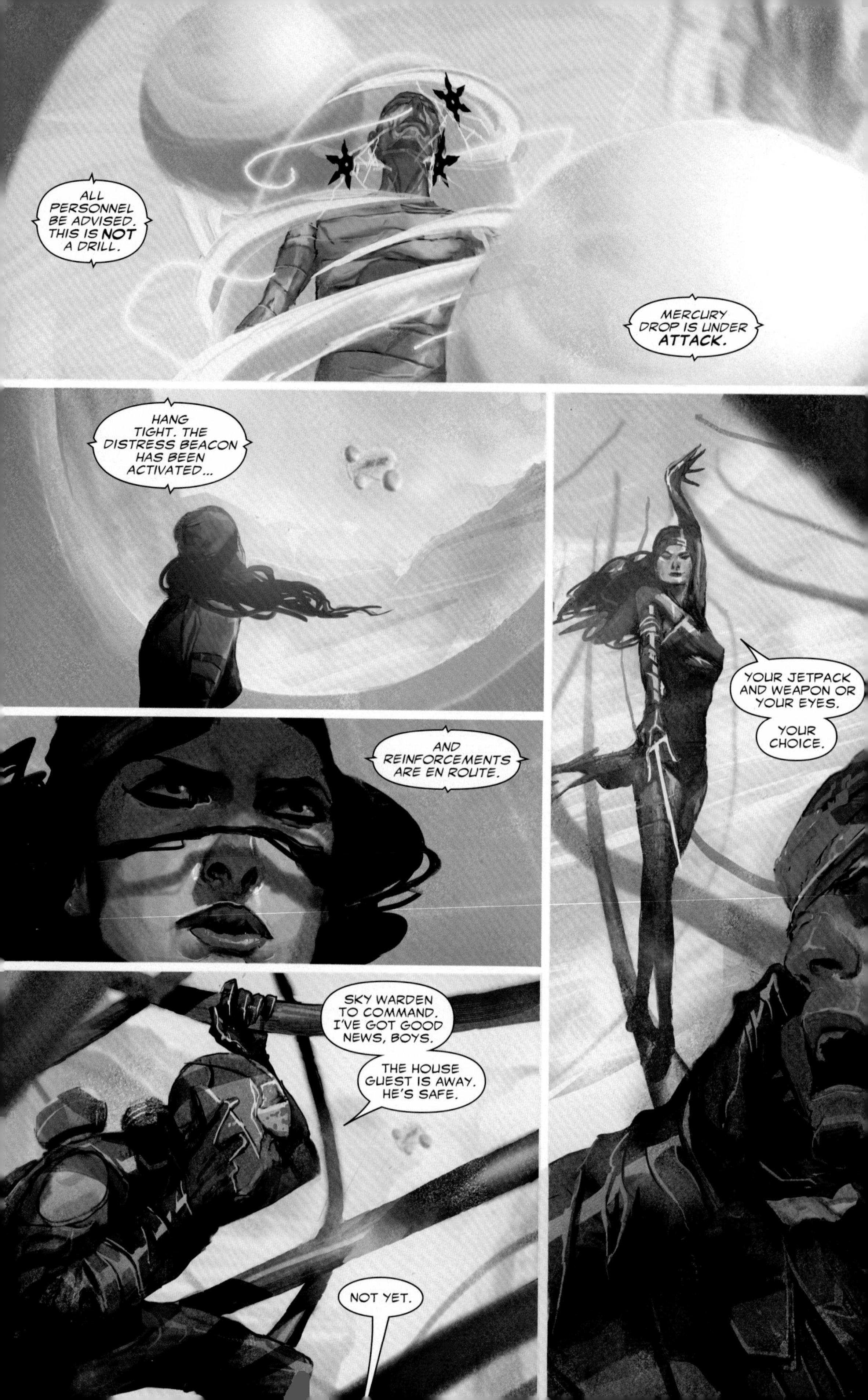
ALL PERSONNEL BE ADVISED. THIS IS **NOT** A DRILL.
MERCURY DROP IS UNDER **ATTACK.**
HANG TIGHT. THE DISTRESS BEACON HAS BEEN ACTIVATED...
AND REINFORCEMENTS ARE EN ROUTE.
SKY WARDEN TO COMMAND. I'VE GOT GOOD NEWS, BOYS.
THE HOUSE GUEST IS AWAY. HE'S SAFE.
NOT YET.
YOUR JETPACK AND WEAPON OR YOUR EYES.
YOUR CHOICE.

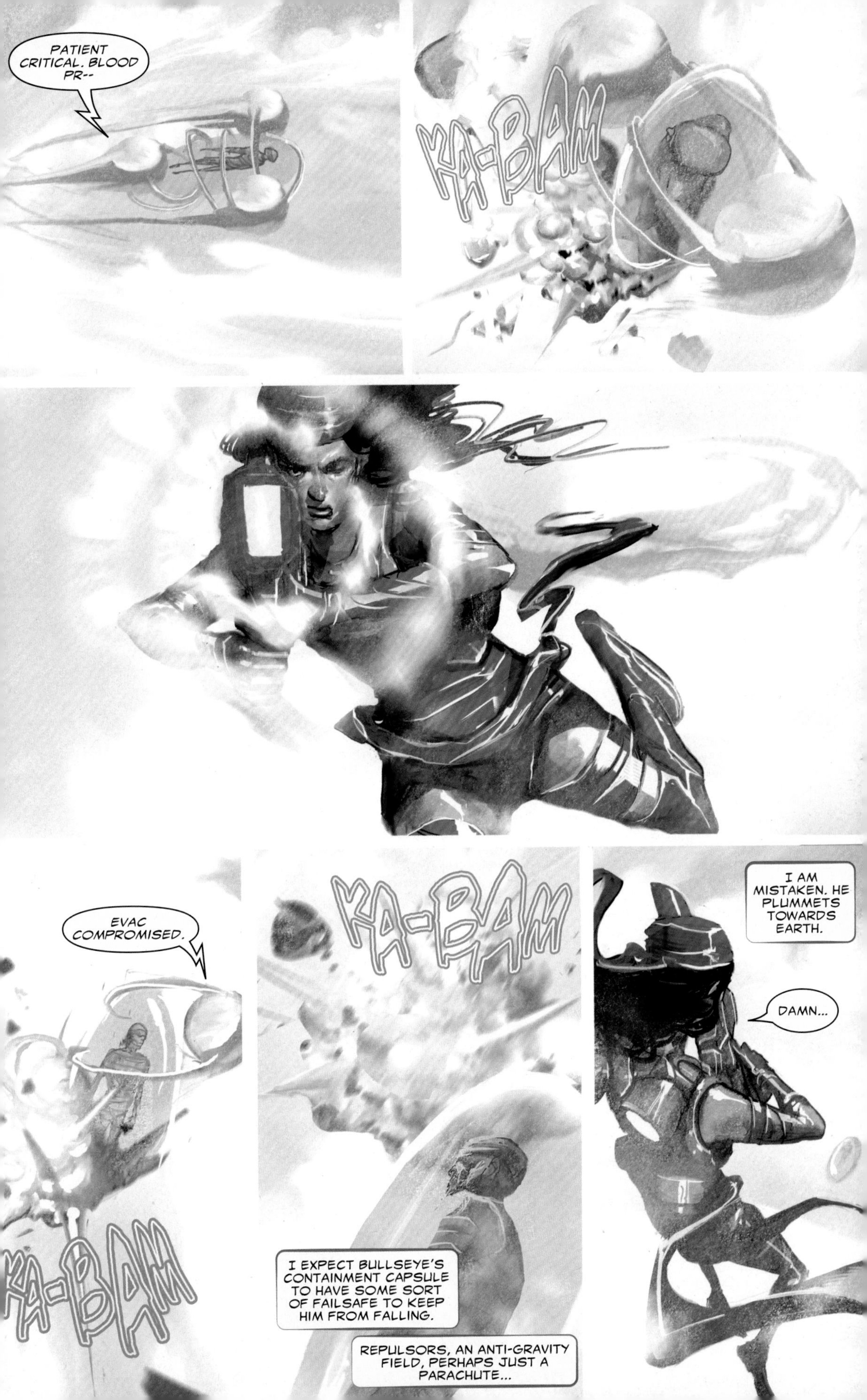
PATIENT CRITICAL. BLOOD PR--
KA-BAM
EVAC COMPROMISED.
KA-BAM
KA-BAM
I EXPECT BULLSEYE'S CONTAINMENT CAPSULE TO HAVE SOME SORT OF FAILSAFE TO KEEP HIM FROM FALLING.
REPULSORS, AN ANTI-GRAVITY FIELD, PERHAPS JUST A PARACHUTE...
I AM MISTAKEN. HE PLUMMETS TOWARDS EARTH.
DAMN...

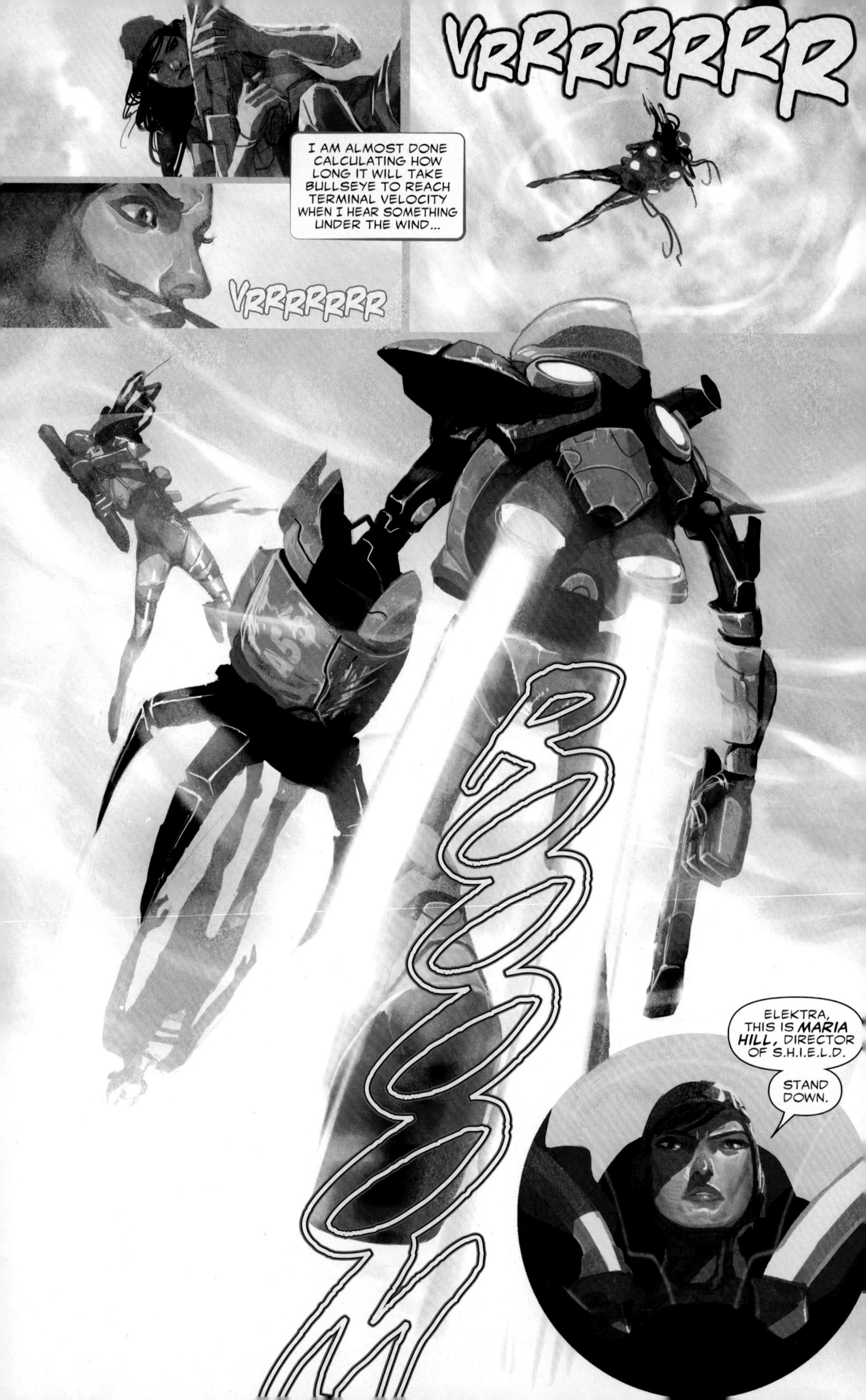
VRRRRRRR
I AM ALMOST DONE CALCULATING HOW LONG IT WILL TAKE BULLSEYE TO REACH TERMINAL VELOCITY WHEN I HEAR SOMETHING UNDER THE WIND...
VRRRRRRR
ELEKTRA, THIS IS MARIA HILL, DIRECTOR OF S.H.I.E.L.D.
STAND DOWN.

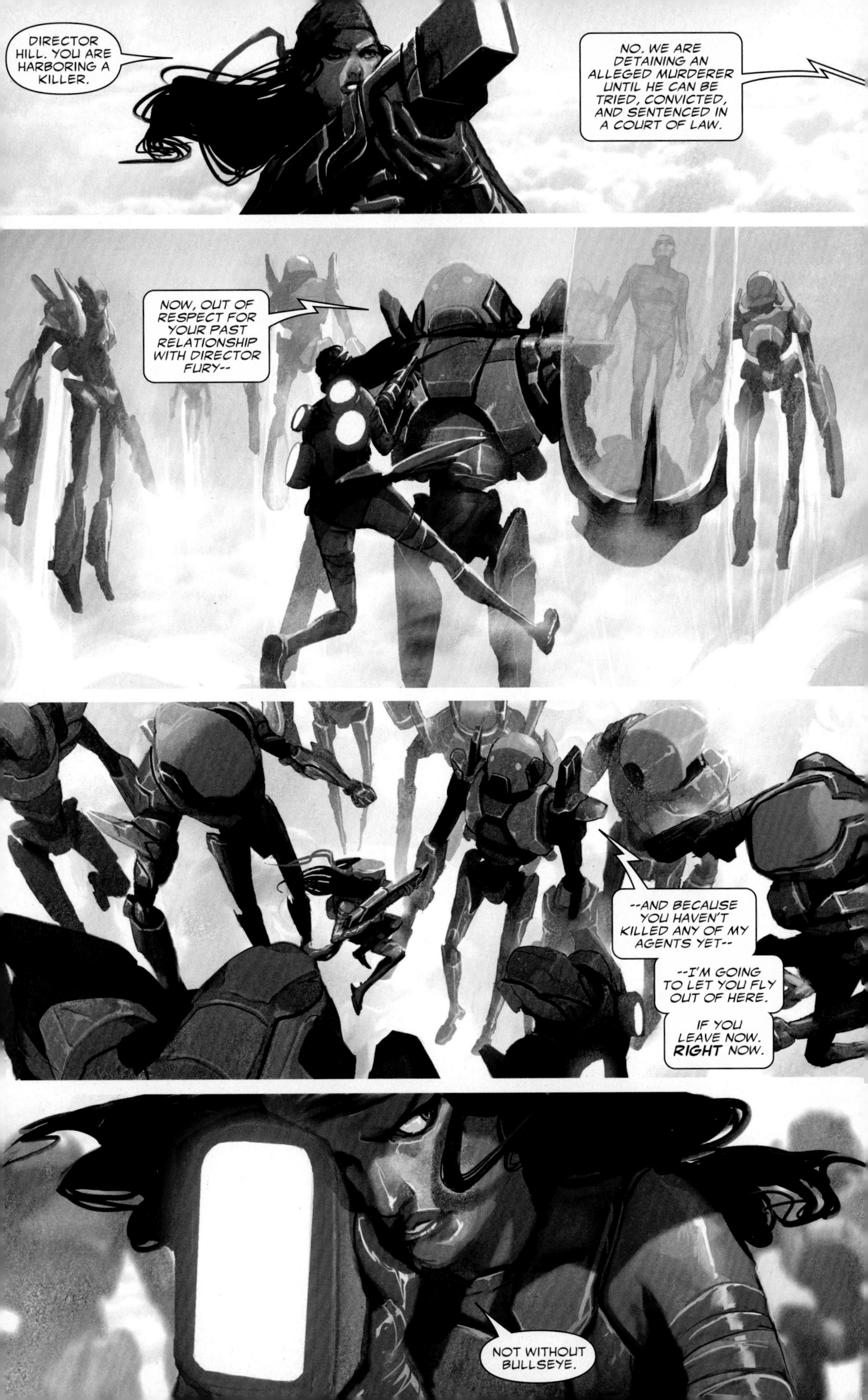
DIRECTOR HILL. YOU ARE HARBORING A KILLER.
NO. WE ARE DETAINING AN ALLEGED MURDERER UNTIL HE CAN BE TRIED, CONVICTED, AND SENTENCED IN A COURT OF LAW.
NOW, OUT OF RESPECT FOR YOUR PAST RELATIONSHIP WITH DIRECTOR FURY--
--AND BECAUSE YOU HAVEN'T KILLED ANY OF MY AGENTS YET--
--I'M GOING TO LET YOU FLY OUT OF HERE.
IF YOU LEAVE NOW. **RIGHT** NOW.
NOT WITHOUT BULLSEYE.

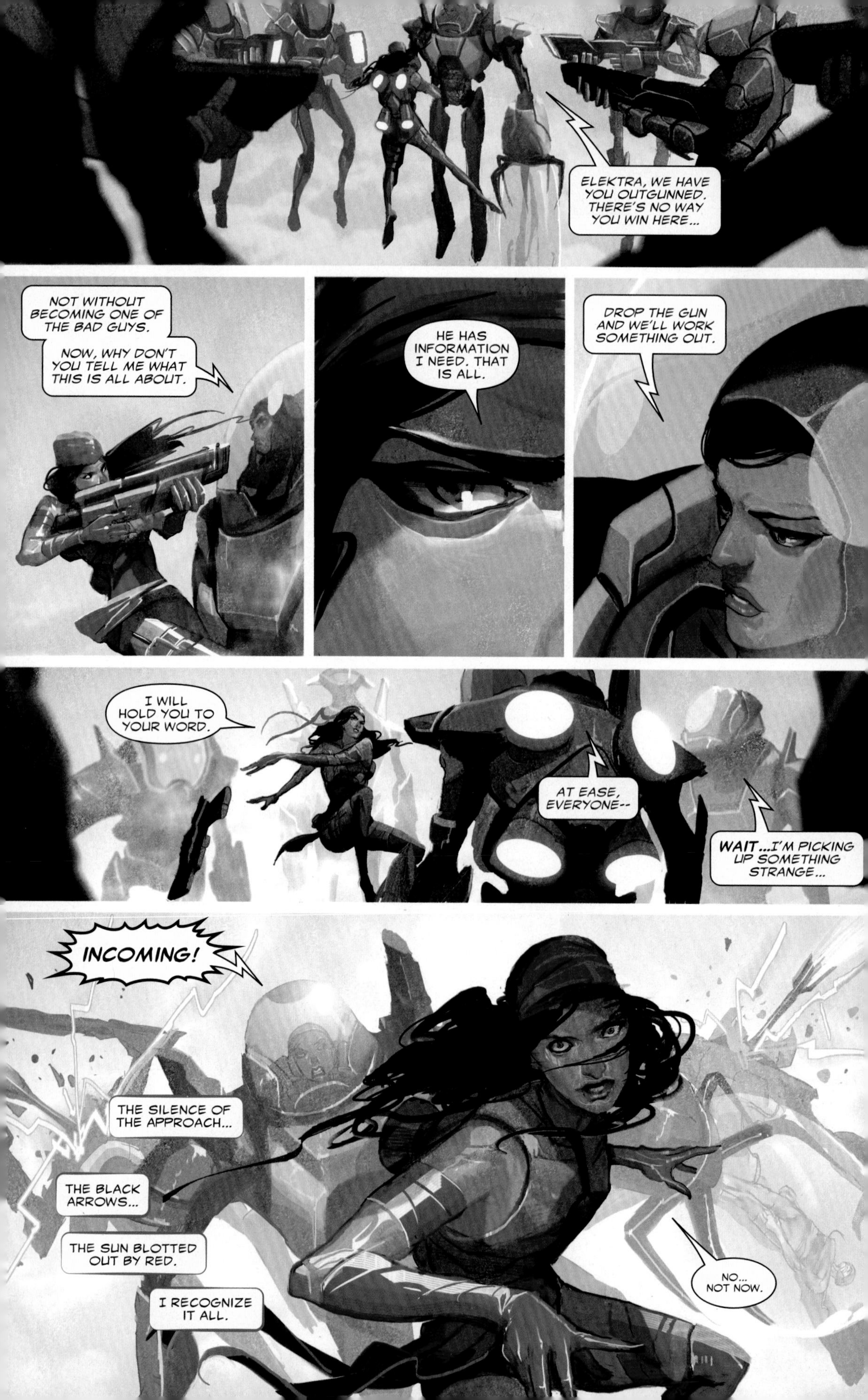

ELEKTRA, WE HAVE YOU OUTGUNNED. THERE'S NO WAY YOU WIN HERE...
NOT WITHOUT BECOMING ONE OF THE BAD GUYS.
NOW, WHY DON'T YOU TELL ME WHAT THIS IS ALL ABOUT.
HE HAS INFORMATION I NEED. THAT IS ALL.
DROP THE GUN AND WE'LL WORK SOMETHING OUT.
I WILL HOLD YOU TO YOUR WORD.
AT EASE, EVERYONE--
WAIT...I'M PICKING UP SOMETHING STRANGE...
INCOMING!
THE SILENCE OF THE APPROACH...
THE BLACK ARROWS...
THE SUN BLOTTED OUT BY RED.
I RECOGNIZE IT ALL.
NO... NOT NOW.

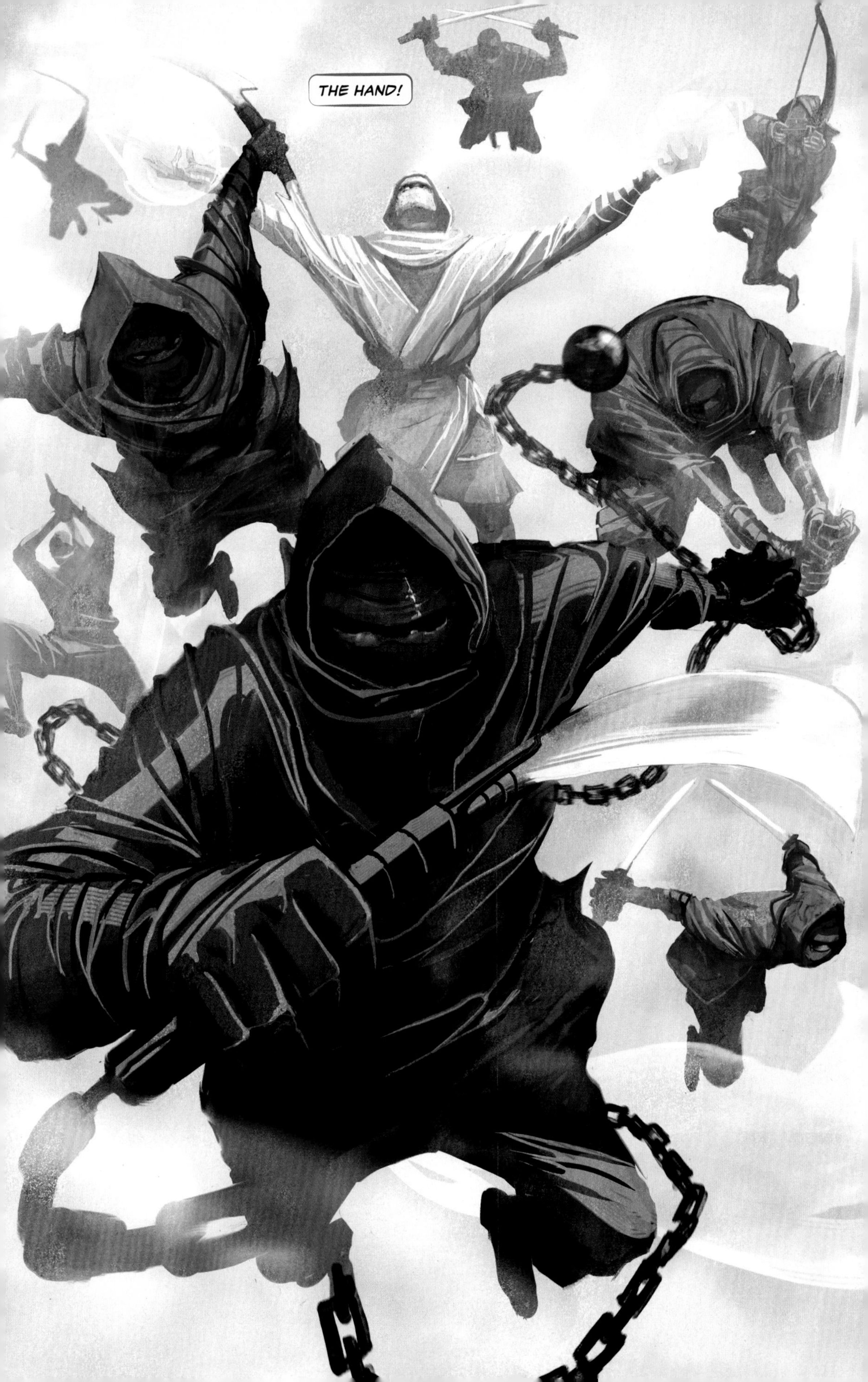
THE HAND!

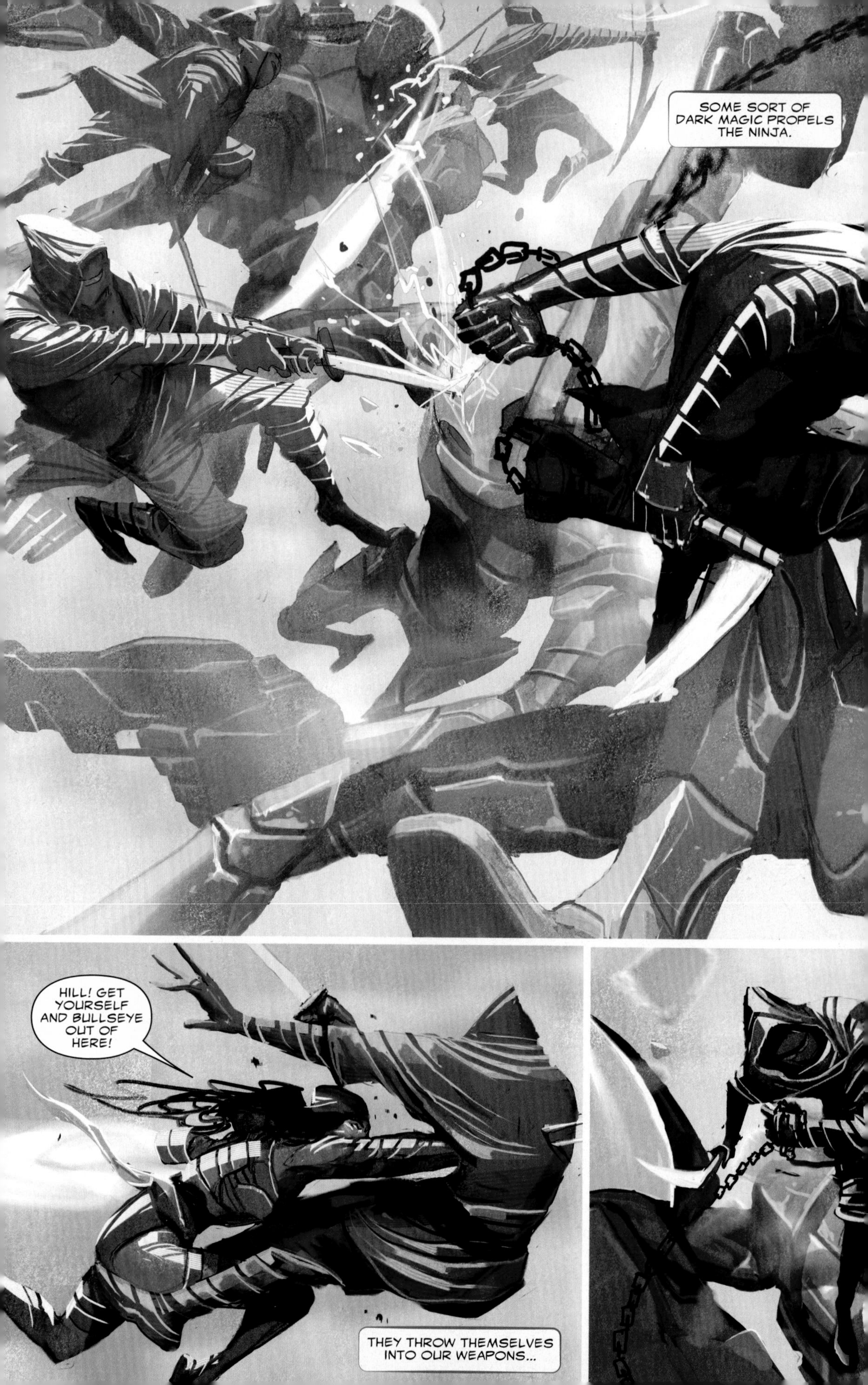
SOME SORT OF DARK MAGIC PROPELS THE NINJA.
HILL! GET YOURSELF AND BULLSEYE OUT OF HERE!
THEY THROW THEMSELVES INTO OUR WEAPONS...

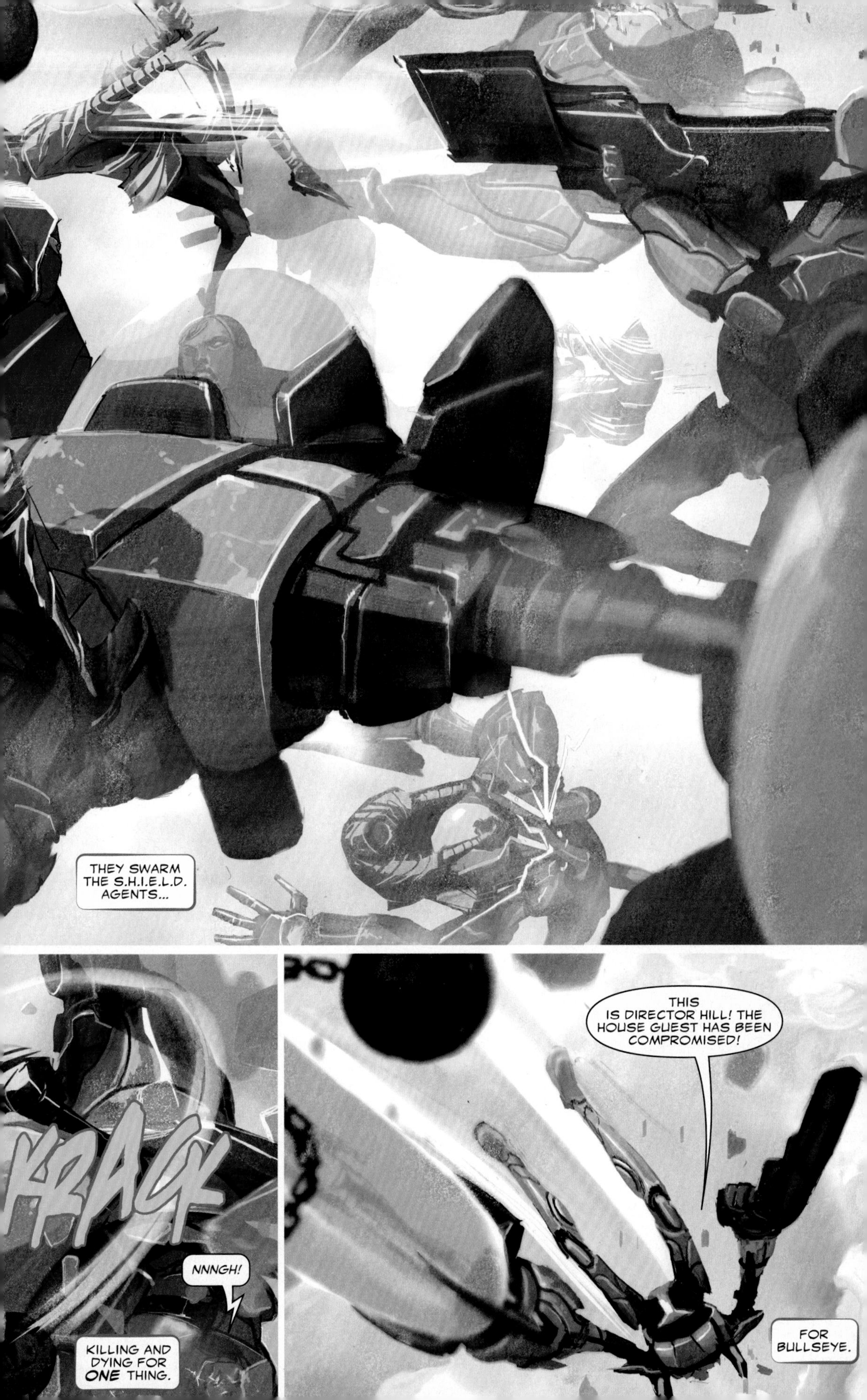
THEY SWARM THE S.H.I.E.L.D. AGENTS...
KRACK
NNNGH!
KILLING AND DYING FOR **ONE** THING.
THIS IS DIRECTOR HILL! THE HOUSE GUEST HAS BEEN COMPROMISED!
FOR BULLSEYE.

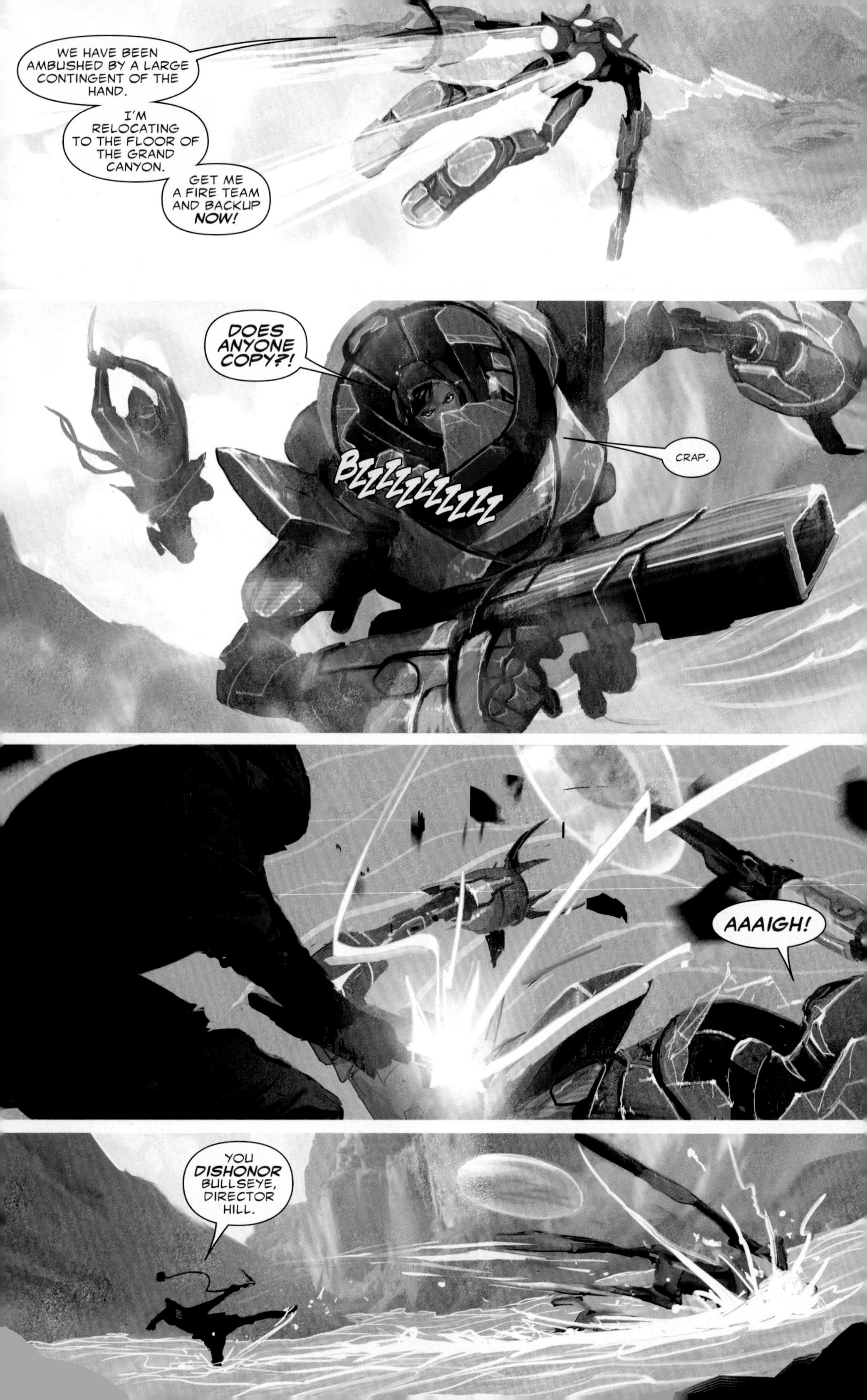
WE HAVE BEEN AMBUSHED BY A LARGE CONTINGENT OF THE HAND.
I'M RELOCATING TO THE FLOOR OF THE GRAND CANYON.
GET ME A FIRE TEAM AND BACKUP NOW!
DOES ANYONE COPY?!
BZZZZZZZZZZZZ
CRAP.
AAAIGH!
YOU DISHONOR BULLSEYE, DIRECTOR HILL.

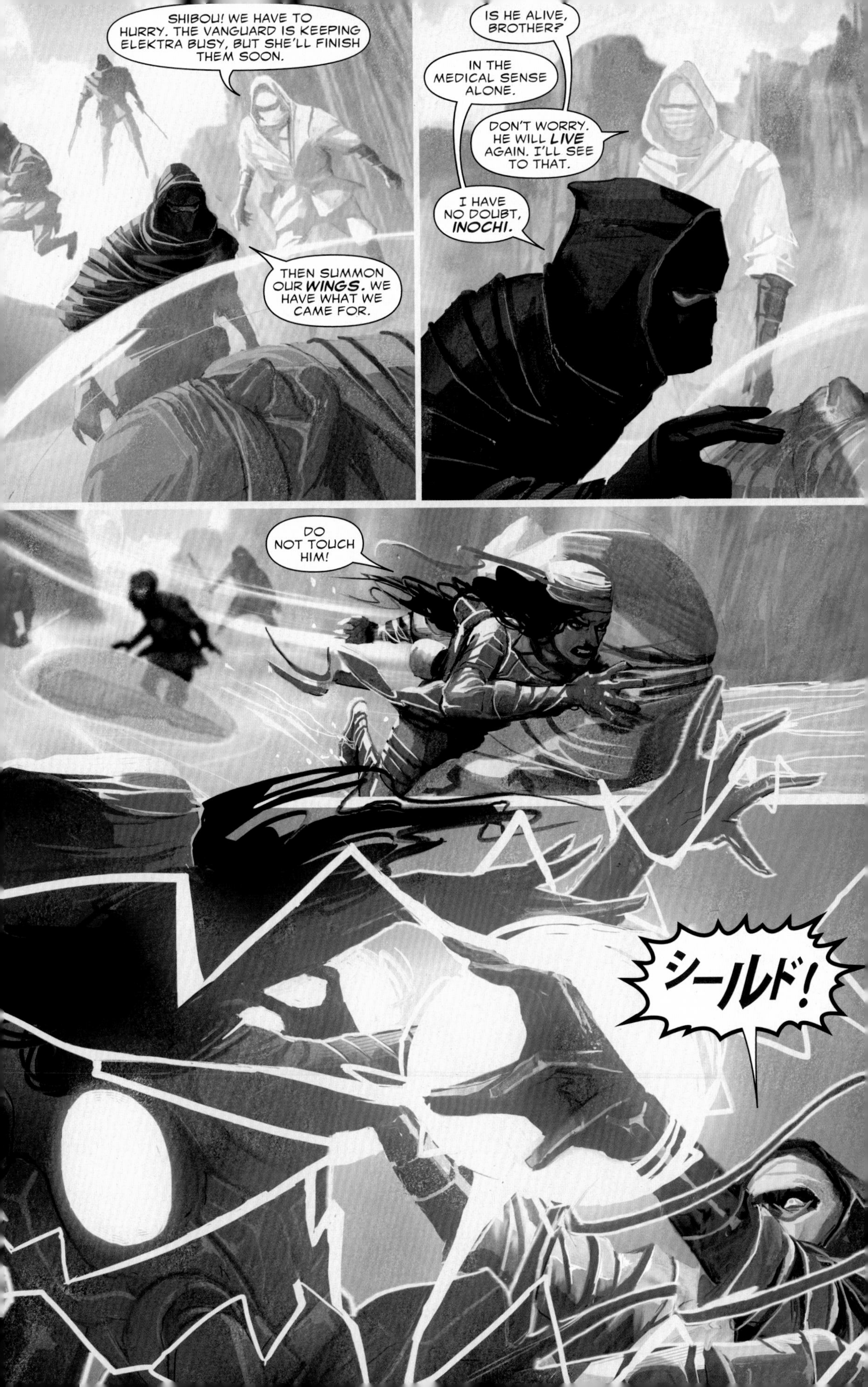
SHIBOU! WE HAVE TO HURRY. THE VANGUARD IS KEEPING ELEKTRA BUSY, BUT SHE'LL FINISH THEM SOON.
THEN SUMMON OUR **WINGS.** WE HAVE WHAT WE CAME FOR.
IS HE ALIVE, BROTHER?
IN THE MEDICAL SENSE ALONE.
DON'T WORRY. HE WILL **LIVE** AGAIN. I'LL SEE TO THAT.
I HAVE NO DOUBT, **INOCHI.**
DO NOT TOUCH HIM!
シールド!

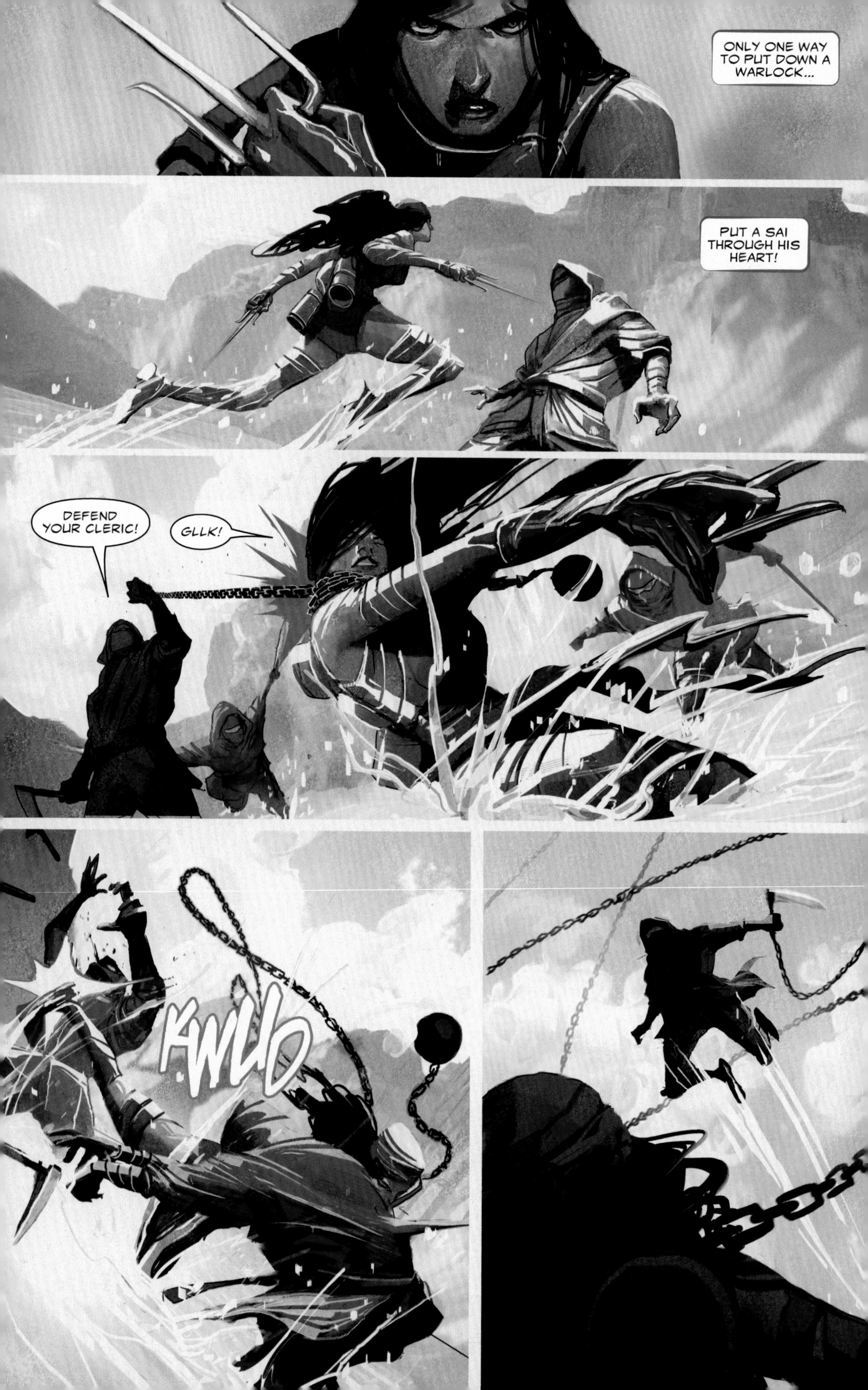
ONLY ONE WAY TO PUT DOWN A WARLOCK...
PUT A SAI THROUGH HIS HEART!
DEFEND YOUR CLERIC!
GLLK!
KWUD

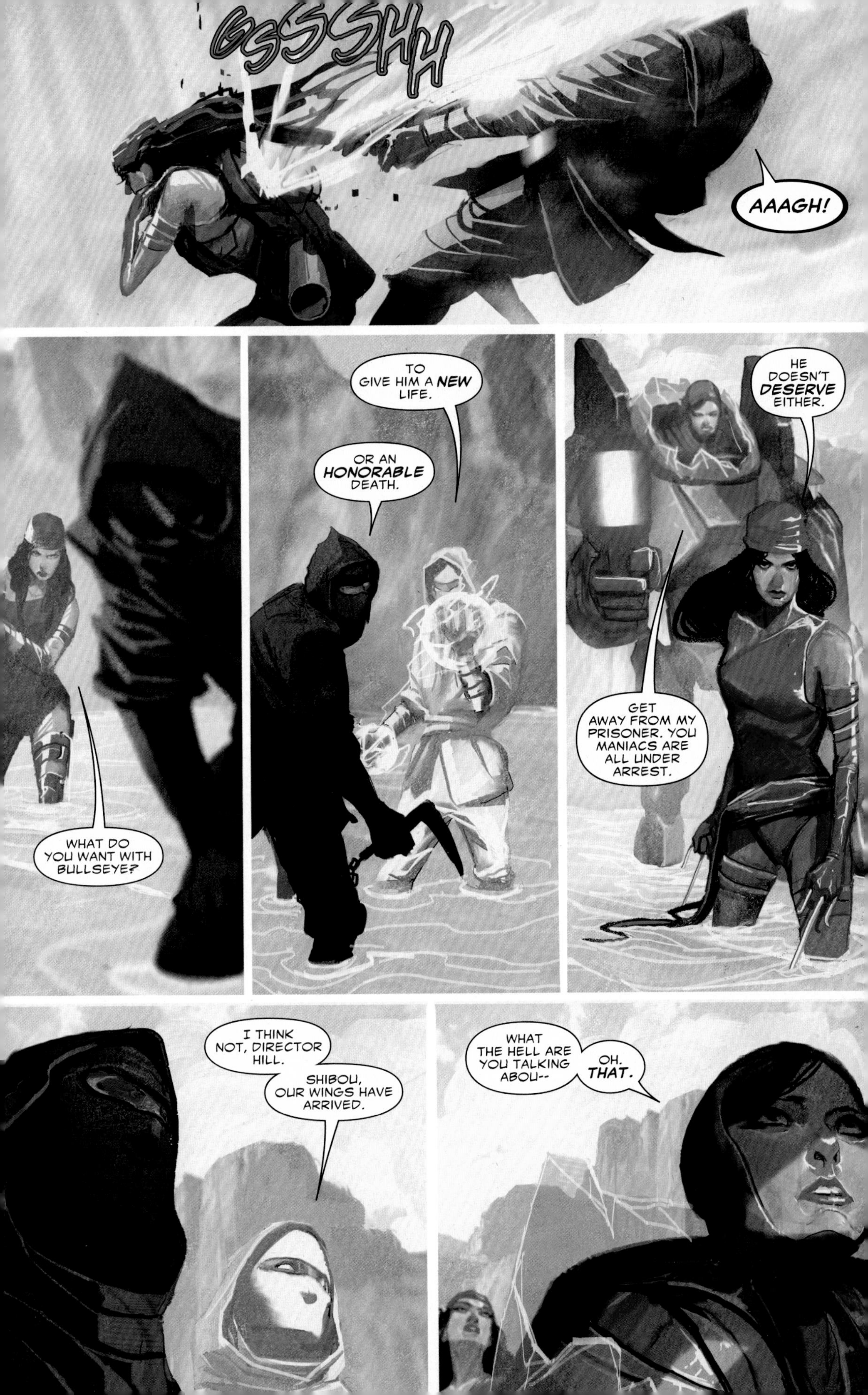
GSSSHH
AAAGH!
WHAT DO YOU WANT WITH BULLSEYE?
TO GIVE HIM A NEW LIFE.
OR AN HONORABLE DEATH.
HE DOESN'T DESERVE EITHER.
GET AWAY FROM MY PRISONER. YOU MANIACS ARE ALL UNDER ARREST.
I THINK NOT, DIRECTOR HILL.
SHIBOU, OUR WINGS HAVE ARRIVED.
WHAT THE HELL ARE YOU TALKING ABOU--
OH. THAT.

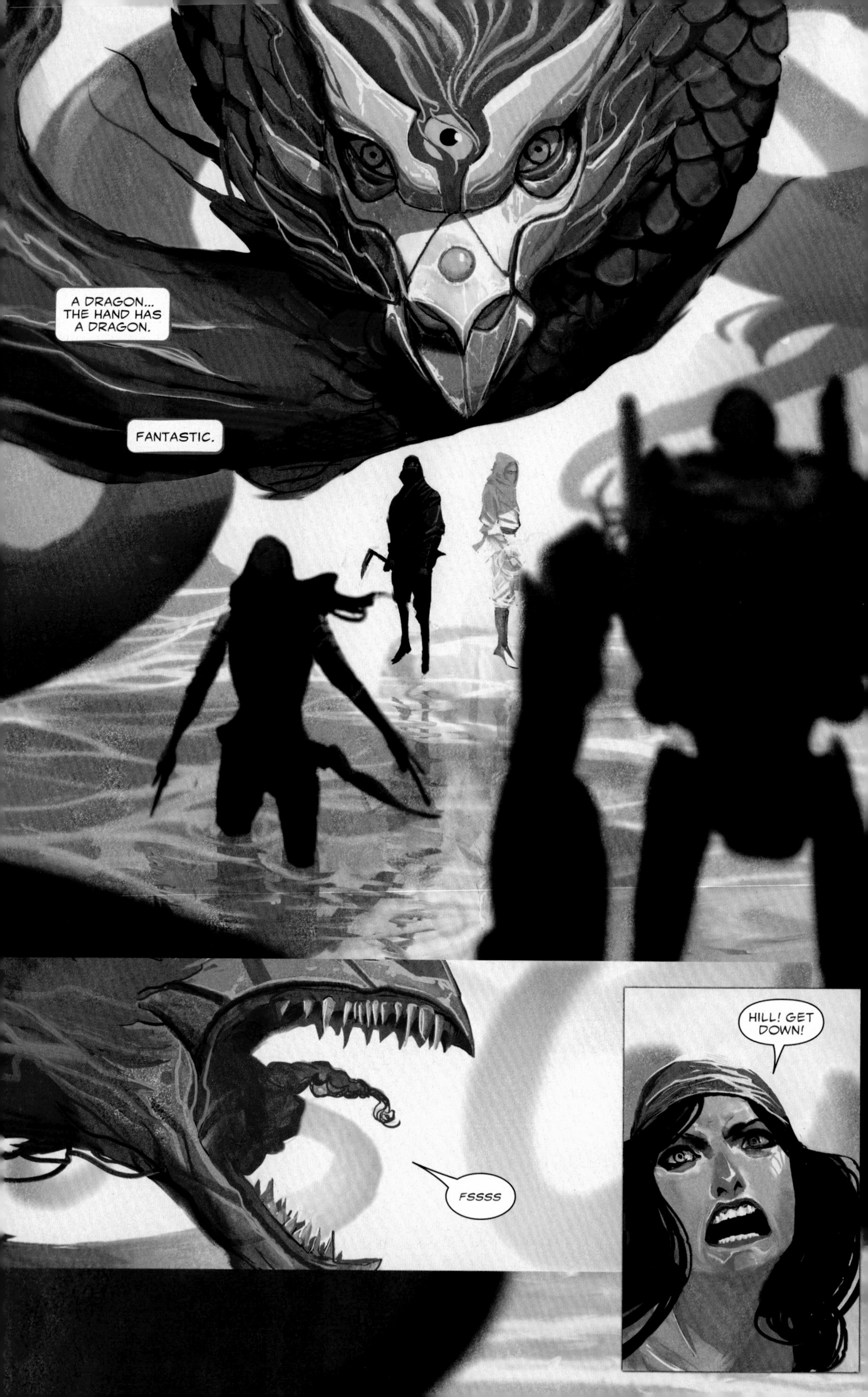
A DRAGON...
THE HAND HAS
A DRAGON.
FANTASTIC.
FSSSS
HILL! GET
DOWN!

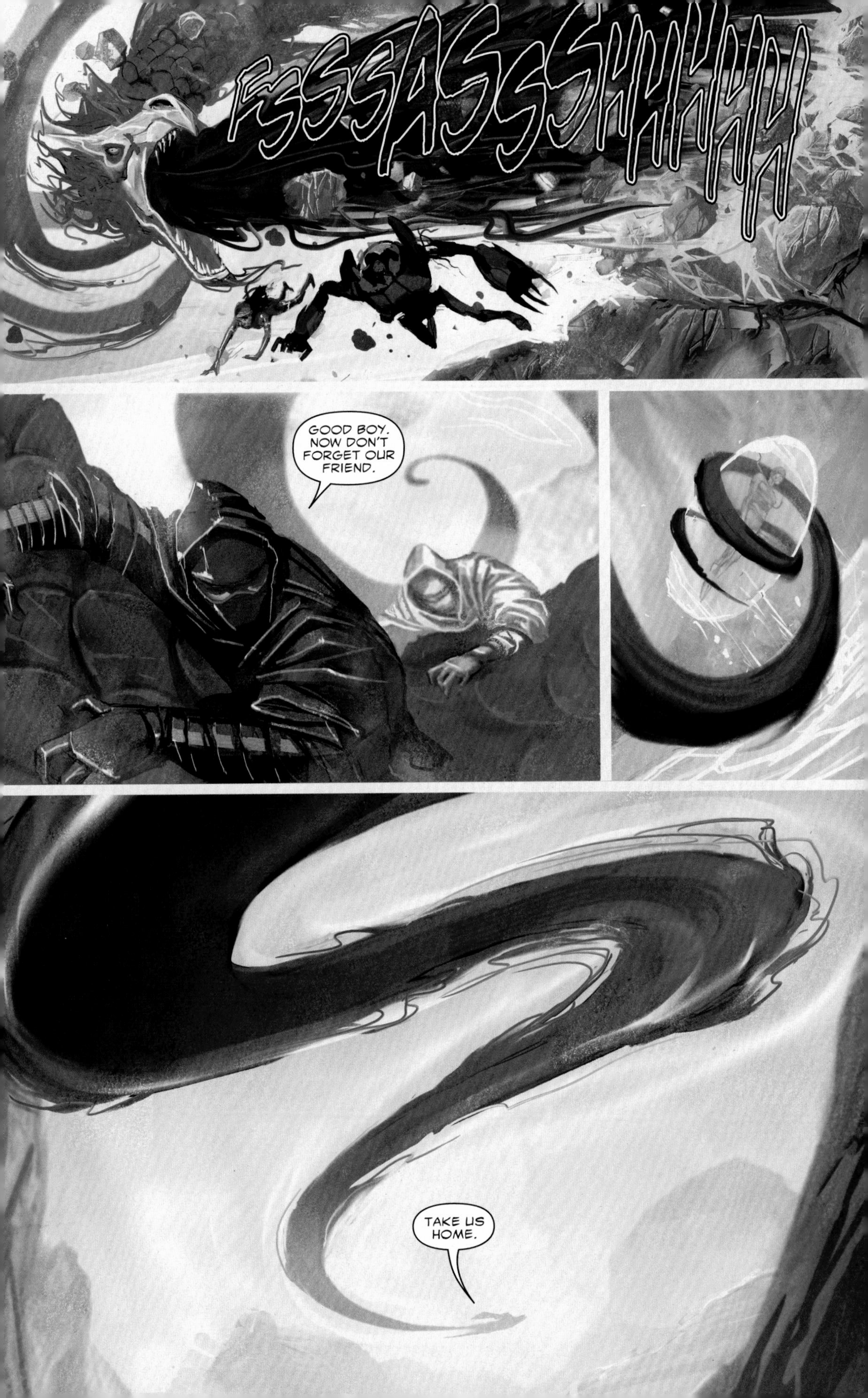
FSSSASSSHHHHH
GOOD BOY. NOW DON'T FORGET OUR FRIEND.
TAKE US HOME.

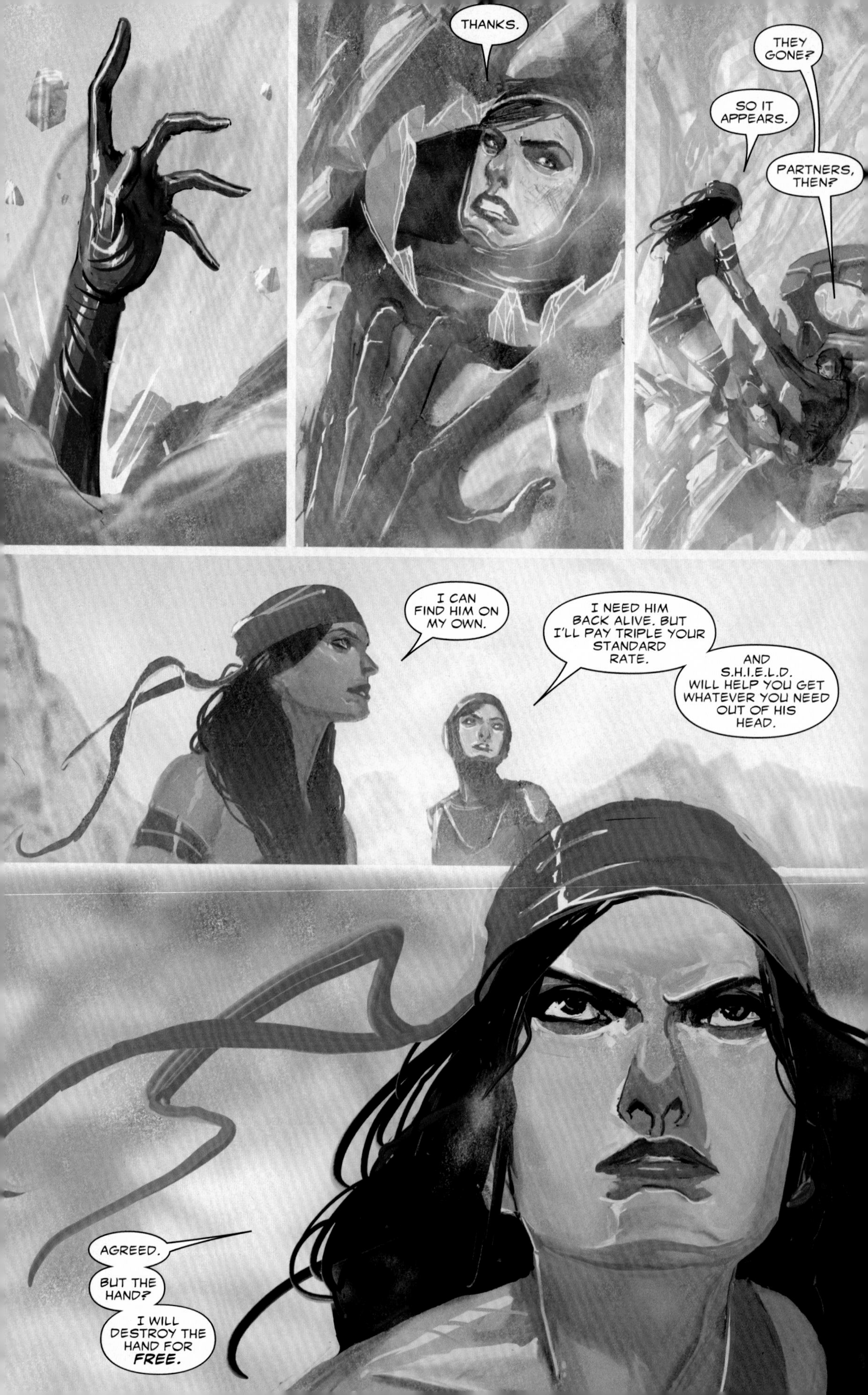
THANKS.
THEY GONE?
SO IT APPEARS.
PARTNERS, THEN?
I CAN FIND HIM ON MY OWN.
I NEED HIM BACK ALIVE. BUT I'LL PAY TRIPLE YOUR STANDARD RATE.
AND S.H.I.E.L.D. WILL HELP YOU GET WHATEVER YOU NEED OUT OF HIS HEAD.
AGREED.
BUT THE HAND?
I WILL DESTROY THE HAND FOR **FREE**.

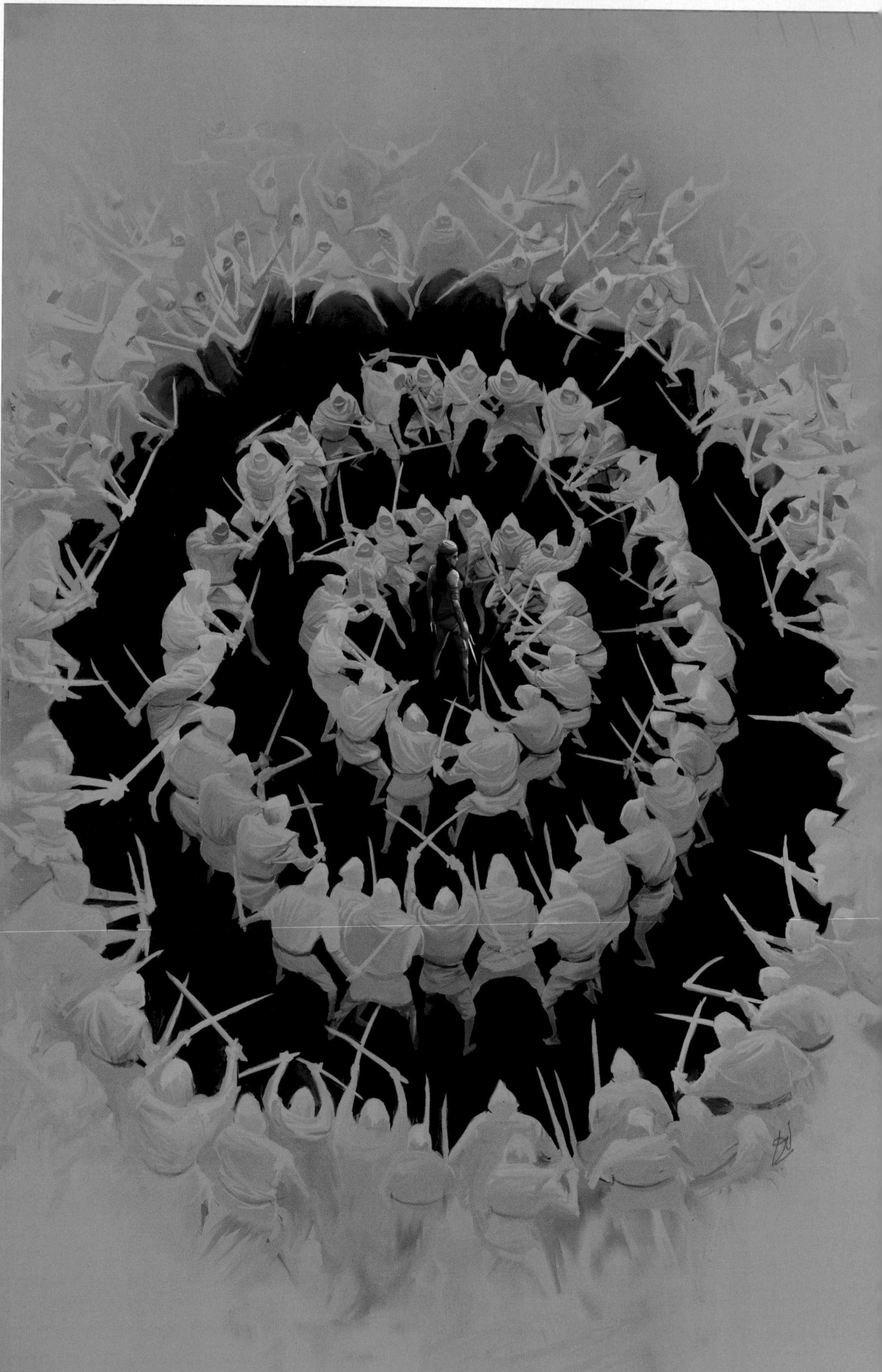

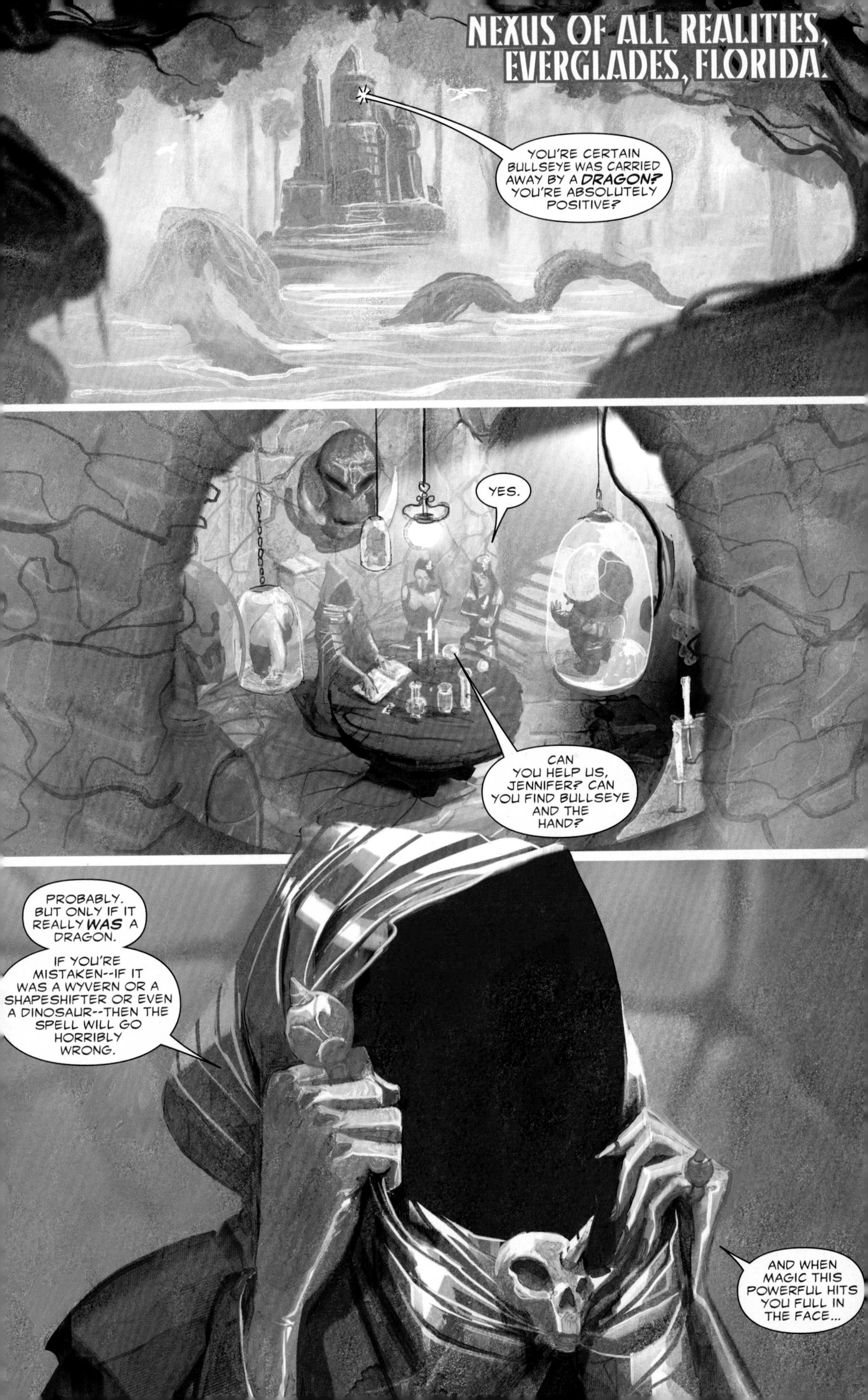
NEXUS OF ALL REALITIES, EVERGLADES, FLORIDA.
YOU'RE CERTAIN BULLSEYE WAS CARRIED AWAY BY A DRAGON? YOU'RE ABSOLUTELY POSITIVE?
YES.
CAN YOU HELP US, JENNIFER? CAN YOU FIND BULLSEYE AND THE HAND?
PROBABLY. BUT ONLY IF IT REALLY WAS A DRAGON.
IF YOU'RE MISTAKEN--IF IT WAS A WYVERN OR A SHAPESHIFTER OR EVEN A DINOSAUR--THEN THE SPELL WILL GO HORRIBLY WRONG.
AND WHEN MAGIC THIS POWERFUL HITS YOU FULL IN THE FACE...

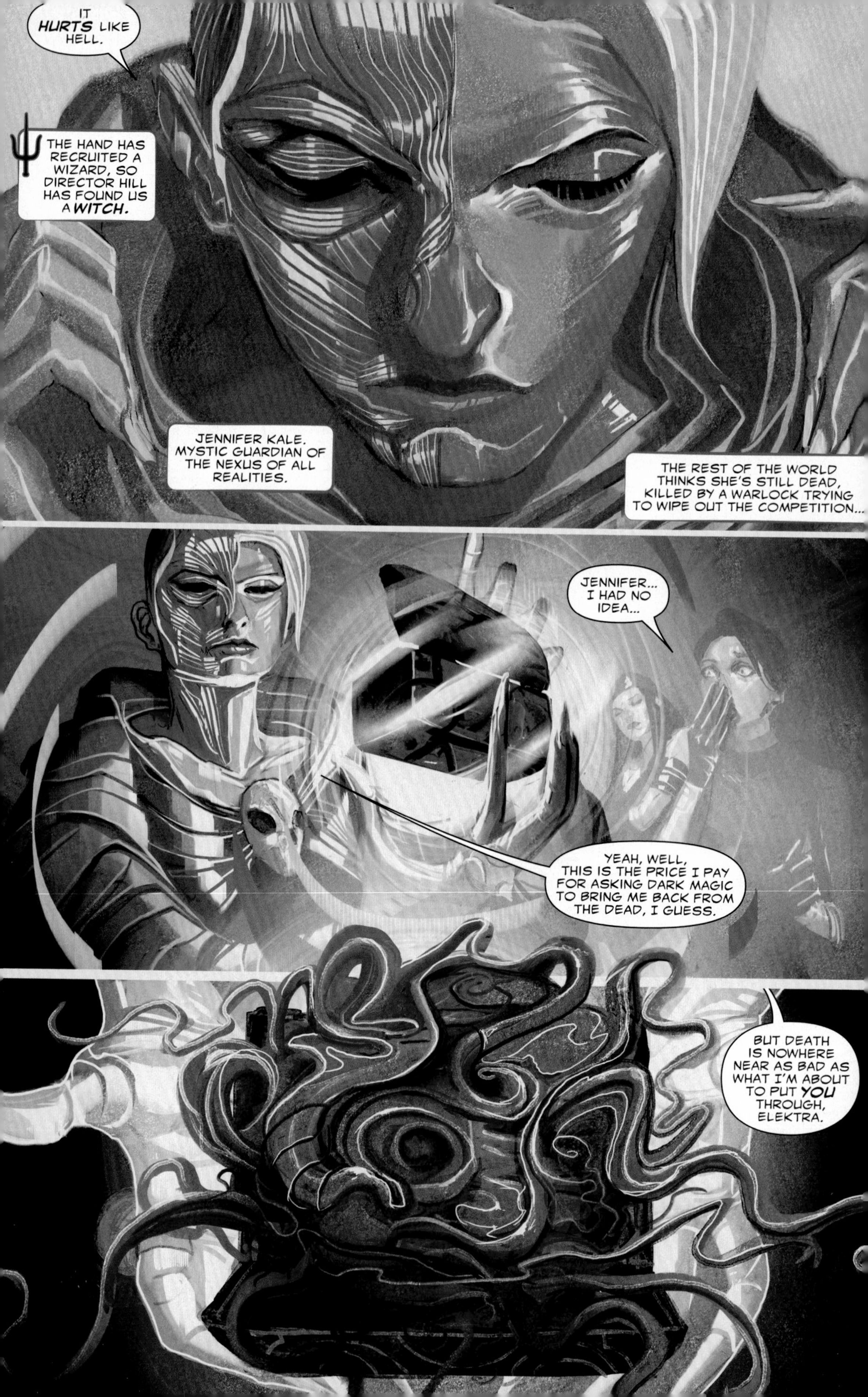
IT HURTS LIKE HELL.
THE HAND HAS RECRUITED A WIZARD, SO DIRECTOR HILL HAS FOUND US A WITCH.
JENNIFER KALE. MYSTIC GUARDIAN OF THE NEXUS OF ALL REALITIES.
THE REST OF THE WORLD THINKS SHE'S STILL DEAD, KILLED BY A WARLOCK TRYING TO WIPE OUT THE COMPETITION...
JENNIFER... I HAD NO IDEA...
YEAH, WELL, THIS IS THE PRICE I PAY FOR ASKING DARK MAGIC TO BRING ME BACK FROM THE DEAD, I GUESS.
BUT DEATH IS NOWHERE NEAR AS BAD AS WHAT I'M ABOUT TO PUT YOU THROUGH, ELEKTRA.

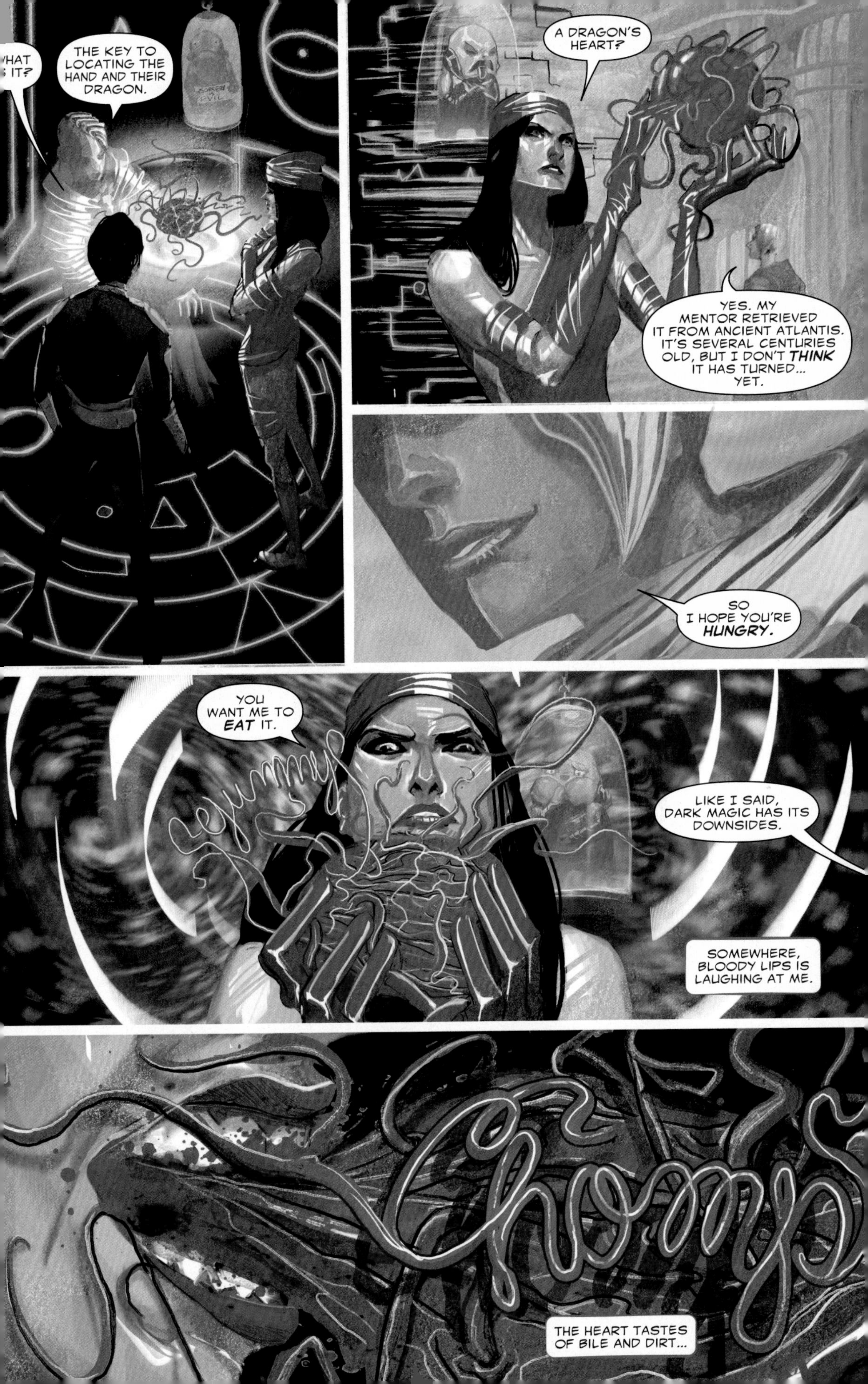
WHAT IS IT?
THE KEY TO LOCATING THE HAND AND THEIR DRAGON.
SORCERY EVIL
A DRAGON'S HEART?
YES. MY MENTOR RETRIEVED IT FROM ANCIENT ATLANTIS. IT'S SEVERAL CENTURIES OLD, BUT I DON'T **THINK** IT HAS TURNED... YET.
SO I HOPE YOU'RE **HUNGRY.**
YOU WANT ME TO **EAT** IT.
LIKE I SAID, DARK MAGIC HAS ITS DOWNSIDES.
SOMEWHERE, BLOODY LIPS IS LAUGHING AT ME.
Chomp
THE HEART TASTES OF BILE AND DIRT...

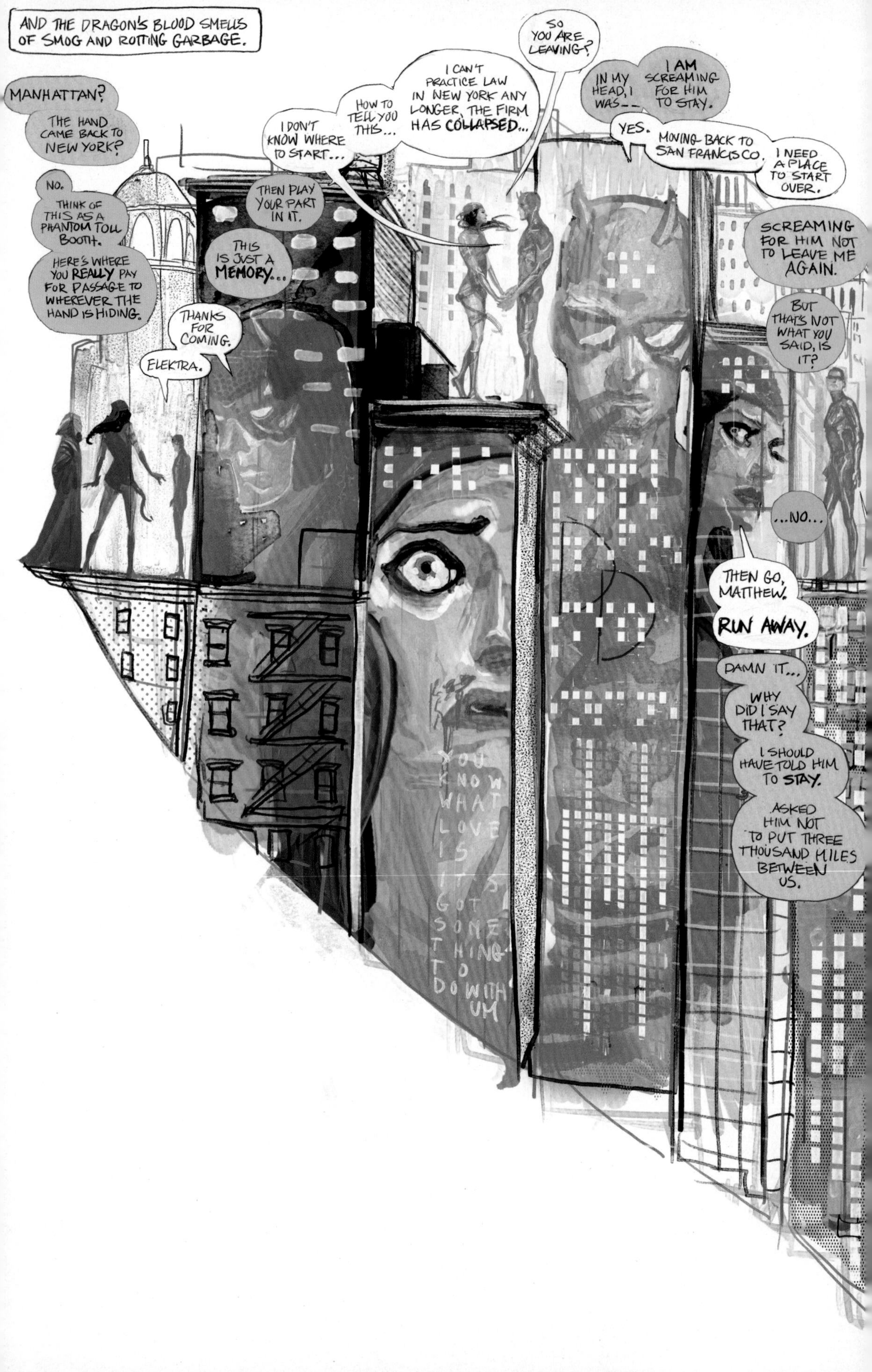

AND THE DRAGON'S BLOOD SMELLS OF SMOG AND ROTTING GARBAGE.
MANHATTAN?
THE HAND CAME BACK TO NEW YORK?
NO.
THINK OF THIS AS A PHANTOM TOLL BOOTH.
HERE'S WHERE YOU **REALLY** PAY FOR PASSAGE TO WHEREVER THE HAND IS HIDING.
THANKS FOR COMING.
ELEKTRA.
THEN PLAY YOUR PART IN IT.
THIS IS JUST A **MEMORY...**
I DON'T KNOW WHERE TO START...
HOW TO TELL YOU THIS...
I CAN'T PRACTICE LAW IN NEW YORK ANY LONGER, THE FIRM HAS **COLLAPSED...**
SO YOU ARE LEAVING?
YES.
MOVING BACK TO SAN FRANCISCO.
I NEED A PLACE TO START OVER.
IN MY HEAD, I WAS--
I AM SCREAMING FOR HIM TO STAY.
SCREAMING FOR HIM NOT TO LEAVE ME AGAIN.
BUT THAT'S NOT WHAT YOU SAID, IS IT?
...NO...
THEN GO, MATTHEW.
RUN AWAY.
DAMN IT...
WHY DID I SAY THAT?
I SHOULD HAVE TOLD HIM TO **STAY.**
ASKED HIM NOT TO PUT THREE THOUSAND MILES BETWEEN US.

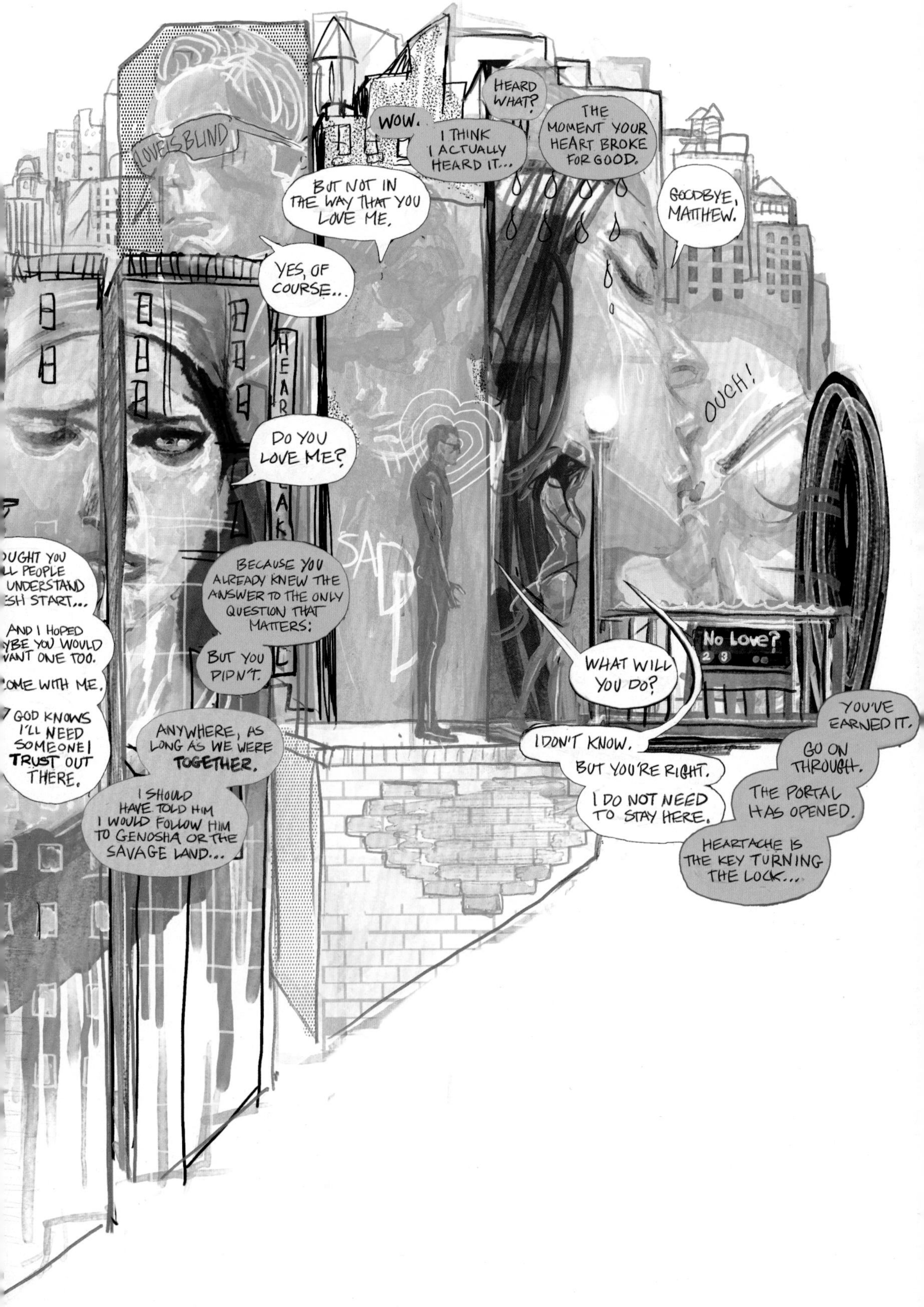
LOVE IS BLIND
OUGHT YOU LL PEOPLE UNDERSTAND ESH START...
AND I HOPED YBE YOU WOULD VANT ONE TOO.
OME WITH ME.
GOD KNOWS I'LL NEED SOMEONE I TRUST OUT THERE.
ANYWHERE, AS LONG AS WE WERE TOGETHER.
I SHOULD HAVE TOLD HIM I WOULD FOLLOW HIM TO GENOSHA OR THE SAVAGE LAND...
DO YOU LOVE ME?
YES, OF COURSE...
BUT NOT IN THE WAY THAT YOU LOVE ME.
BECAUSE YOU ALREADY KNEW THE ANSWER TO THE ONLY QUESTION THAT MATTERS:
BUT YOU DIDN'T.
WOW.
I THINK I ACTUALLY HEARD IT...
HEARD WHAT?
THE MOMENT YOUR HEART BROKE FOR GOOD.
GOODBYE, MATTHEW.
OUCH!
No Love?
WHAT WILL YOU DO?
I DON'T KNOW.
BUT YOU'RE RIGHT.
I DO NOT NEED TO STAY HERE.
YOU'VE EARNED IT.
GO ON THROUGH.
THE PORTAL HAS OPENED.
HEARTACHE IS THE KEY TURNING THE LOCK...

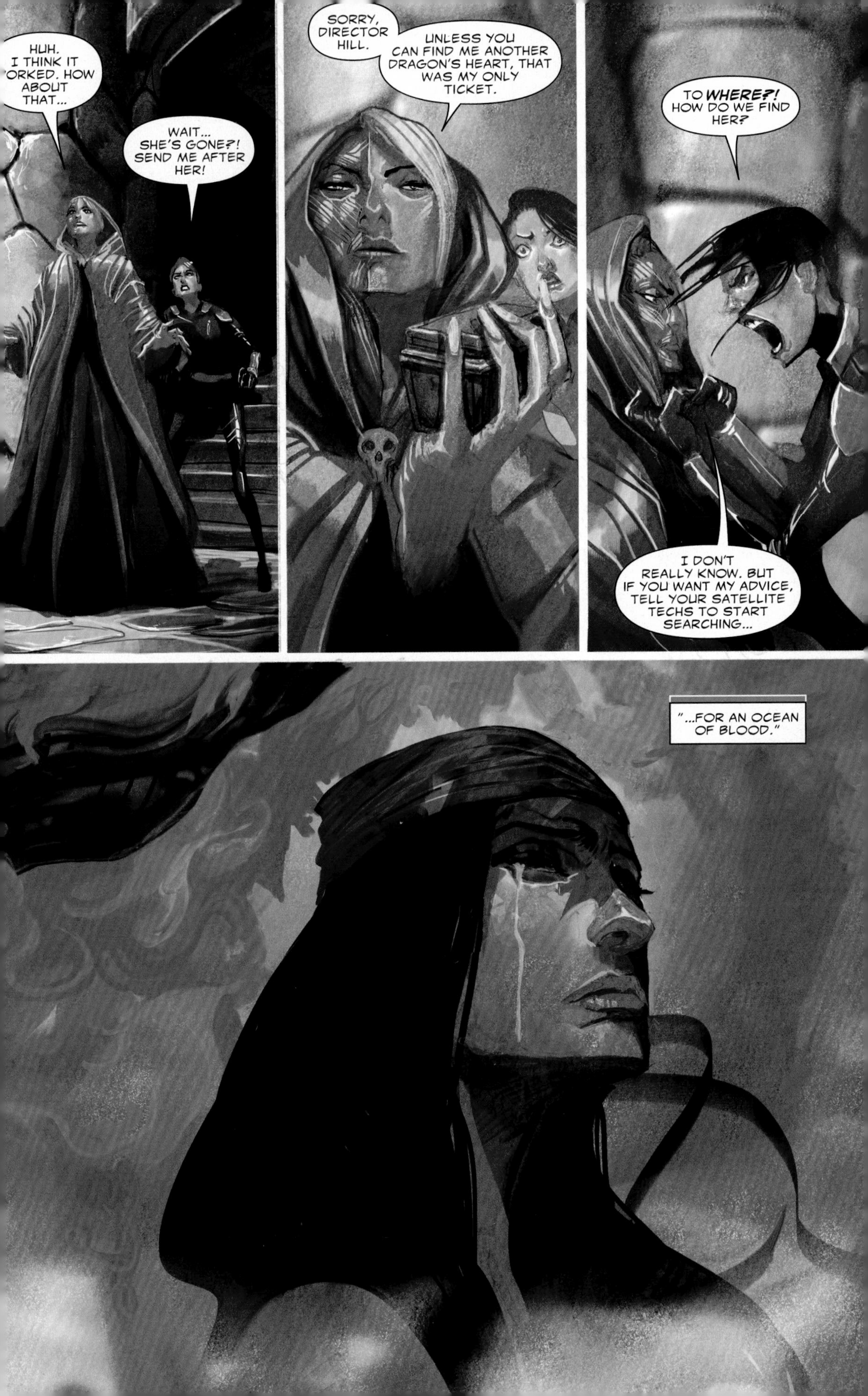
HUH. I THINK IT WORKED. HOW ABOUT THAT...
WAIT... SHE'S GONE?! SEND ME AFTER HER!
SORRY, DIRECTOR HILL.
UNLESS YOU CAN FIND ME ANOTHER DRAGON'S HEART, THAT WAS MY ONLY TICKET.
TO WHERE?! HOW DO WE FIND HER?
I DON'T REALLY KNOW. BUT IF YOU WANT MY ADVICE, TELL YOUR SATELLITE TECHS TO START SEARCHING...
"...FOR AN OCEAN OF BLOOD."

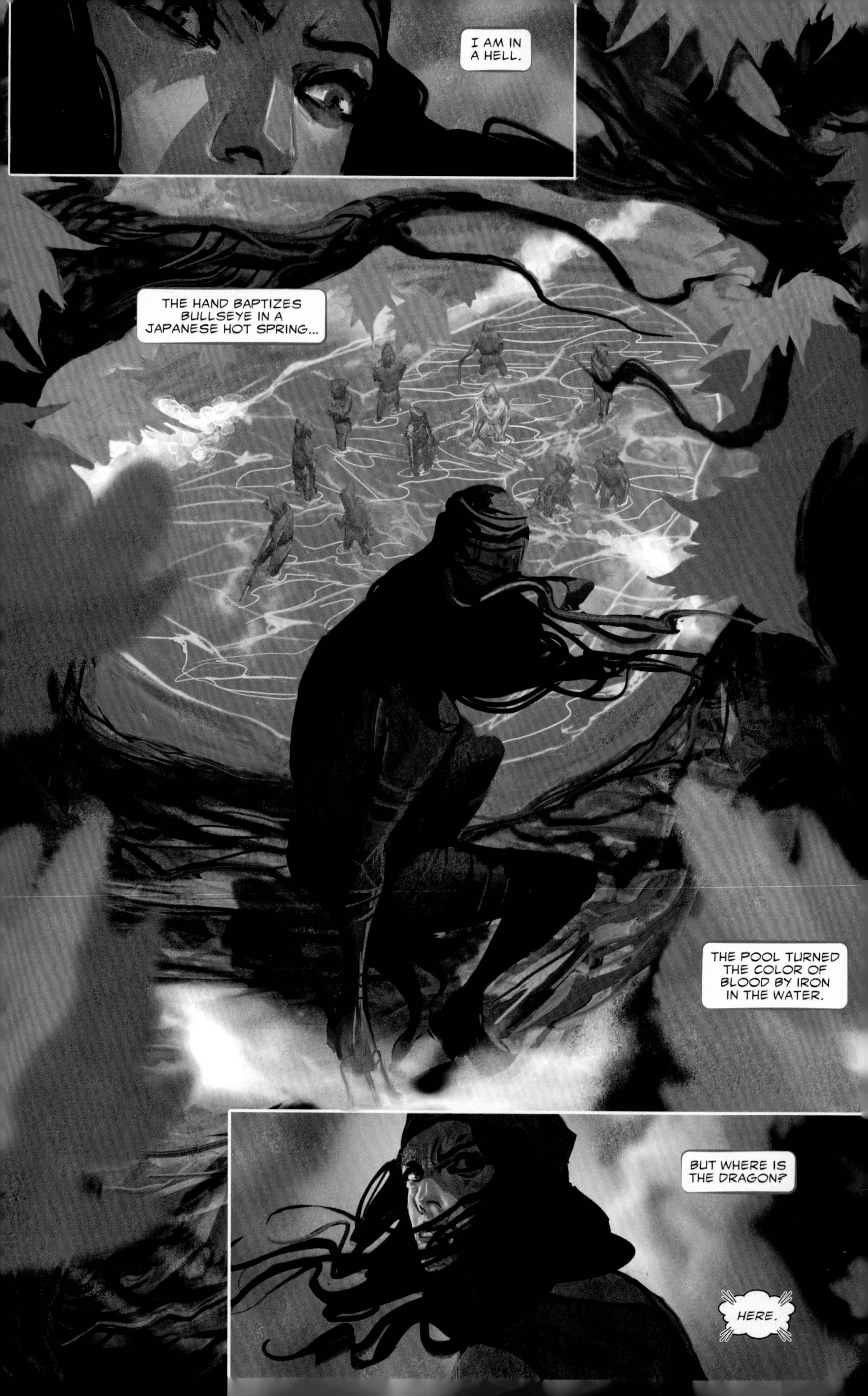
I AM IN A HELL.
THE HAND BAPTIZES BULLSEYE IN A JAPANESE HOT SPRING...
THE POOL TURNED THE COLOR OF BLOOD BY IRON IN THE WATER.
BUT WHERE IS THE DRAGON?
HERE.

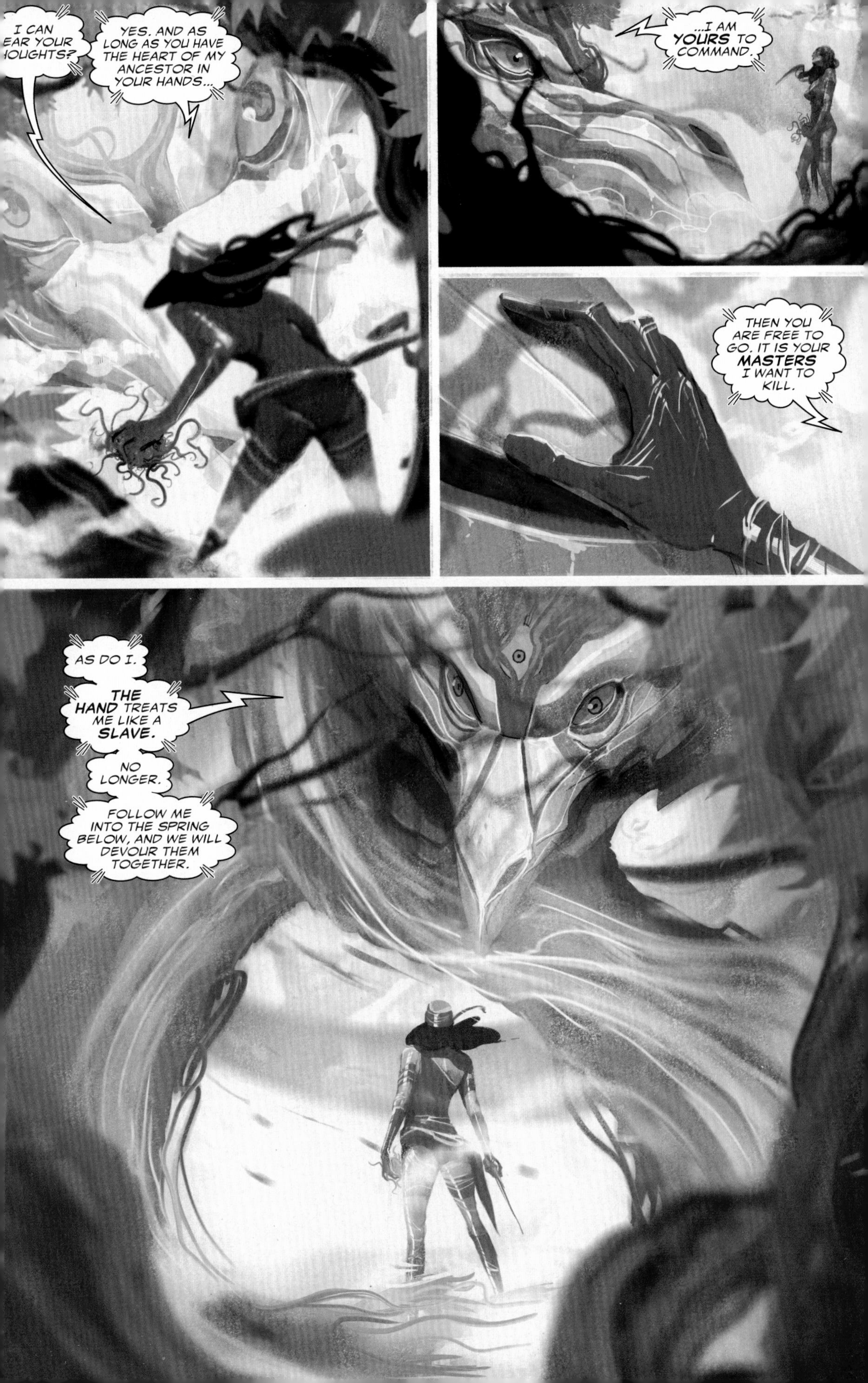
I CAN
EAR YOUR
HOUGHTS?
YES. AND AS LONG AS YOU HAVE THE HEART OF MY ANCESTOR IN YOUR HANDS...
...I AM YOURS TO COMMAND.
THEN YOU ARE FREE TO GO. IT IS YOUR MASTERS I WANT TO KILL.
AS DO I.
THE HAND TREATS ME LIKE A SLAVE.
NO LONGER.
FOLLOW ME INTO THE SPRING BELOW, AND WE WILL DEVOUR THEM TOGETHER.

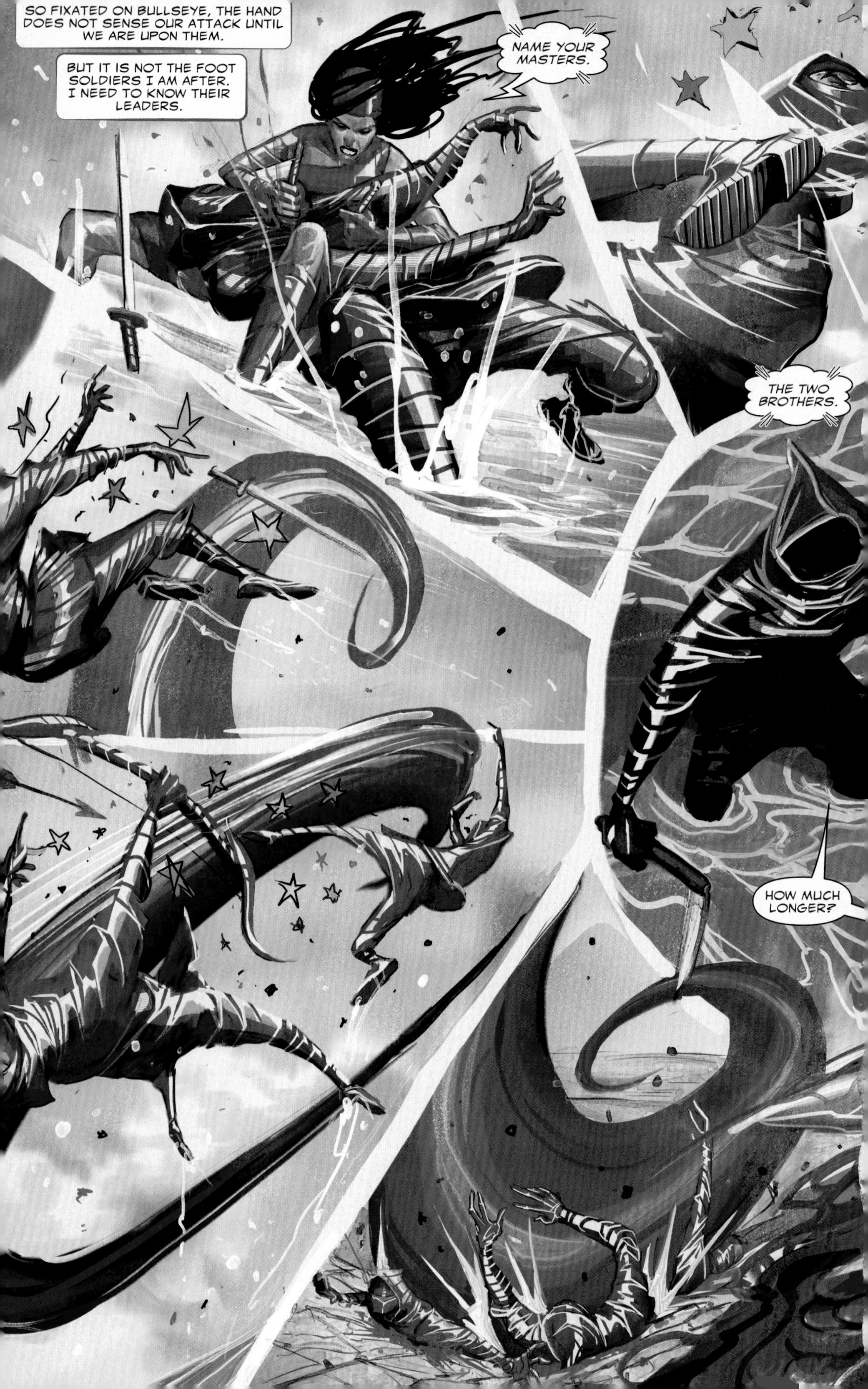
SO FIXATED ON BULLSEYE, THE HAND DOES NOT SENSE OUR ATTACK UNTIL WE ARE UPON THEM.
BUT IT IS NOT THE FOOT SOLDIERS I AM AFTER. I NEED TO KNOW THEIR LEADERS.
NAME YOUR MASTERS.
THE TWO BROTHERS.
HOW MUCH LONGER?

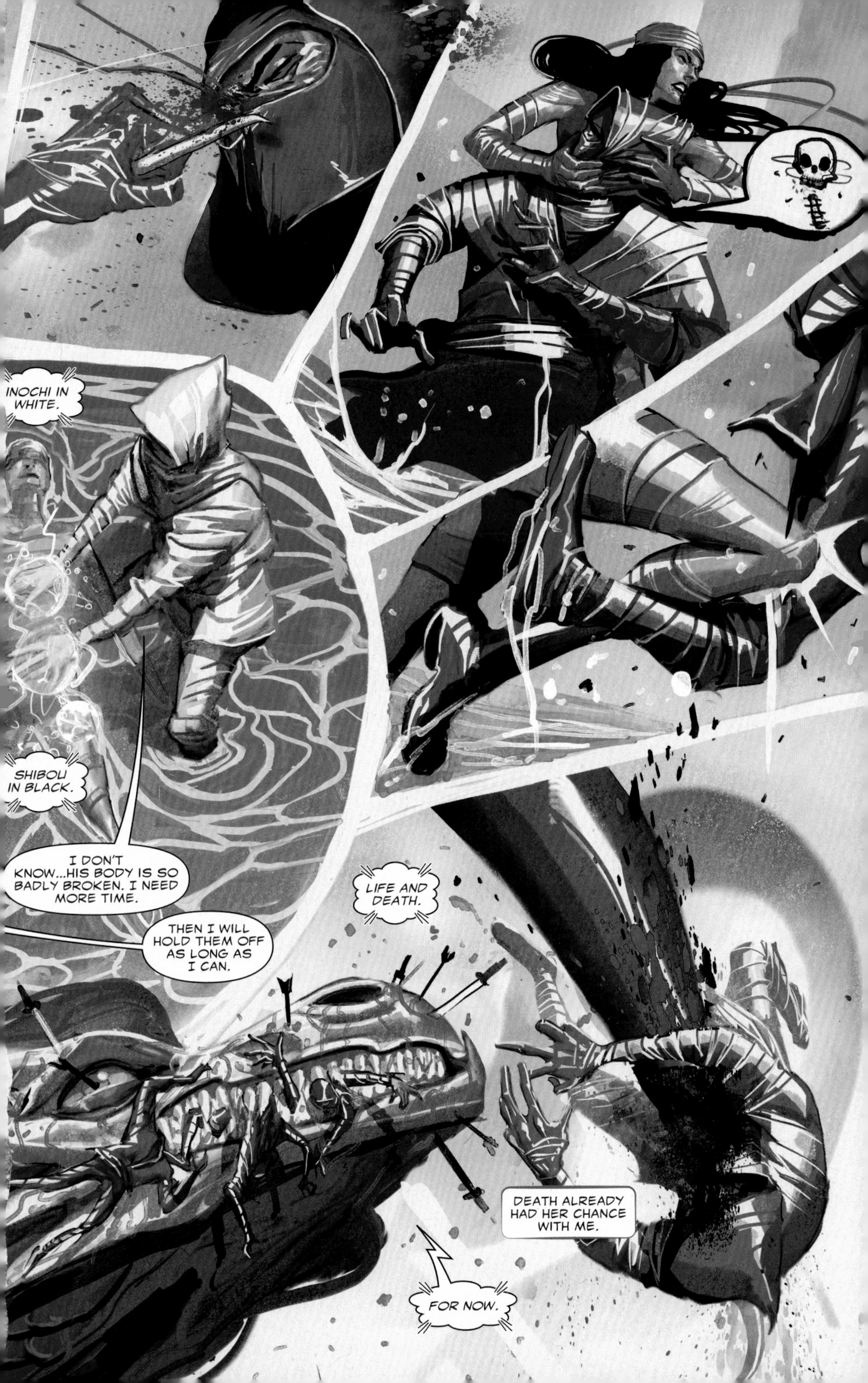
INOCHI IN WHITE.
SHIBOU IN BLACK.
I DON'T KNOW...HIS BODY IS SO BADLY BROKEN. I NEED MORE TIME.
THEN I WILL HOLD THEM OFF AS LONG AS I CAN.
LIFE AND DEATH.
DEATH ALREADY HAD HER CHANCE WITH ME.
FOR NOW.

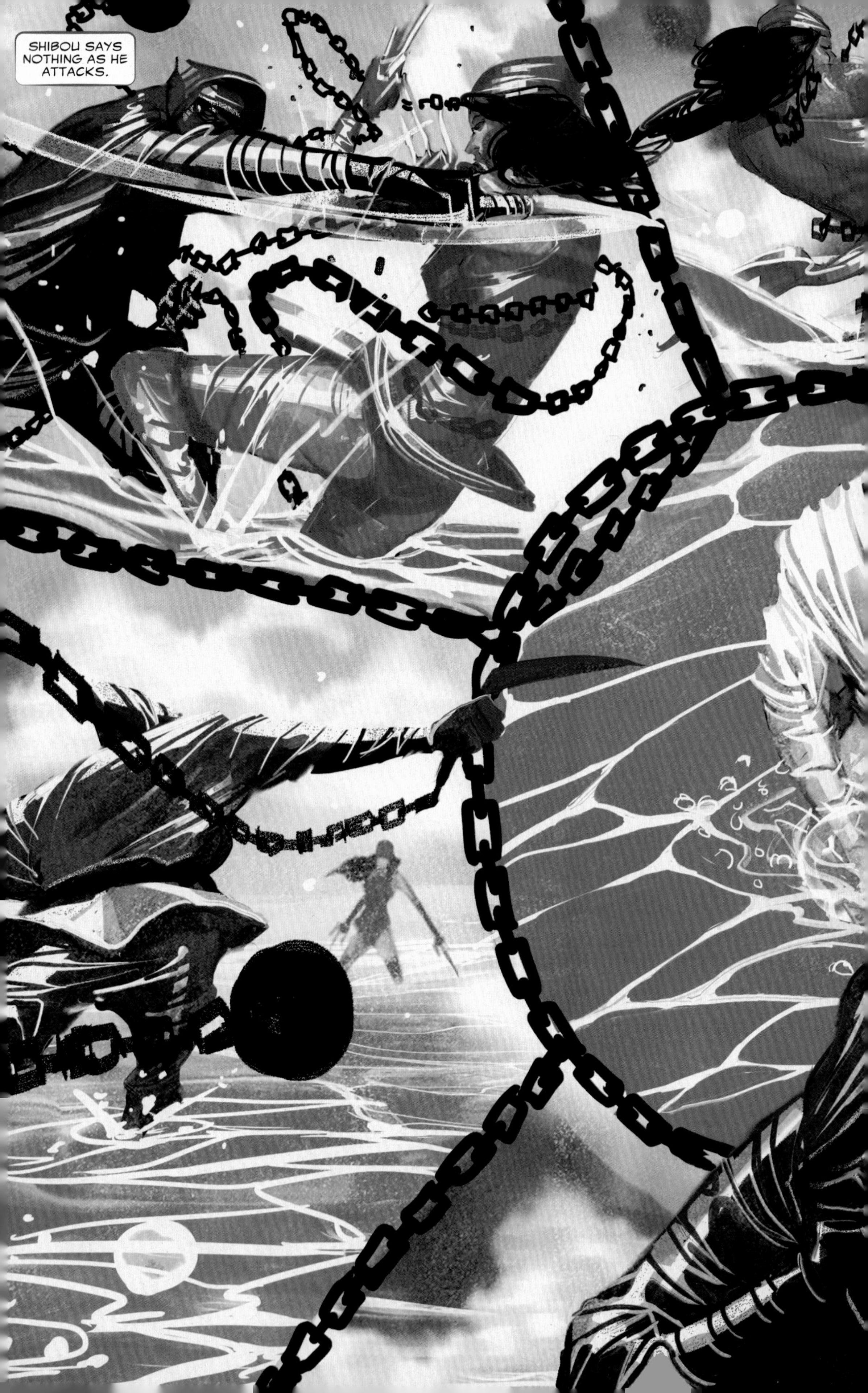
SHIBOU SAYS NOTHING AS HE ATTACKS.

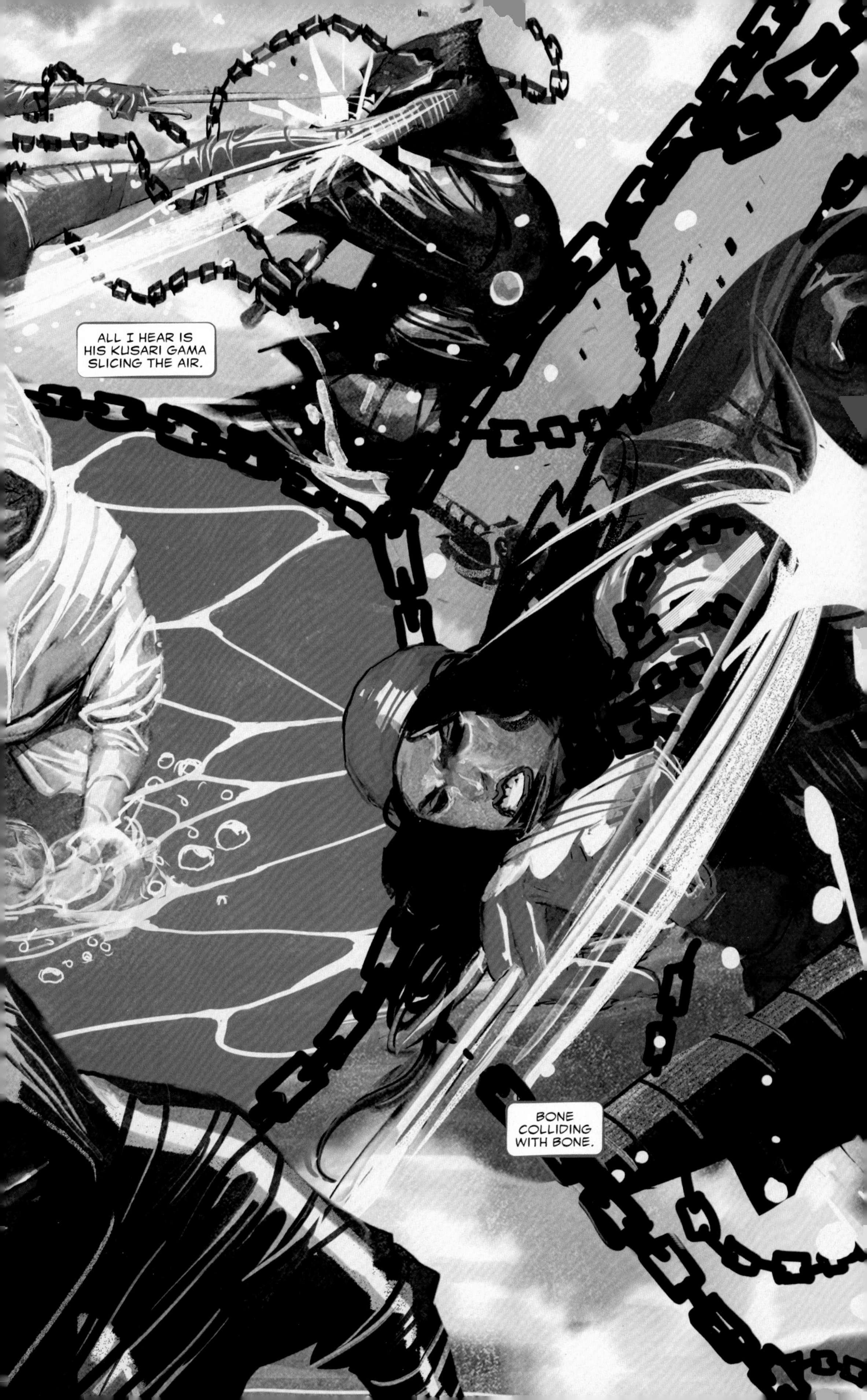
ALL I HEAR IS HIS KUSARI GAMA SLICING THE AIR.
BONE COLLIDING WITH BONE.

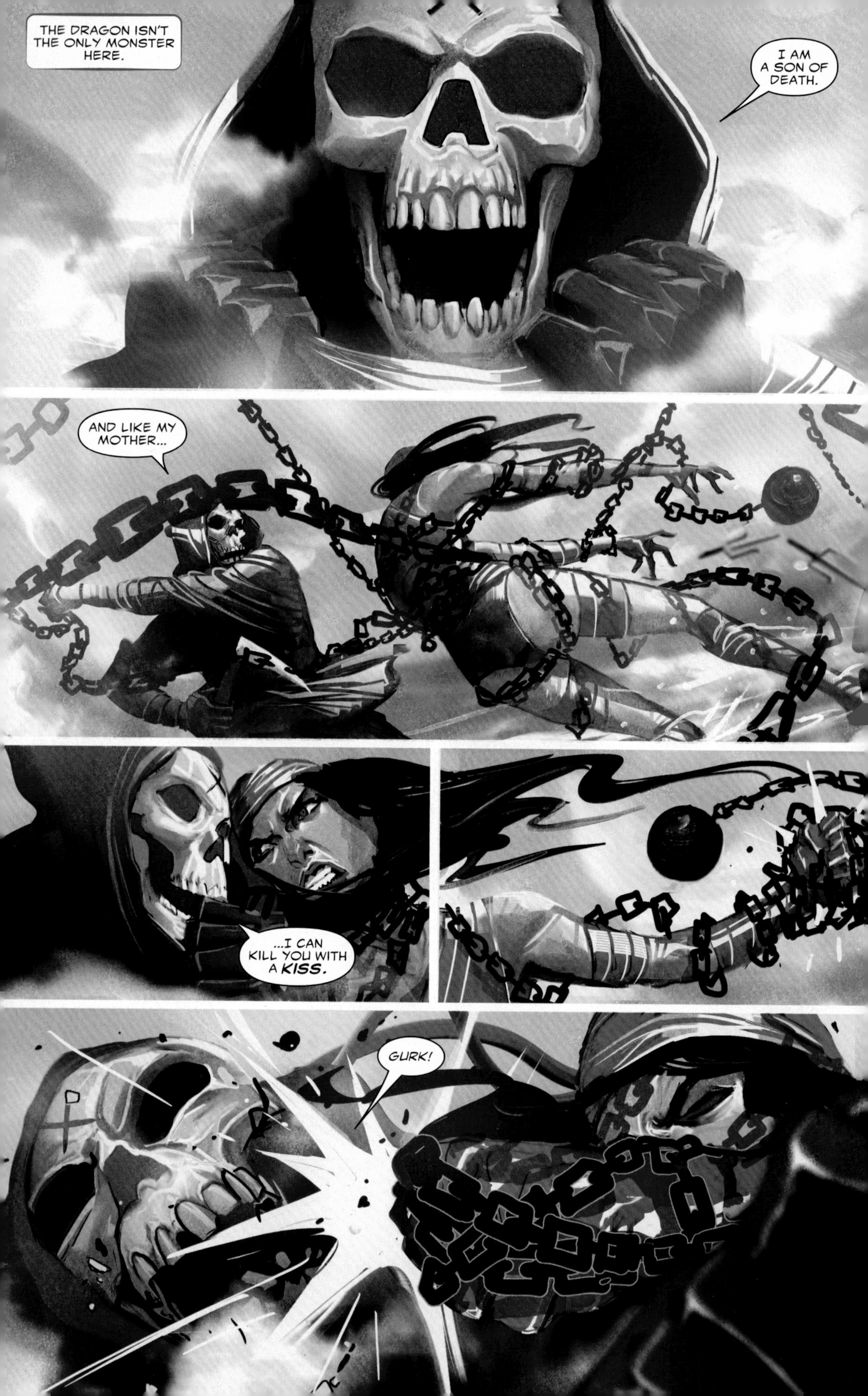
THE DRAGON ISN'T THE ONLY MONSTER HERE.
I AM A SON OF DEATH.
AND LIKE MY MOTHER...
...I CAN KILL YOU WITH A **KISS.**
GURK!

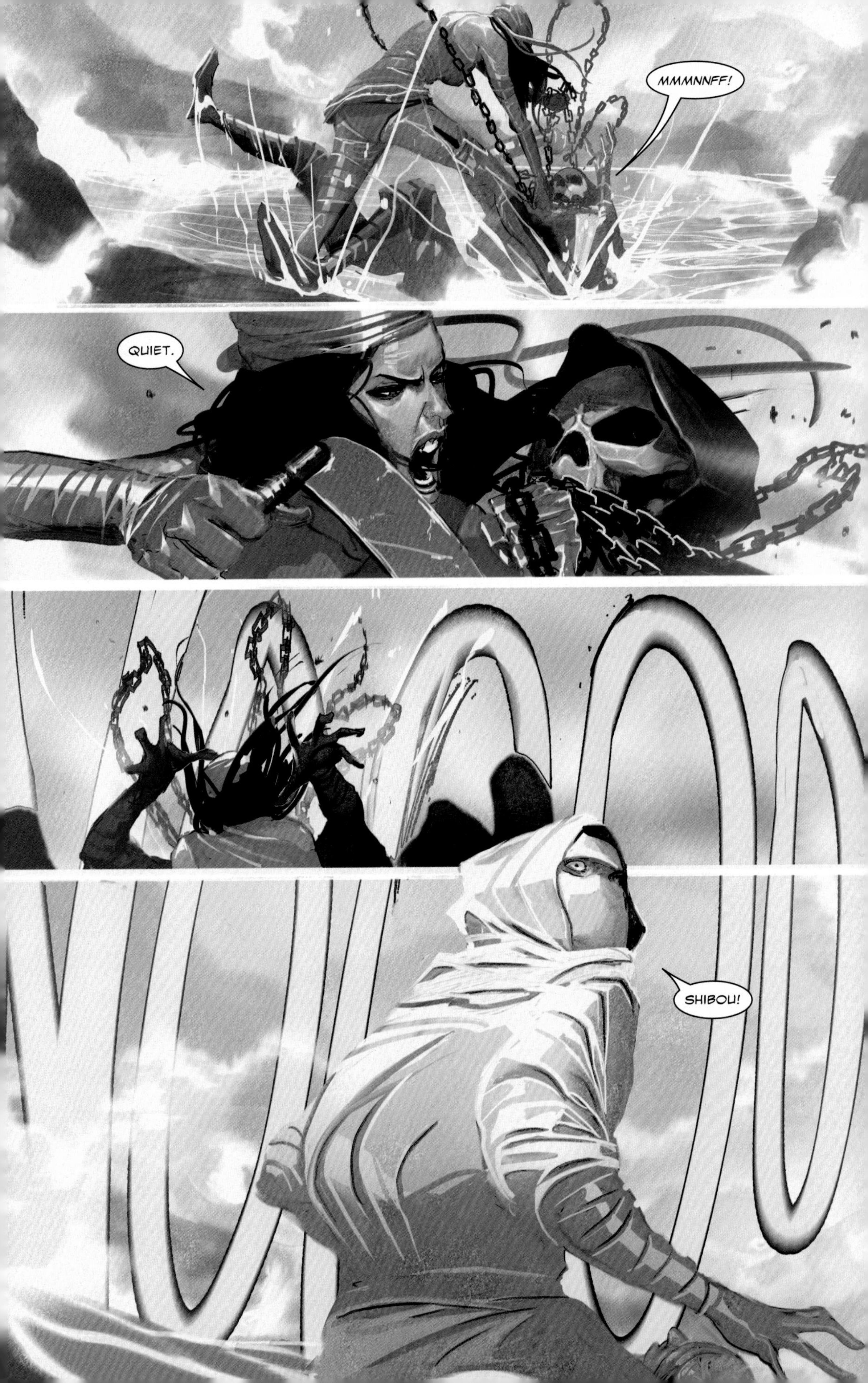
MMMNNFF!
QUIET.
SHIBOU!

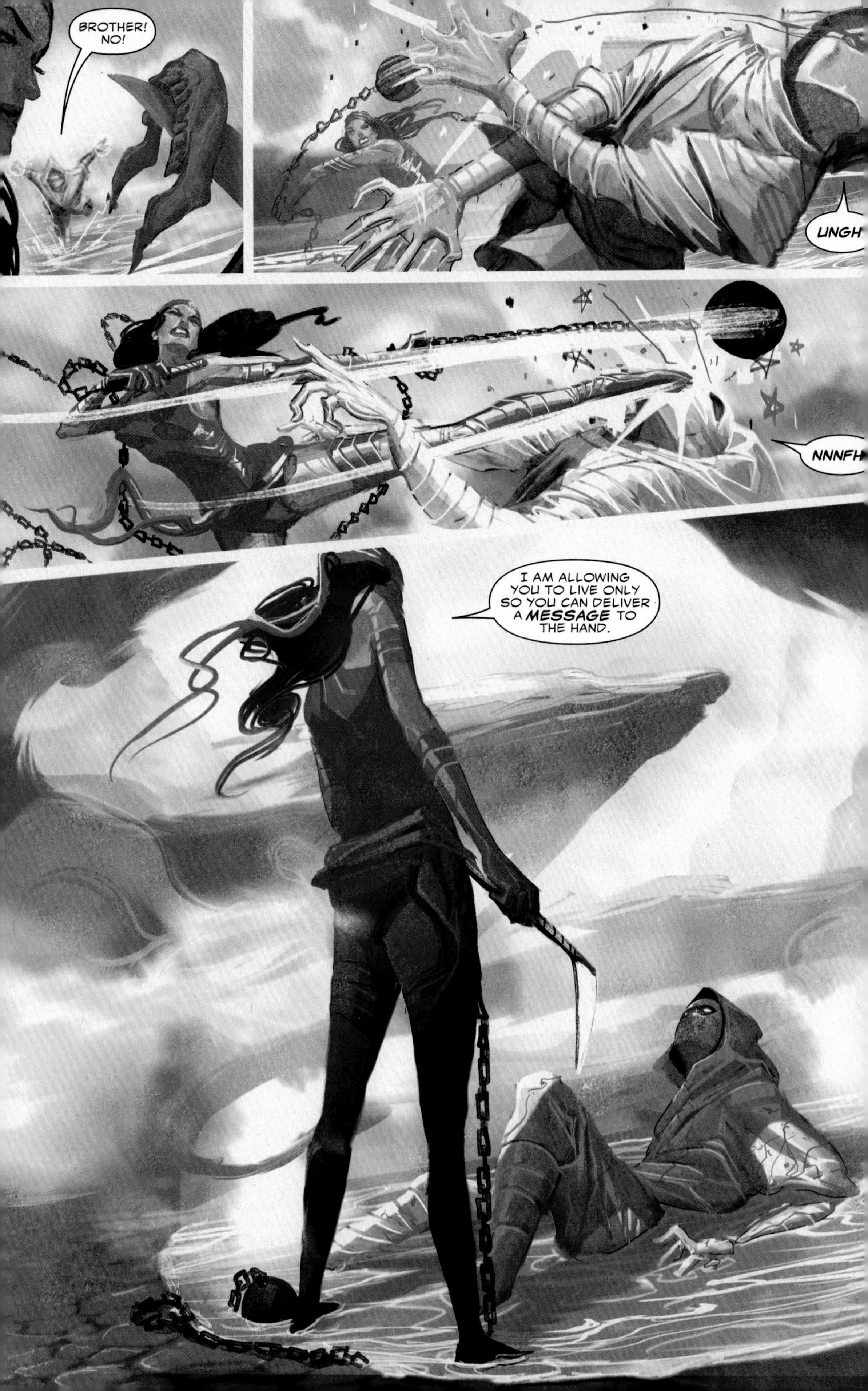
BROTHER! NO!
UNGH
NNNFH
I AM ALLOWING YOU TO LIVE ONLY SO YOU CAN DELIVER A MESSAGE TO THE HAND.

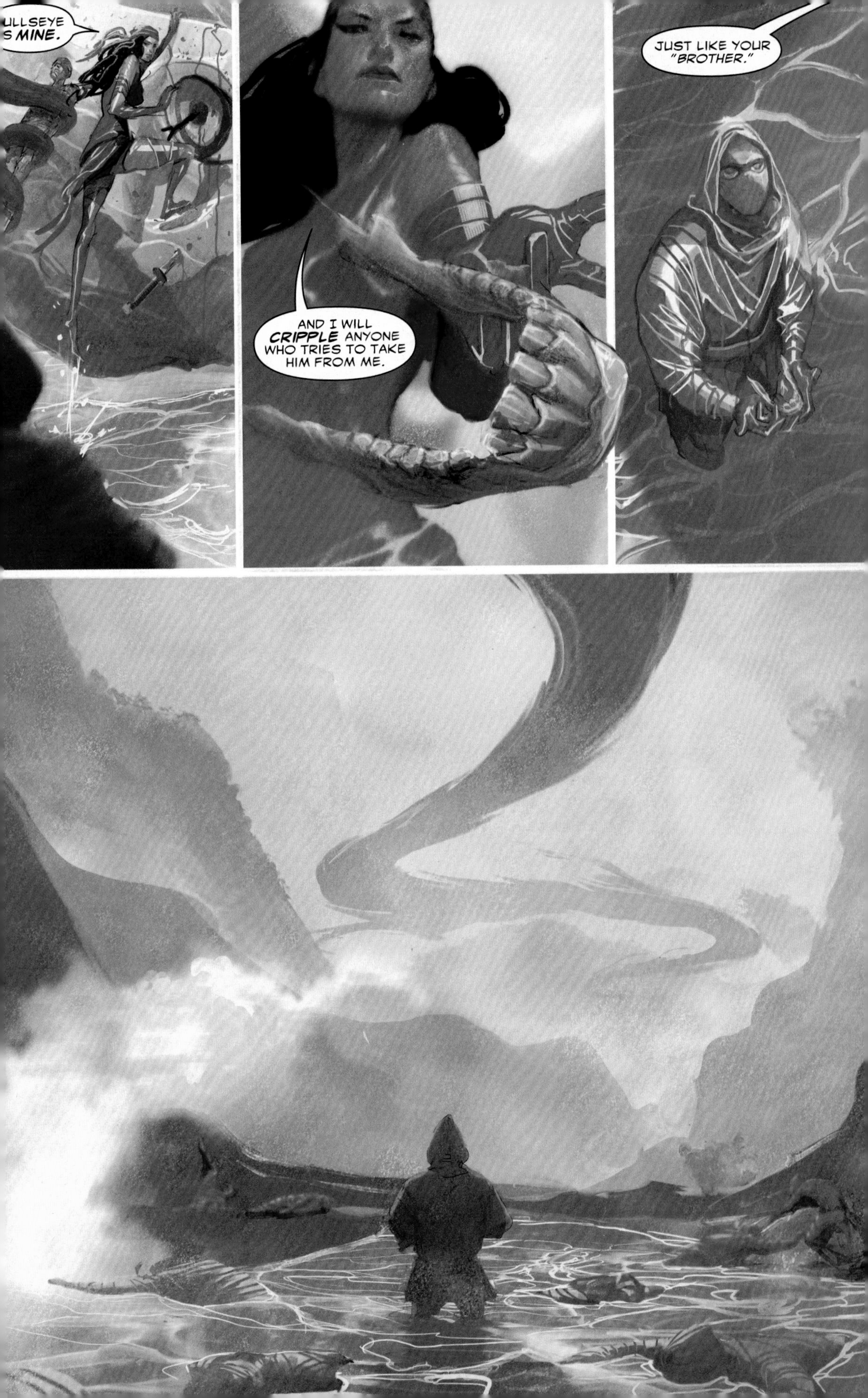
ULLSEYE
S MINE.
AND I WILL CRIPPLE ANYONE WHO TRIES TO TAKE HIM FROM ME.
JUST LIKE YOUR "BROTHER."

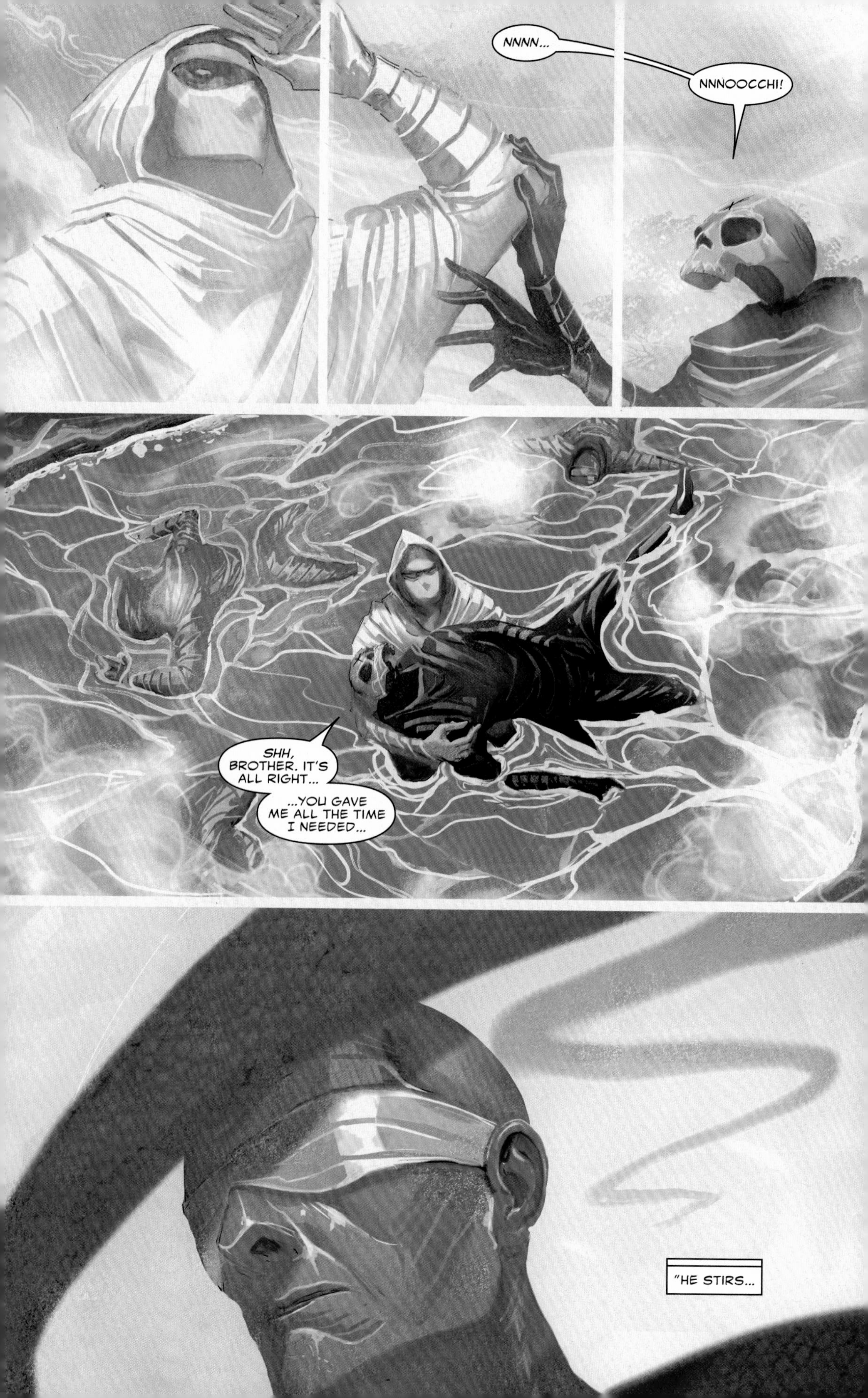
NNNN...
NNNOOCCHI!
SHH, BROTHER. IT'S ALL RIGHT...
...YOU GAVE ME ALL THE TIME I NEEDED...
"HE STIRS...

"...BULLSEYE IS ALREADY ON THE *MEND*."

BOGEY COMING IN FAST, DAD.

ASSASSINS' GUILD?

KENTO AND CAPE CROW. THE HIMALAYAS.

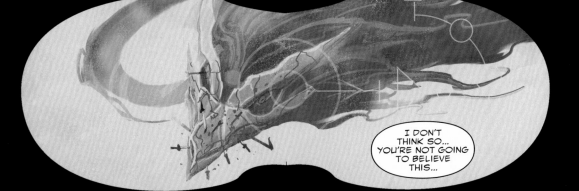

I DON'T THINK SO... YOU'RE NOT GOING TO BELIEVE THIS...

I SEE IT. ANOTHER KILOMETER AND I CAN PUT A BULLET THROUGH ITS GOOD EYE.

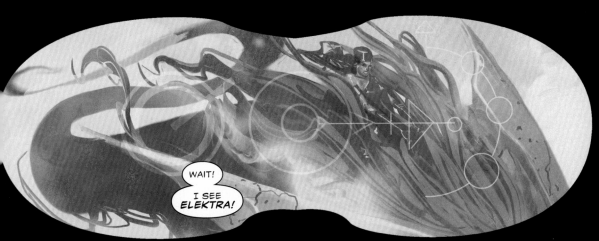

WAIT! I SEE *ELEKTRA*!

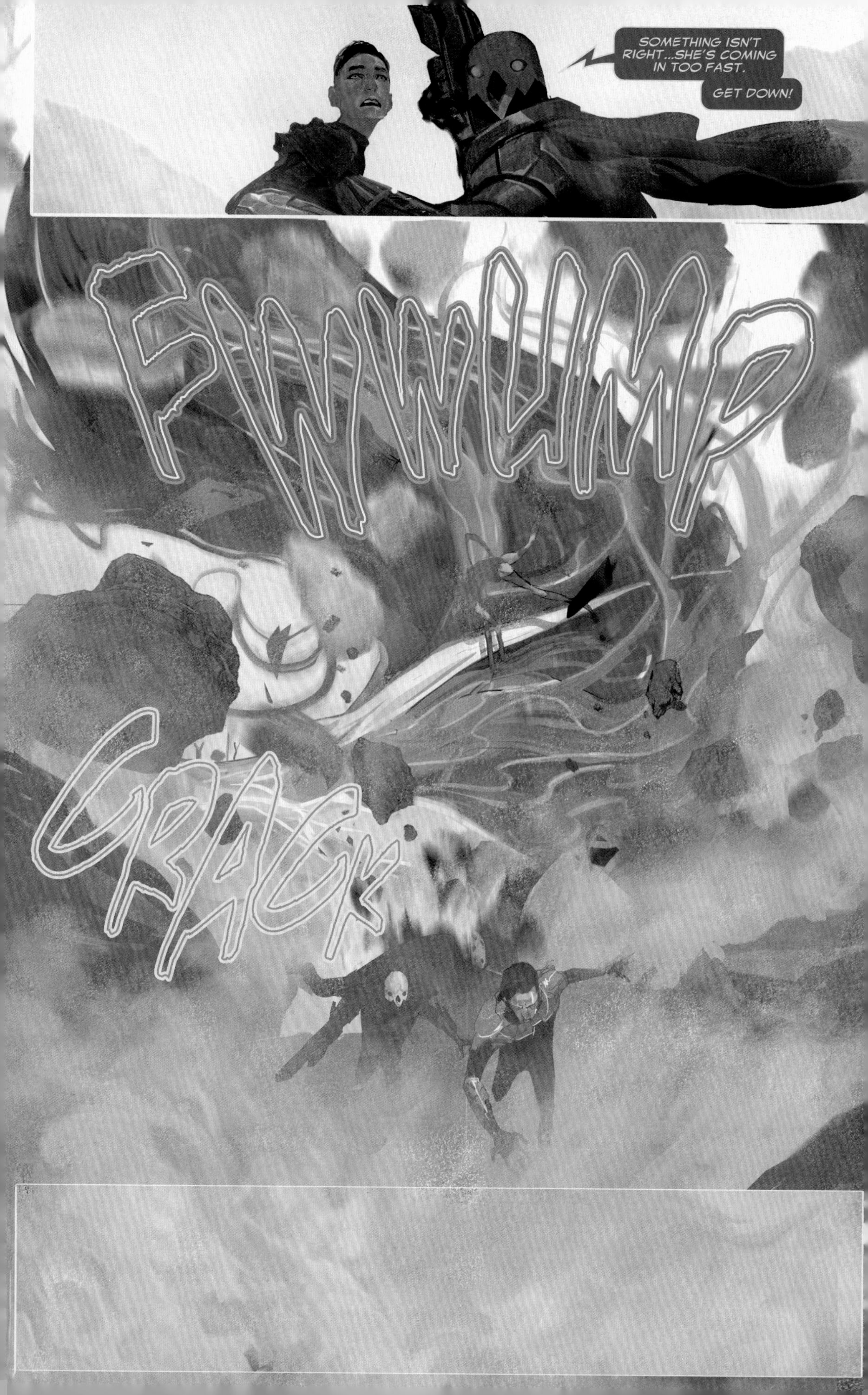
SOMETHING ISN'T RIGHT...SHE'S COMING IN TOO FAST.
GET DOWN!

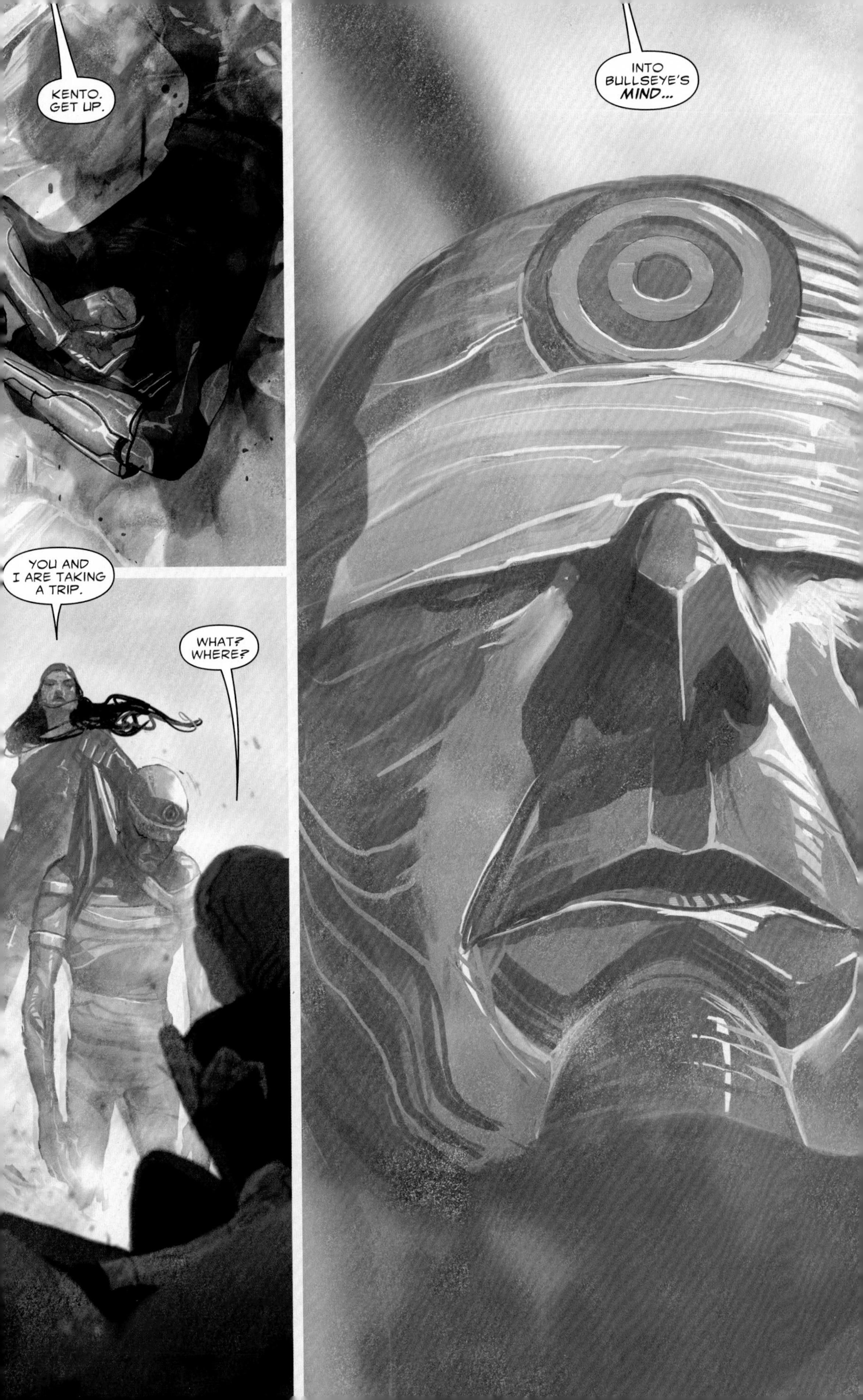
KENTO. GET UP.
YOU AND I ARE TAKING A TRIP.
WHAT? WHERE?
INTO BULLSEYE'S MIND...

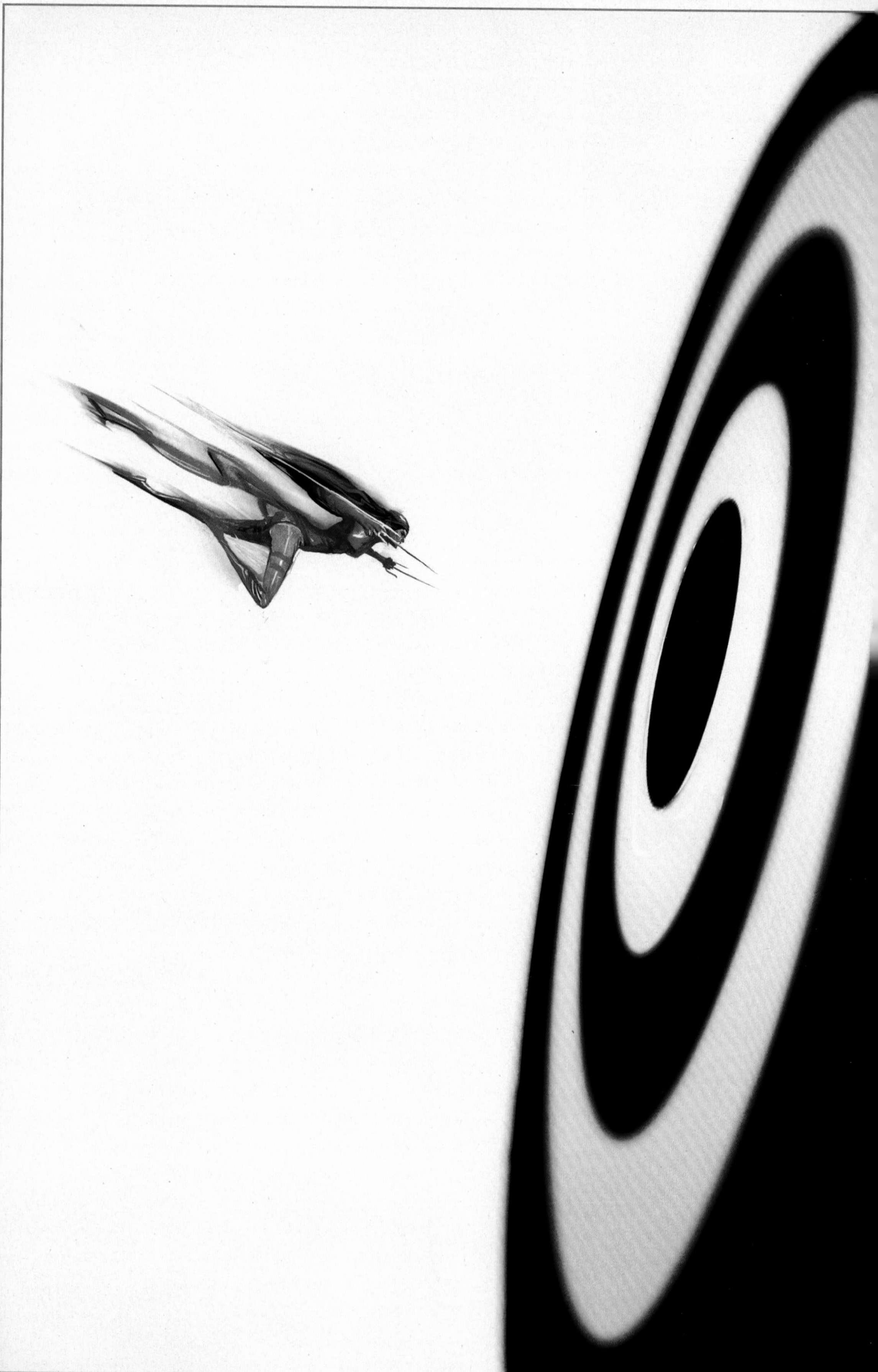

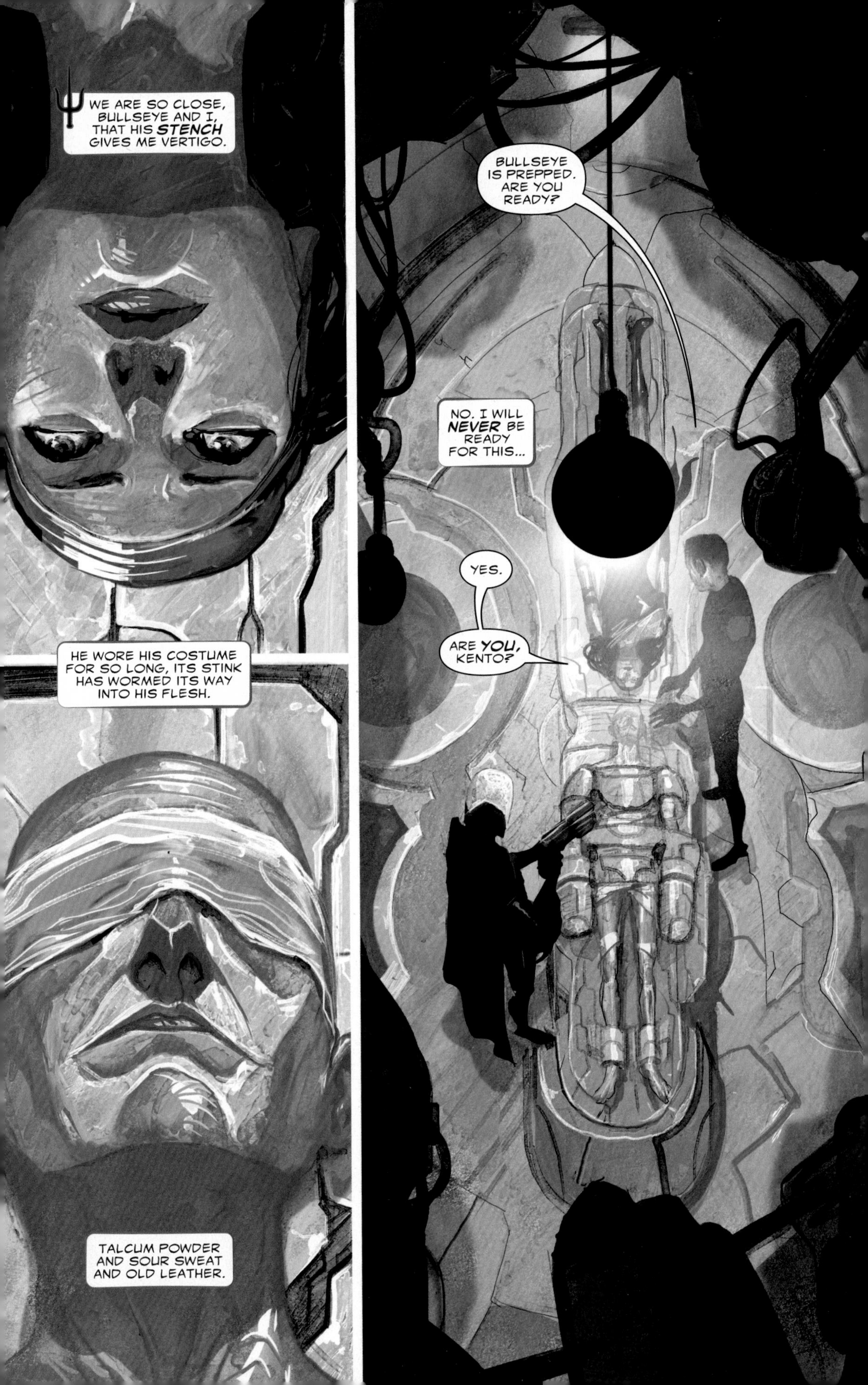
WE ARE SO CLOSE, BULLSEYE AND I, THAT HIS STENCH GIVES ME VERTIGO.
HE WORE HIS COSTUME FOR SO LONG, ITS STINK HAS WORMED ITS WAY INTO HIS FLESH.
TALCUM POWDER AND SOUR SWEAT AND OLD LEATHER.
BULLSEYE IS PREPPED. ARE YOU READY?
NO. I WILL NEVER BE READY FOR THIS...
YES.
ARE YOU, KENTO?

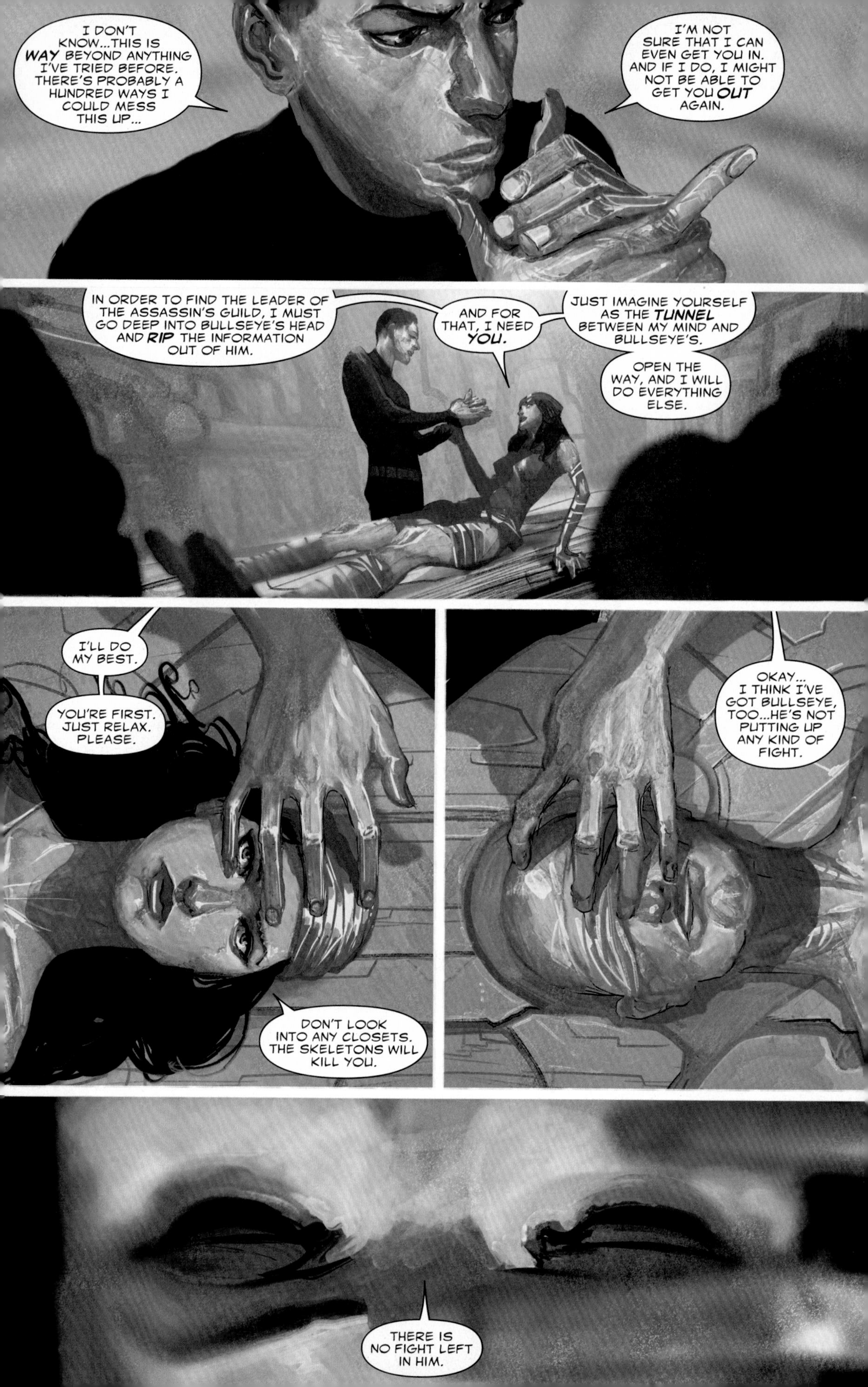
I DON'T KNOW...THIS IS WAY BEYOND ANYTHING I'VE TRIED BEFORE. THERE'S PROBABLY A HUNDRED WAYS I COULD MESS THIS UP...
I'M NOT SURE THAT I CAN EVEN GET YOU IN. AND IF I DO, I MIGHT NOT BE ABLE TO GET YOU OUT AGAIN.
IN ORDER TO FIND THE LEADER OF THE ASSASSIN'S GUILD, I MUST GO DEEP INTO BULLSEYE'S HEAD AND RIP THE INFORMATION OUT OF HIM.
AND FOR THAT, I NEED YOU.
JUST IMAGINE YOURSELF AS THE TUNNEL BETWEEN MY MIND AND BULLSEYE'S.
OPEN THE WAY, AND I WILL DO EVERYTHING ELSE.
I'LL DO MY BEST.
YOU'RE FIRST. JUST RELAX. PLEASE.
DON'T LOOK INTO ANY CLOSETS. THE SKELETONS WILL KILL YOU.
OKAY... I THINK I'VE GOT BULLSEYE, TOO...HE'S NOT PUTTING UP ANY KIND OF FIGHT.
THERE IS NO FIGHT LEFT IN HIM.

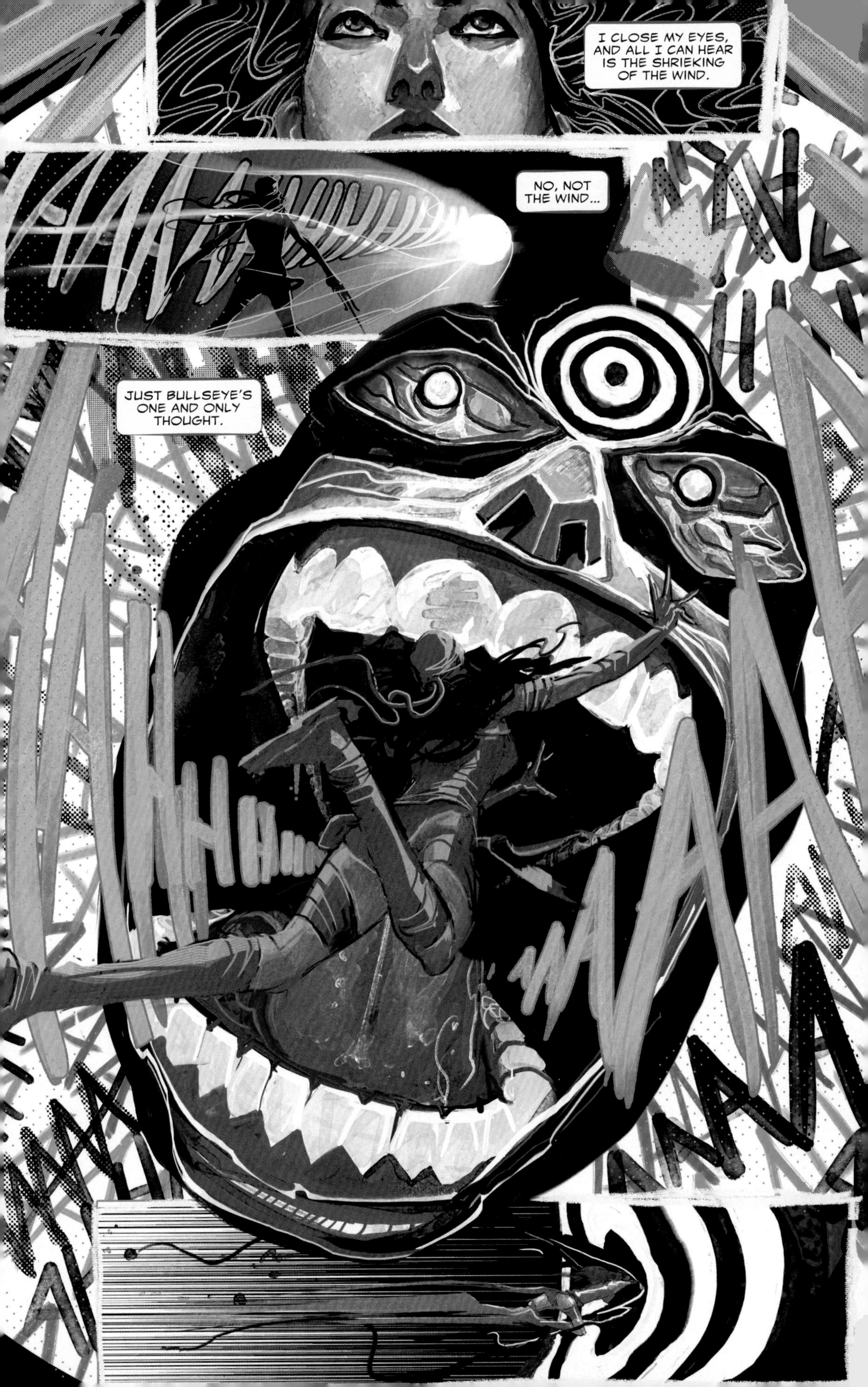
I CLOSE MY EYES, AND ALL I CAN HEAR IS THE SHRIEKING OF THE WIND.
NO, NOT THE WIND...
JUST BULLSEYE'S ONE AND ONLY THOUGHT.

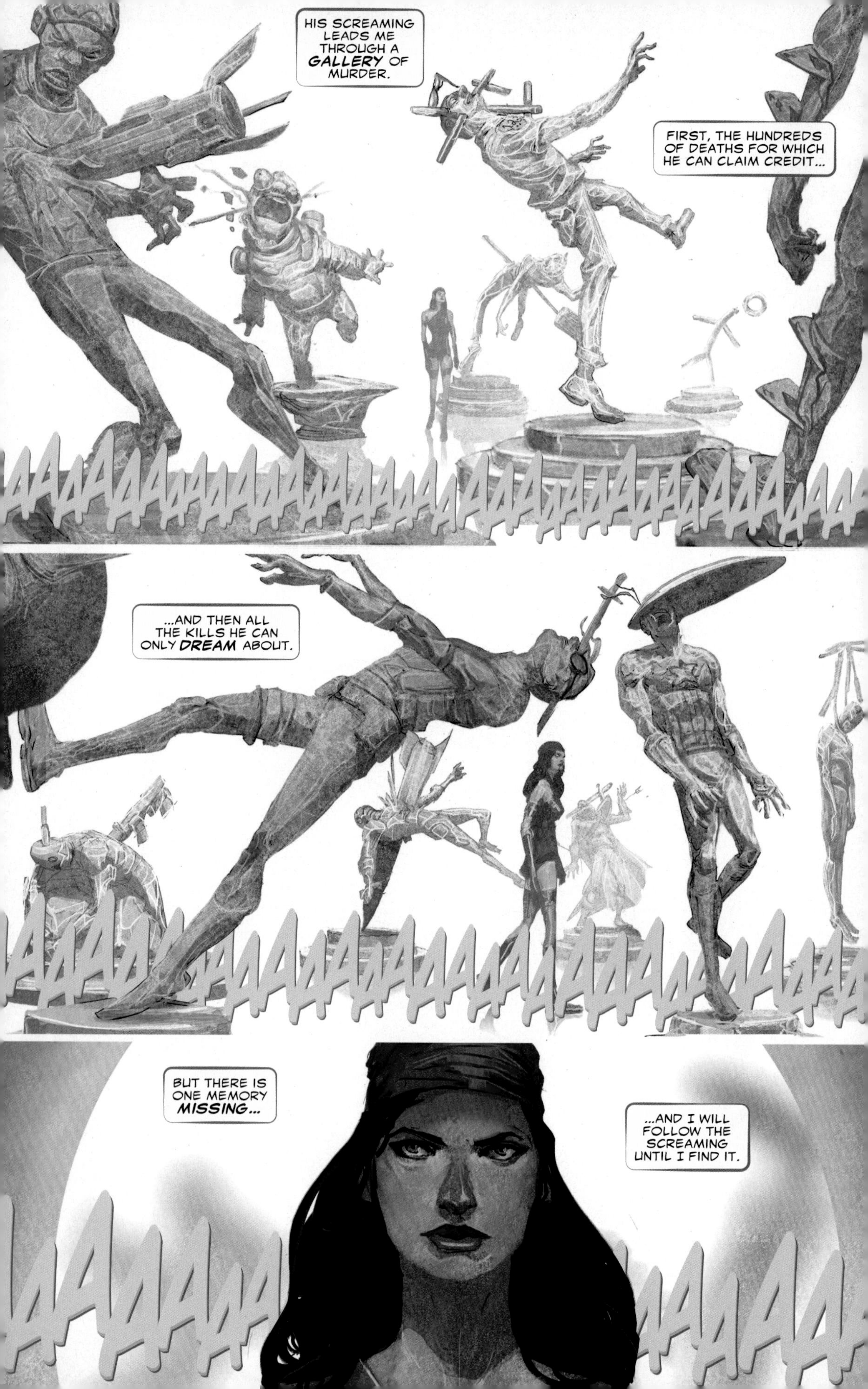
HIS SCREAMING LEADS ME THROUGH A GALLERY OF MURDER.
FIRST, THE HUNDREDS OF DEATHS FOR WHICH HE CAN CLAIM CREDIT...
AAAAAAAAAAAAAAAAAAAAAAAAAAAAAAAAAAAAAAAA
...AND THEN ALL THE KILLS HE CAN ONLY DREAM ABOUT.
AAAAAAAAAAAAAAAAAAAAAAAAAAAAAAAAAAAAAAAA
BUT THERE IS ONE MEMORY MISSING...
...AND I WILL FOLLOW THE SCREAMING UNTIL I FIND IT.
AAAAAAAAAAAAAAAA

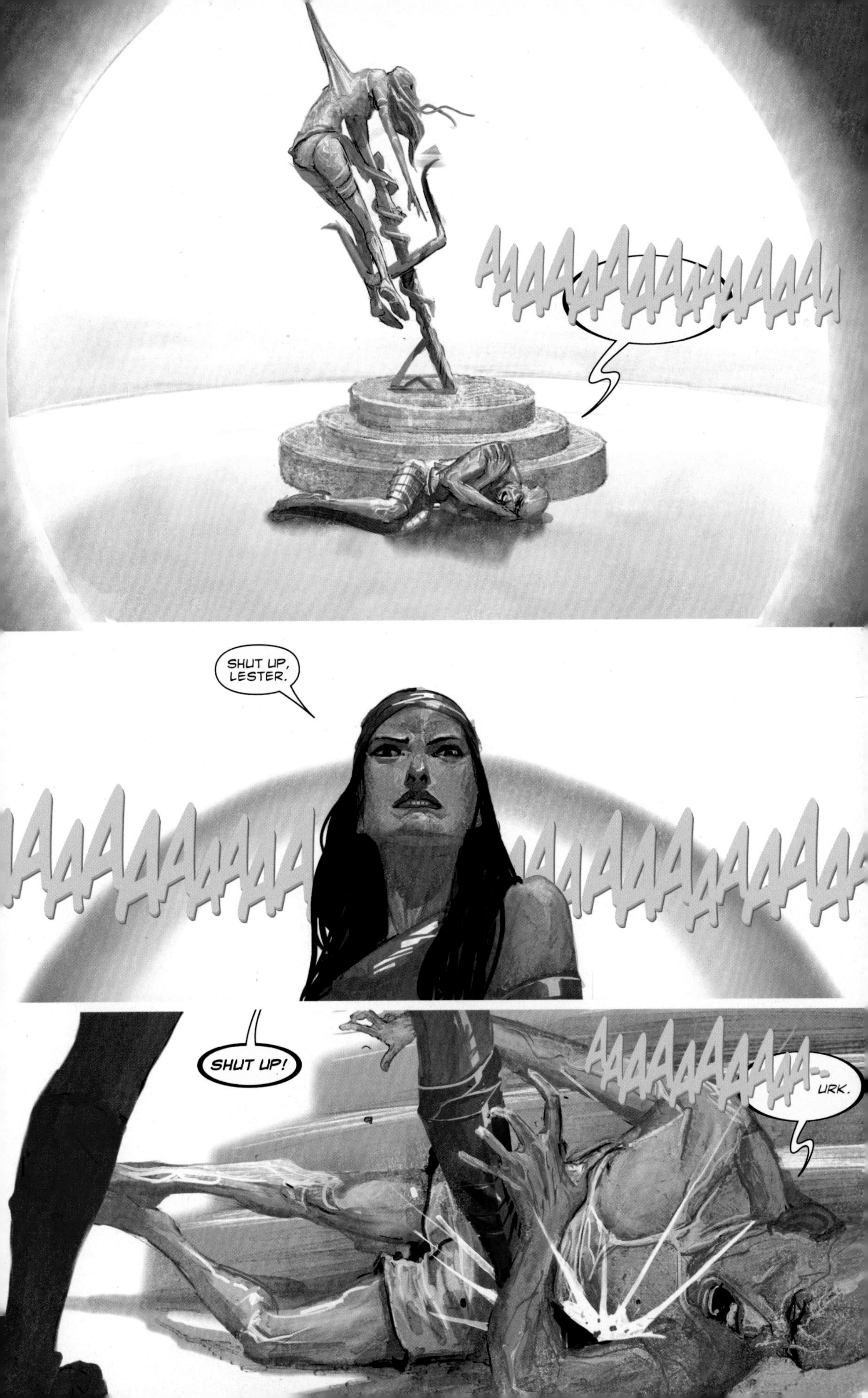
AAAAAAAAAAAAAAAAA
SHUT UP, LESTER.
AAAAAAAAAAAAAAAAAAAAAAAAAA
SHUT UP!
AAAAAAAAAA--
URK.

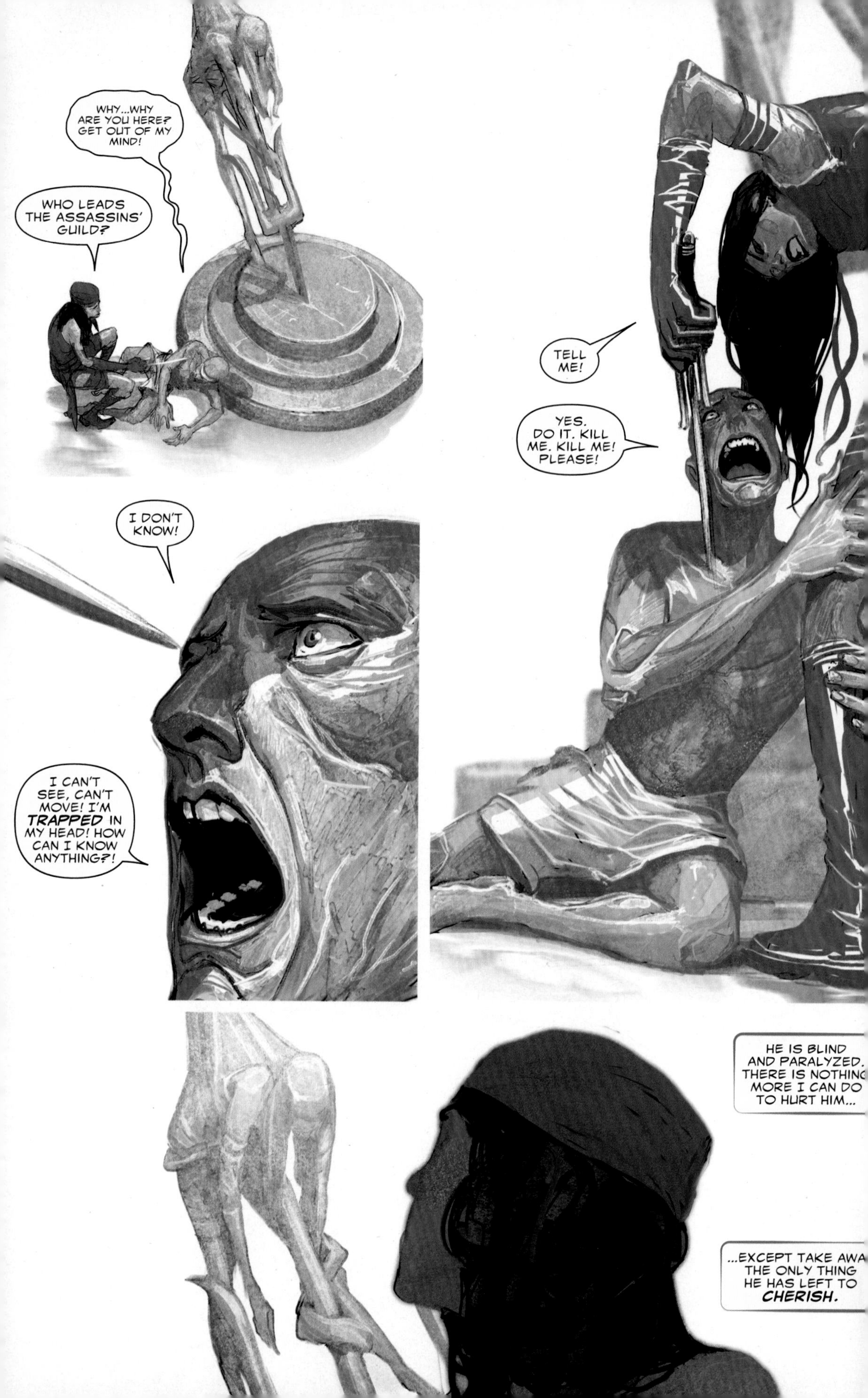
WHY...WHY ARE YOU HERE? GET OUT OF MY MIND!
WHO LEADS THE ASSASSINS' GUILD?
TELL ME!
YES. DO IT. KILL ME. KILL ME! PLEASE!
I DON'T KNOW!
I CAN'T SEE, CAN'T MOVE! I'M TRAPPED IN MY HEAD! HOW CAN I KNOW ANYTHING?!
HE IS BLIND AND PARALYZED. THERE IS NOTHING MORE I CAN DO TO HURT HIM...
...EXCEPT TAKE AWAY THE ONLY THING HE HAS LEFT TO CHERISH.

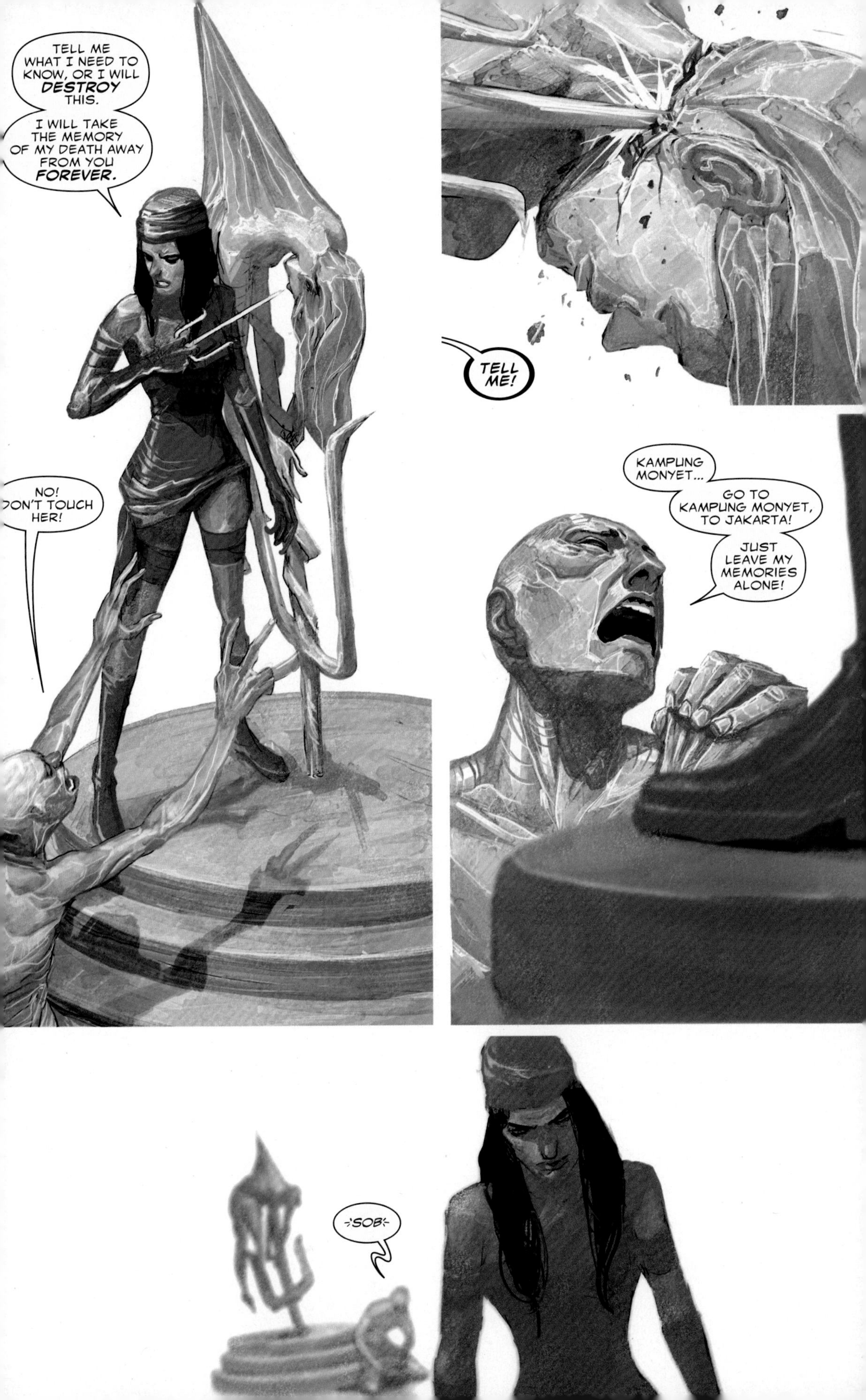
TELL ME WHAT I NEED TO KNOW, OR I WILL DESTROY THIS.
I WILL TAKE THE MEMORY OF MY DEATH AWAY FROM YOU FOREVER.
TELL ME!
NO! DON'T TOUCH HER!
KAMPUNG MONYET...
GO TO KAMPUNG MONYET, TO JAKARTA!
JUST LEAVE MY MEMORIES ALONE!
-SOB-

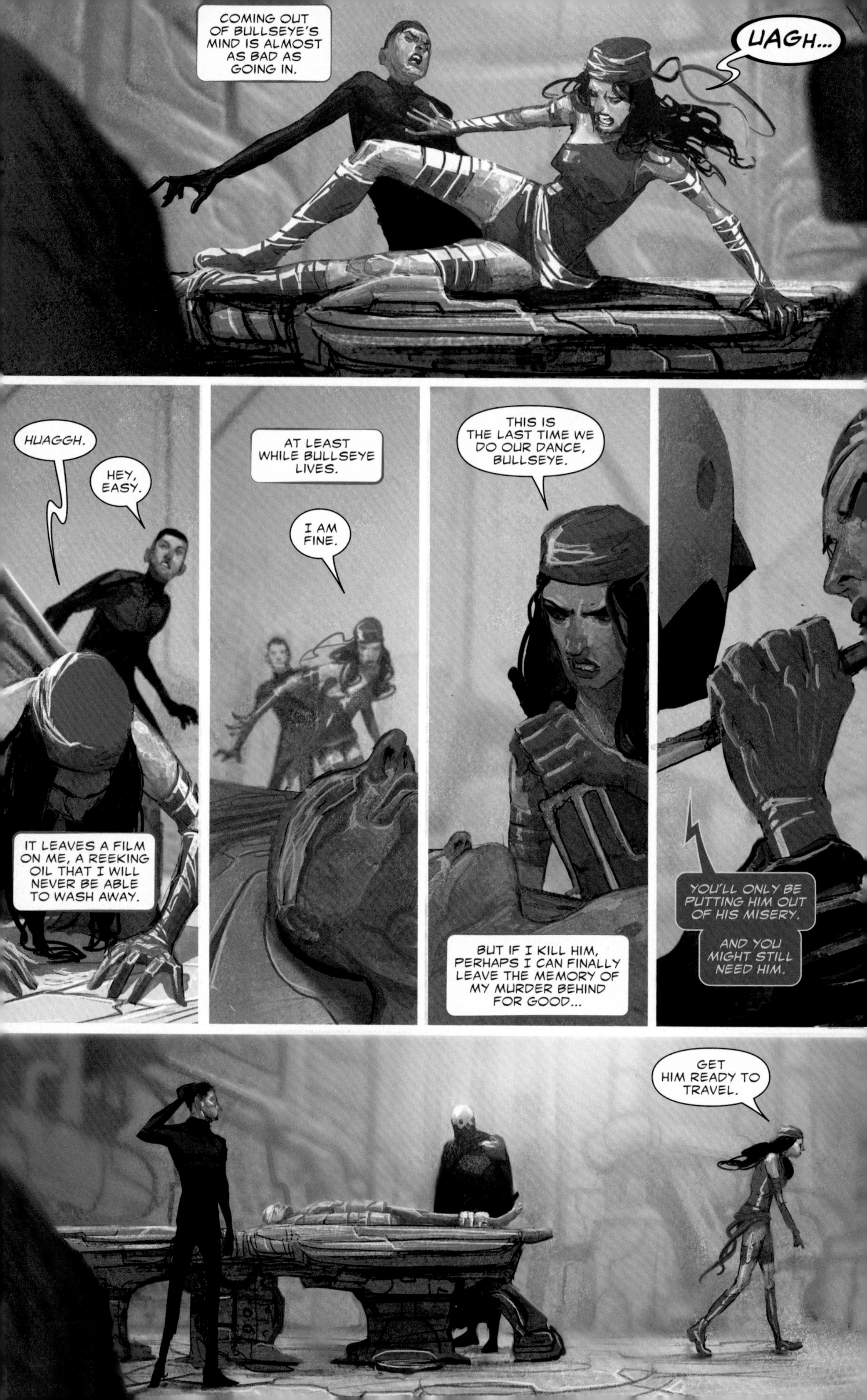
COMING OUT OF BULLSEYE'S MIND IS ALMOST AS BAD AS GOING IN.
UAGH...
HUAGGH.
HEY, EASY.
IT LEAVES A FILM ON ME, A REEKING OIL THAT I WILL NEVER BE ABLE TO WASH AWAY.
AT LEAST WHILE BULLSEYE LIVES.
I AM FINE.
THIS IS THE LAST TIME WE DO OUR DANCE, BULLSEYE.
BUT IF I KILL HIM, PERHAPS I CAN FINALLY LEAVE THE MEMORY OF MY MURDER BEHIND FOR GOOD...
YOU'LL ONLY BE PUTTING HIM OUT OF HIS MISERY.
AND YOU MIGHT STILL NEED HIM.
GET HIM READY TO TRAVEL.

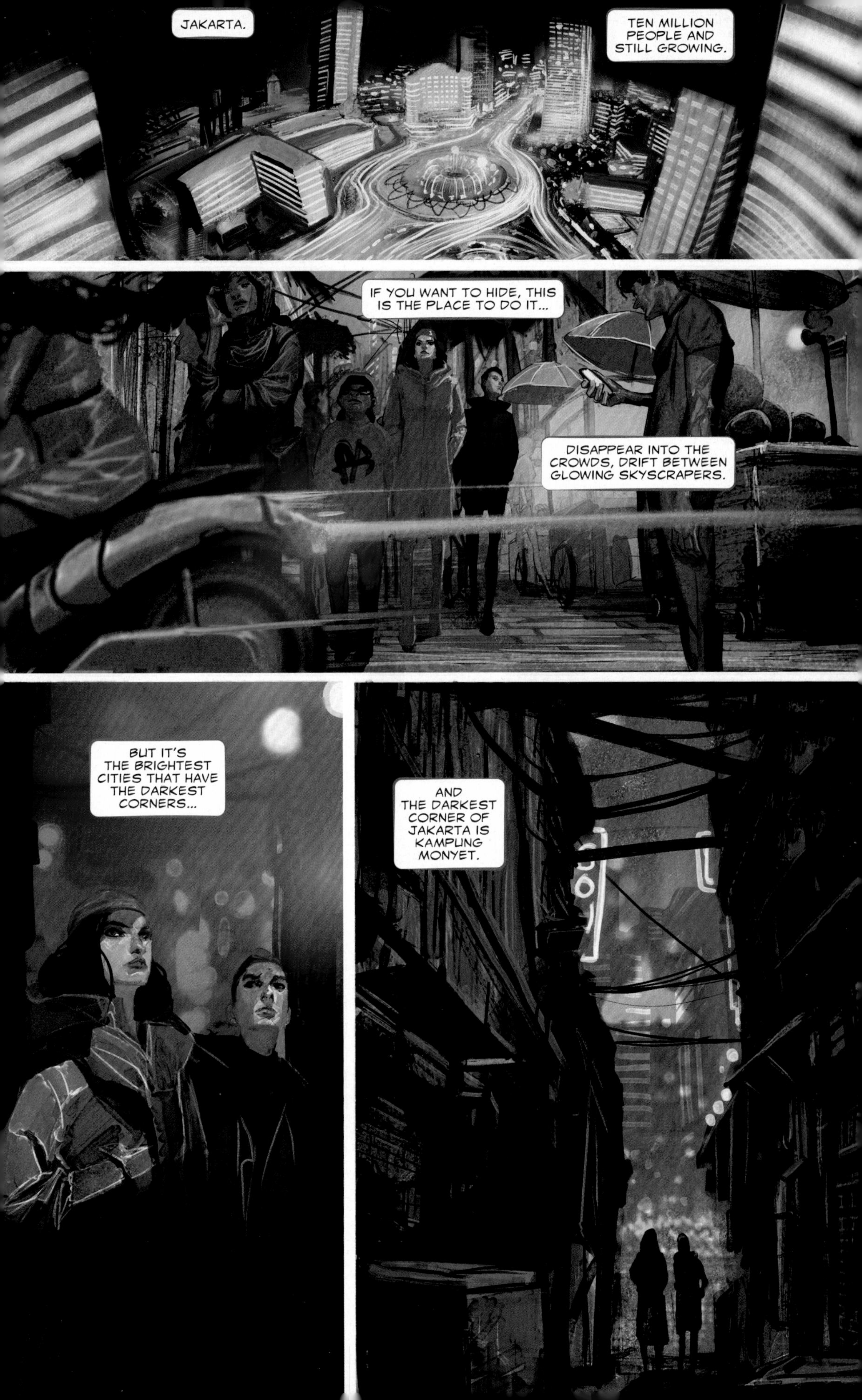
JAKARTA.
TEN MILLION PEOPLE AND STILL GROWING.
IF YOU WANT TO HIDE, THIS IS THE PLACE TO DO IT...
DISAPPEAR INTO THE CROWDS, DRIFT BETWEEN GLOWING SKYSCRAPERS.
BUT IT'S THE BRIGHTEST CITIES THAT HAVE THE DARKEST CORNERS...
AND THE DARKEST CORNER OF JAKARTA IS KAMPUNG MONYET.

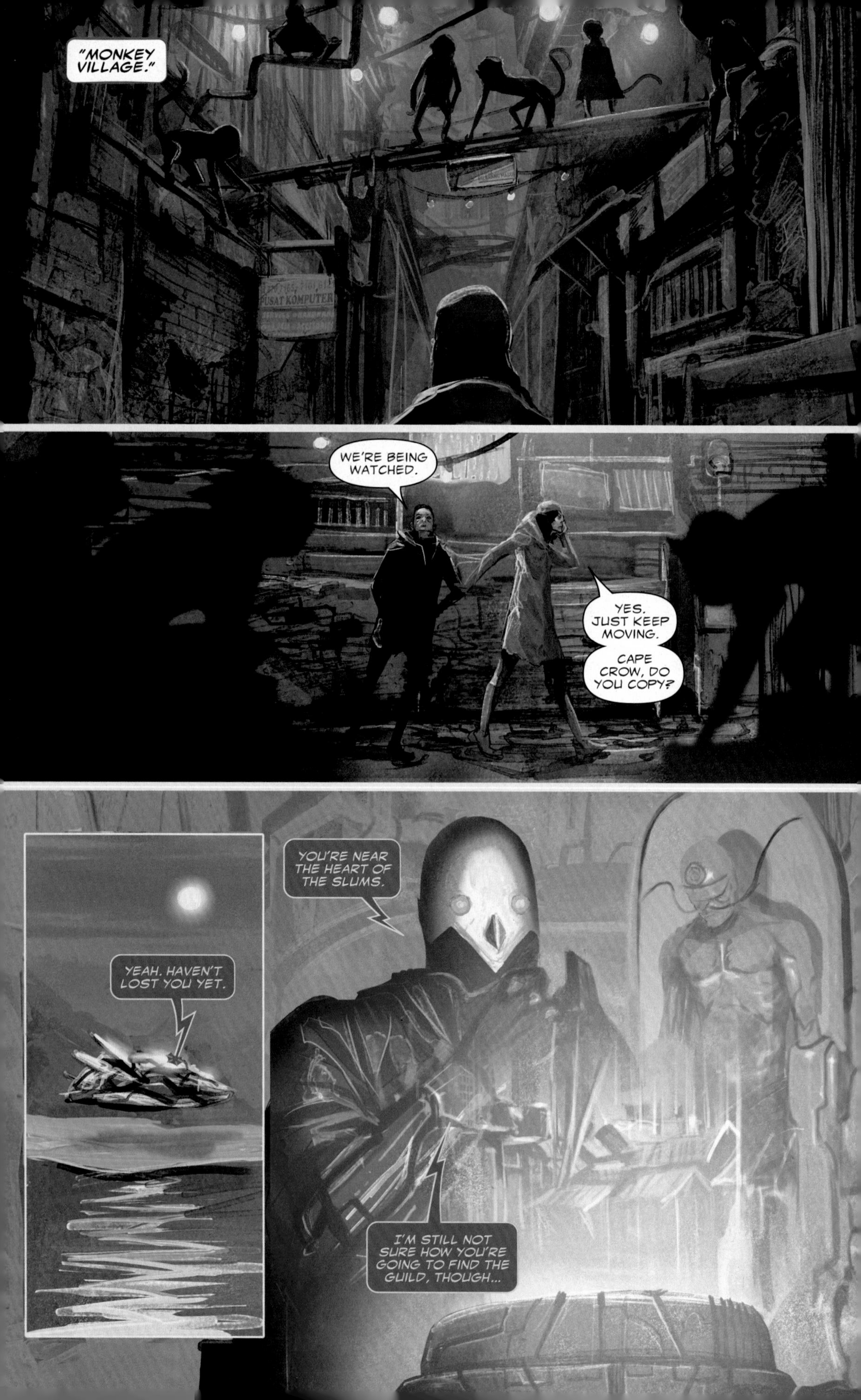
"MONKEY VILLAGE."
PUSAT KOMPUTER
WE'RE BEING WATCHED.
YES. JUST KEEP MOVING.
CAPE CROW, DO YOU COPY?
YEAH. HAVEN'T LOST YOU YET.
YOU'RE NEAR THE HEART OF THE SLUMS.
I'M STILL NOT SURE HOW YOU'RE GOING TO FIND THE GUILD, THOUGH...

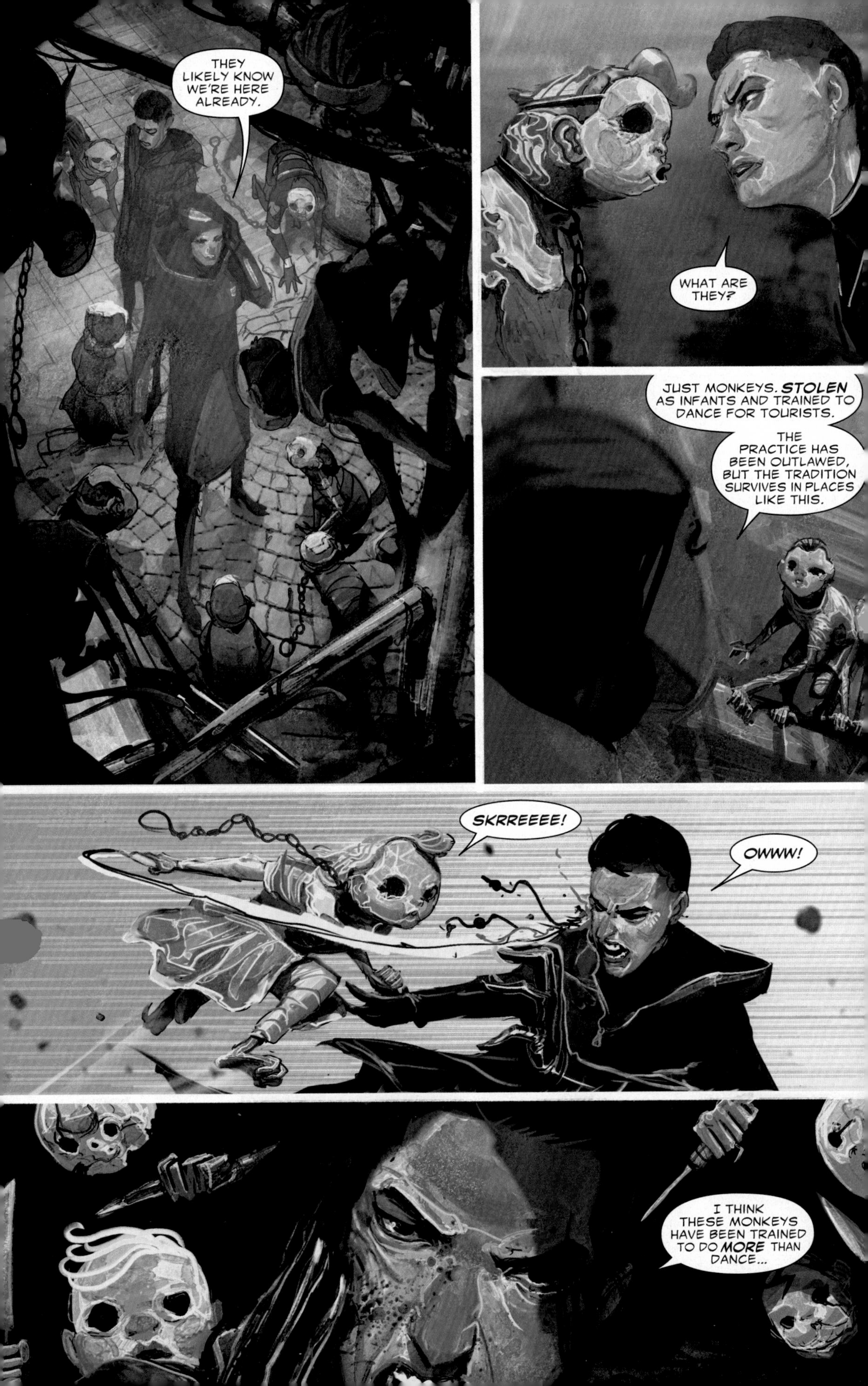
THEY LIKELY KNOW WE'RE HERE ALREADY.
WHAT ARE THEY?
JUST MONKEYS. STOLEN AS INFANTS AND TRAINED TO DANCE FOR TOURISTS.
THE PRACTICE HAS BEEN OUTLAWED, BUT THE TRADITION SURVIVES IN PLACES LIKE THIS.
SKRREEEE!
OWWW!
I THINK THESE MONKEYS HAVE BEEN TRAINED TO DO MORE THAN DANCE...

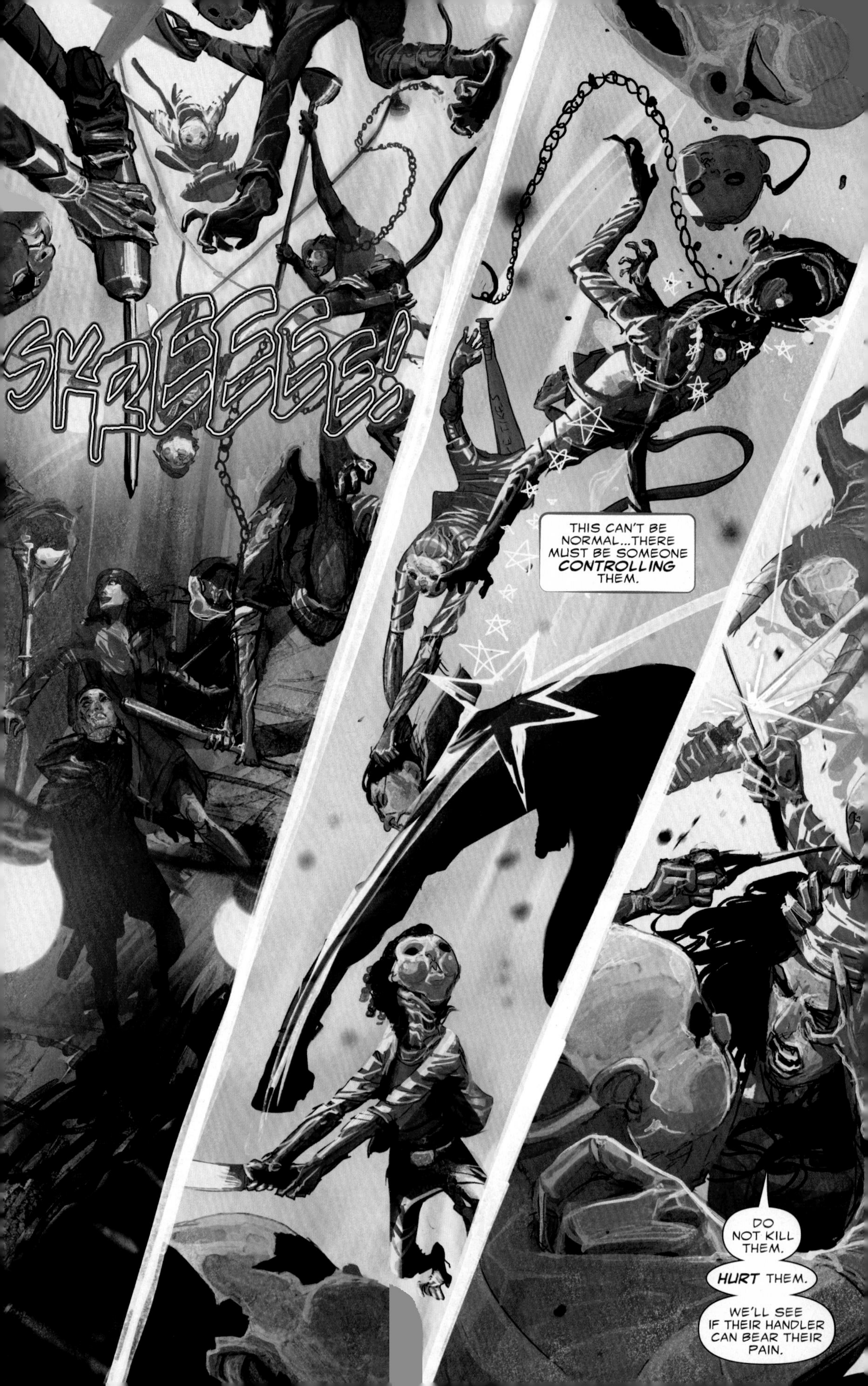
SKREEEE!
THIS CAN'T BE NORMAL...THERE MUST BE SOMEONE CONTROLLING THEM.
DO NOT KILL THEM.
HURT THEM.
WE'LL SEE IF THEIR HANDLER CAN BEAR THEIR PAIN.

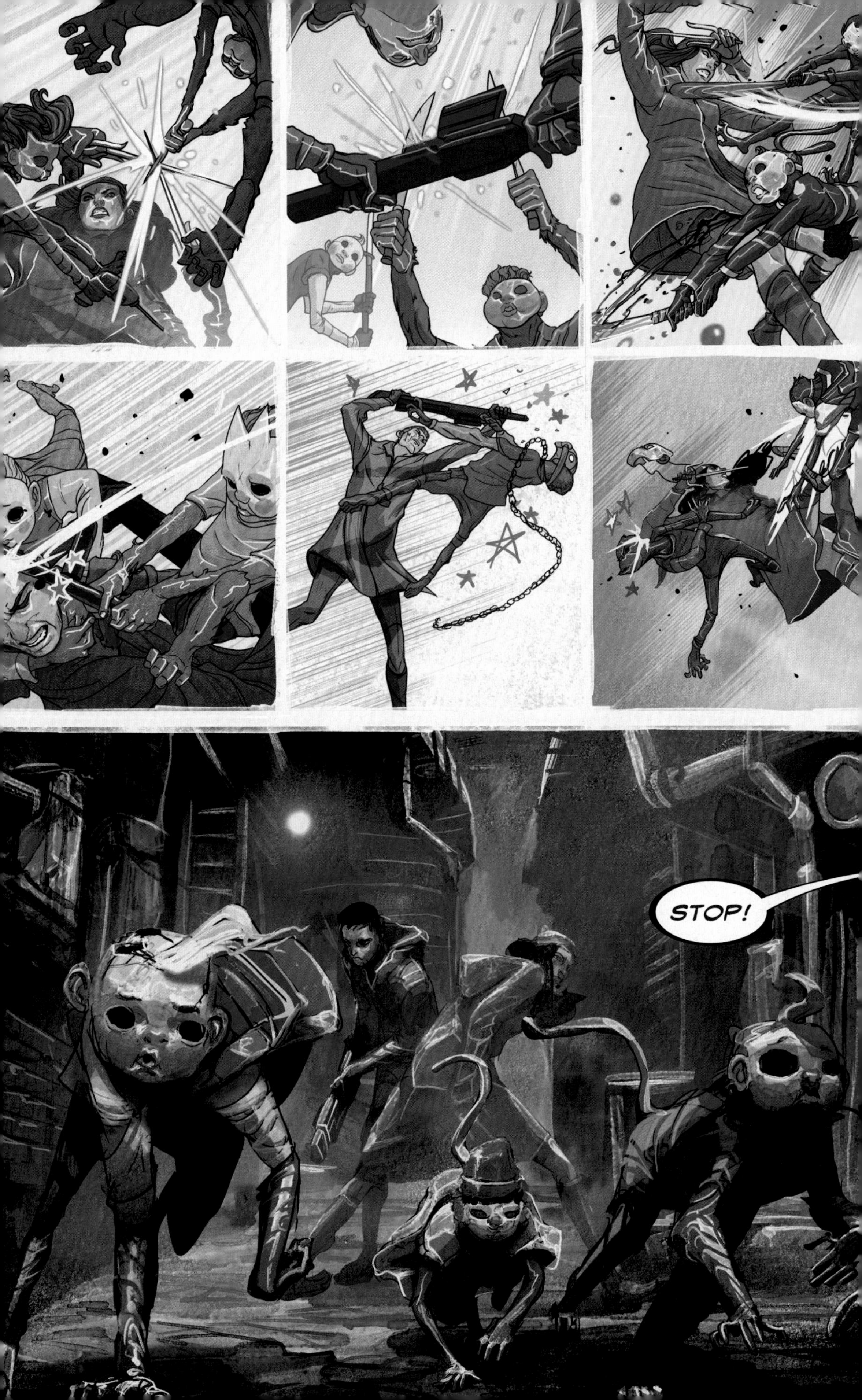
STOP!

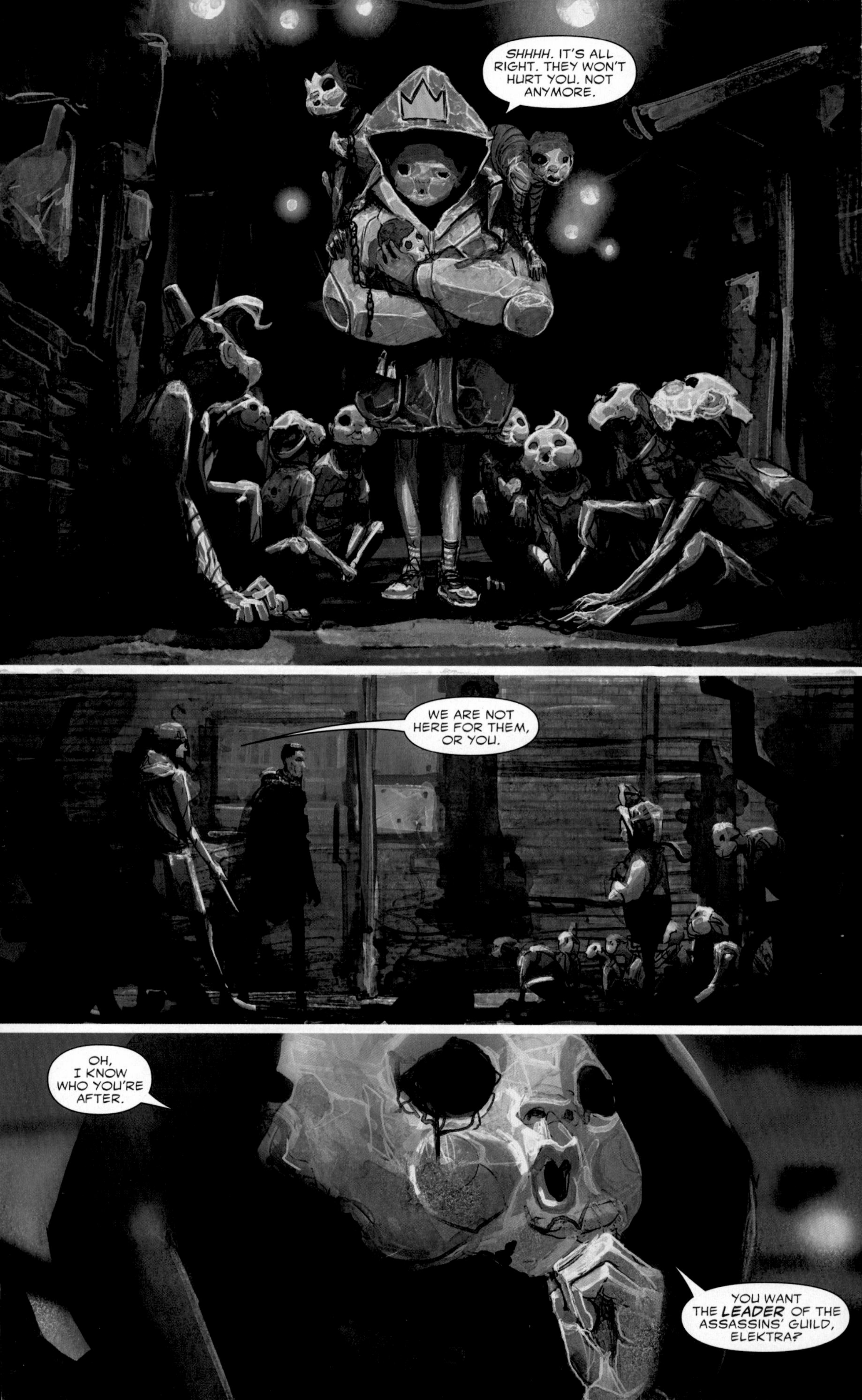
SHHHH. IT'S ALL RIGHT. THEY WON'T HURT YOU. NOT ANYMORE.
WE ARE NOT HERE FOR THEM, OR YOU.
OH, I KNOW WHO YOU'RE AFTER.
YOU WANT THE LEADER OF THE ASSASSINS' GUILD, ELEKTRA?

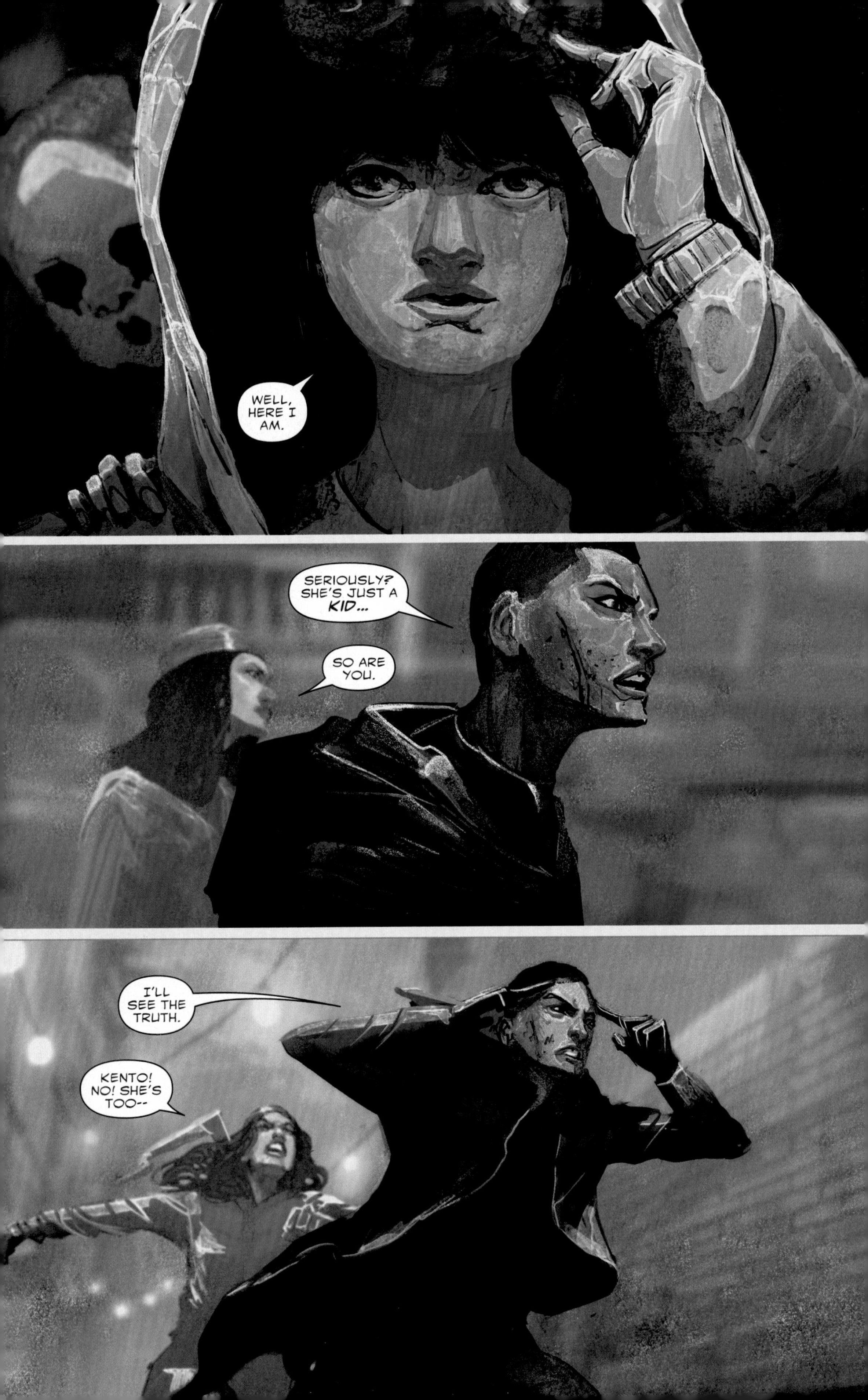
WELL, HERE I AM.
SERIOUSLY? SHE'S JUST A KID...
SO ARE YOU.
I'LL SEE THE TRUTH.
KENTO! NO! SHE'S TOO--

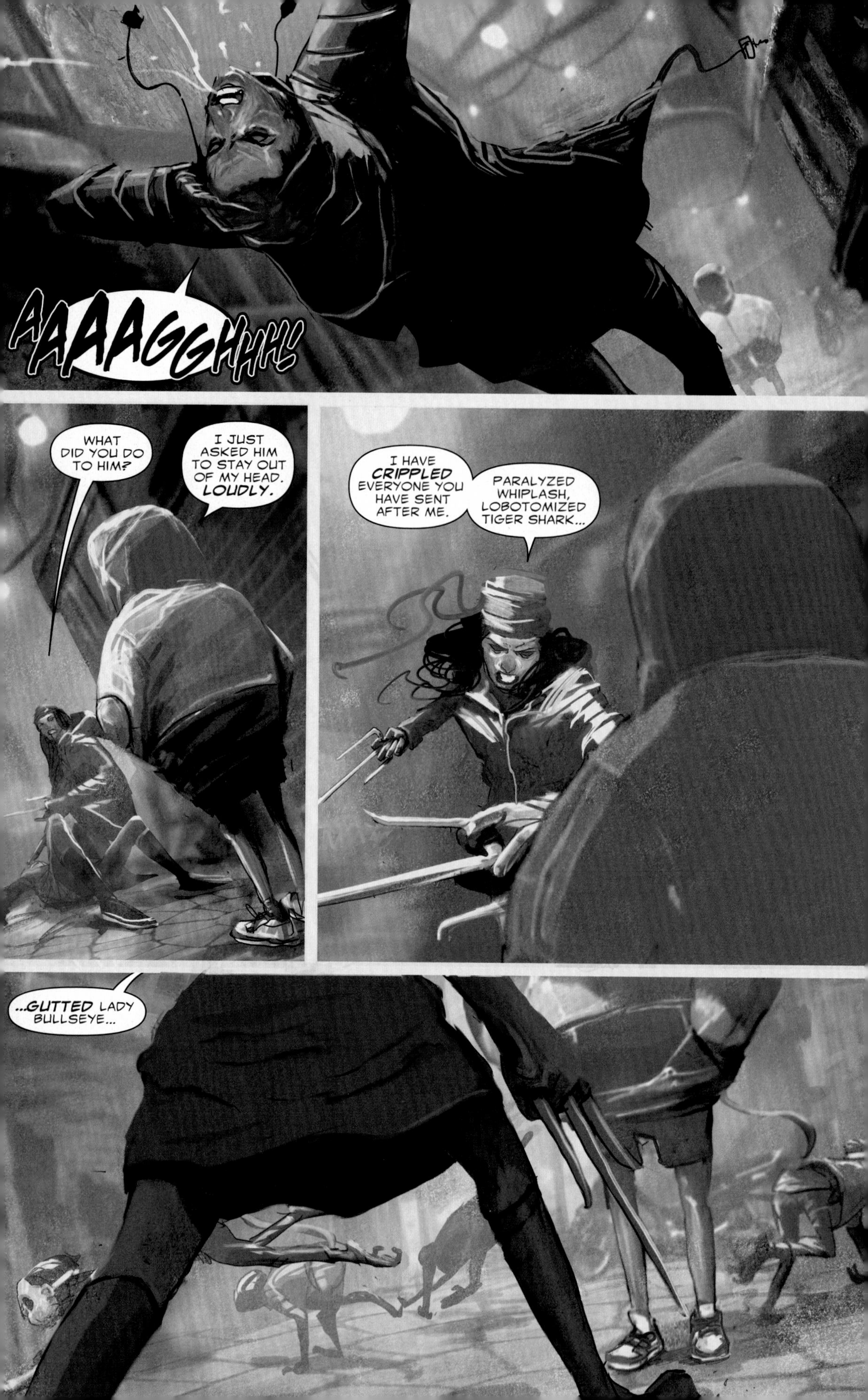
AAAAGGHHH!
WHAT DID YOU DO TO HIM?
I JUST ASKED HIM TO STAY OUT OF MY HEAD. LOUDLY.
I HAVE CRIPPLED EVERYONE YOU HAVE SENT AFTER ME.
PARALYZED WHIPLASH, LOBOTOMIZED TIGER SHARK...
...GUTTED LADY BULLSEYE...

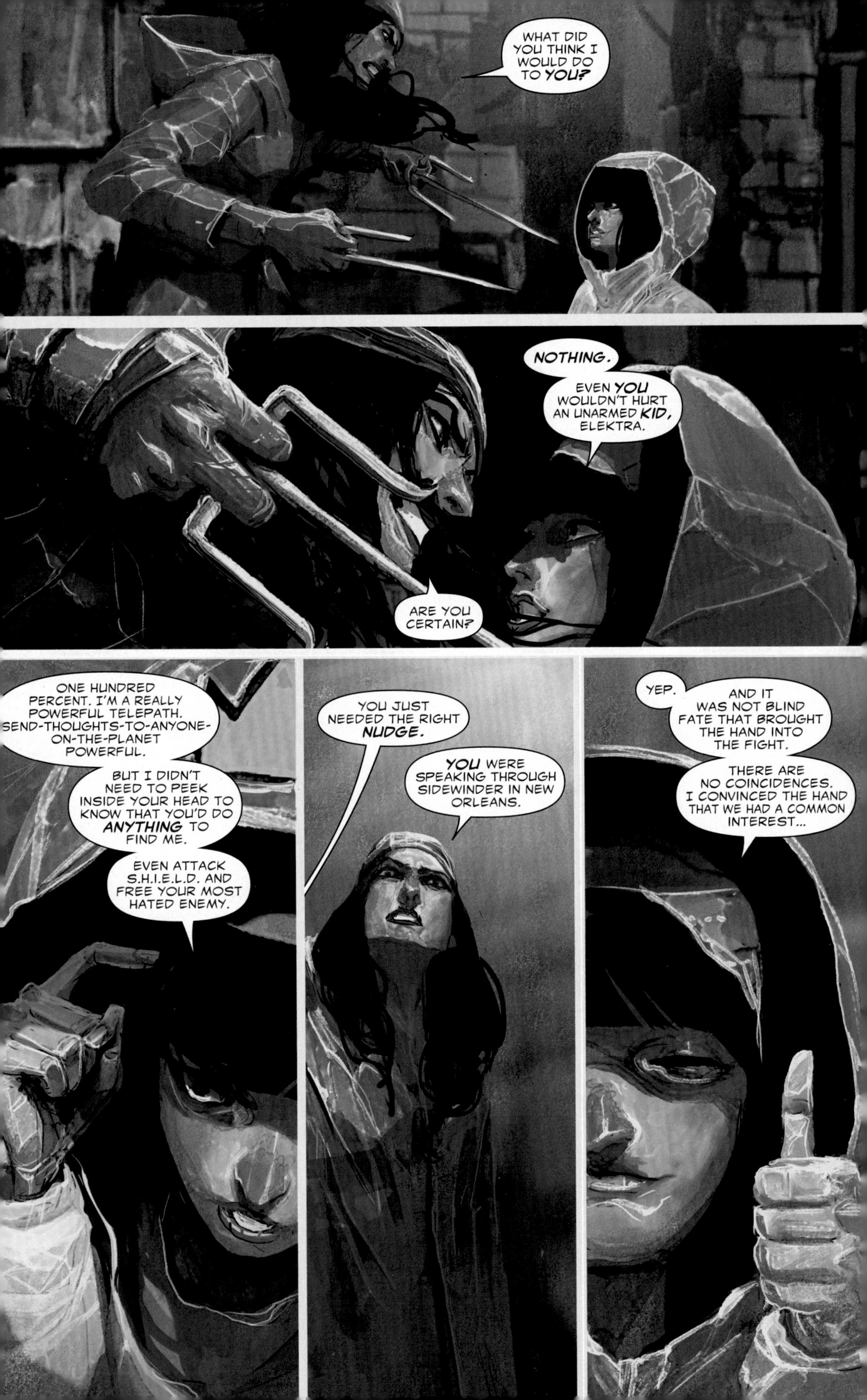

WHAT DID YOU THINK I WOULD DO TO YOU?
NOTHING.
EVEN YOU WOULDN'T HURT AN UNARMED KID, ELEKTRA.
ARE YOU CERTAIN?
ONE HUNDRED PERCENT. I'M A REALLY POWERFUL TELEPATH. SEND-THOUGHTS-TO-ANYONE-ON-THE-PLANET POWERFUL.
BUT I DIDN'T NEED TO PEEK INSIDE YOUR HEAD TO KNOW THAT YOU'D DO ANYTHING TO FIND ME.
EVEN ATTACK S.H.I.E.L.D. AND FREE YOUR MOST HATED ENEMY.
YOU JUST NEEDED THE RIGHT NUDGE.
YOU WERE SPEAKING THROUGH SIDEWINDER IN NEW ORLEANS.
YEP.
AND IT WAS NOT BLIND FATE THAT BROUGHT THE HAND INTO THE FIGHT.
THERE ARE NO COINCIDENCES. I CONVINCED THE HAND THAT WE HAD A COMMON INTEREST...

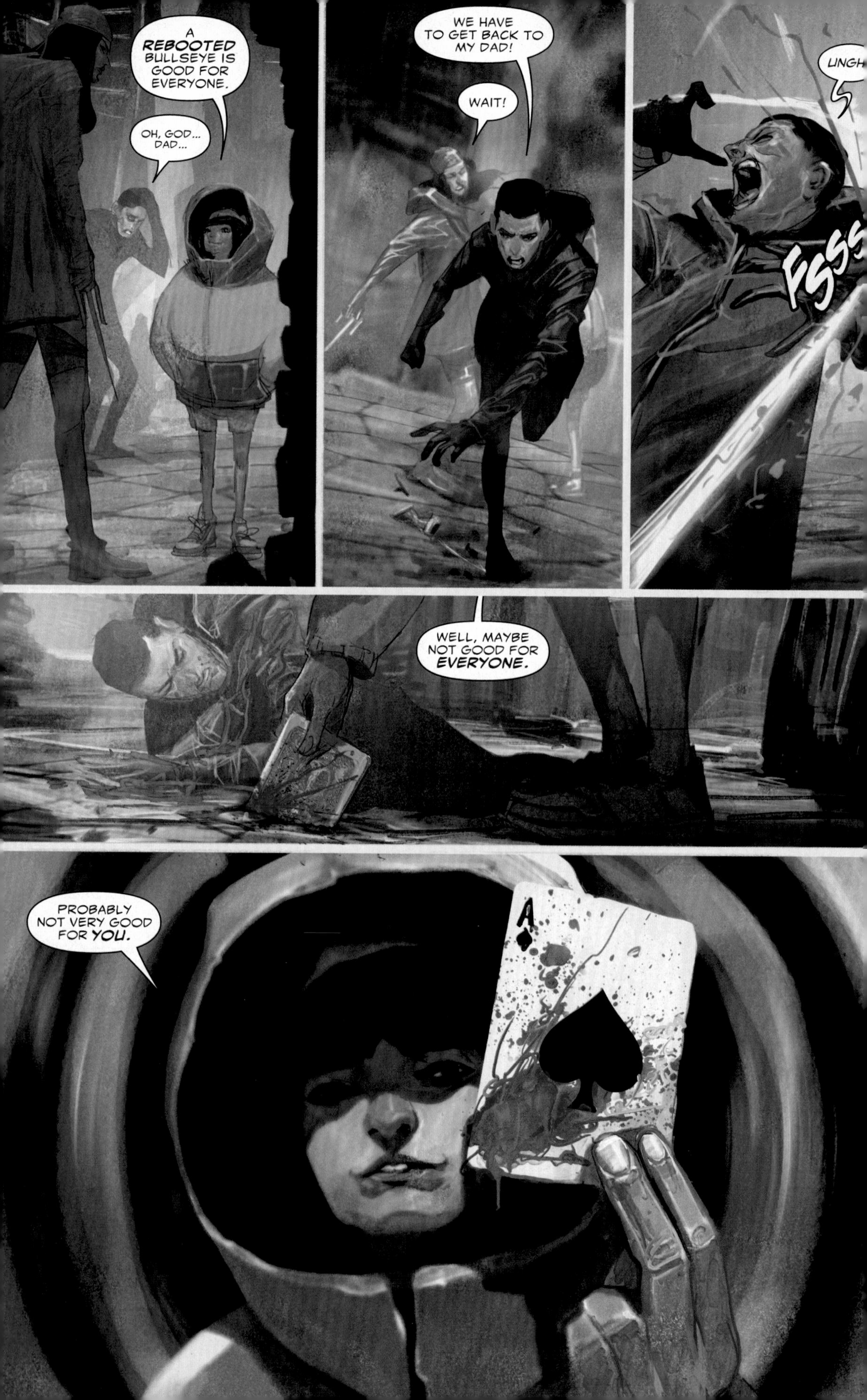
A REBOOTED BULLSEYE IS GOOD FOR EVERYONE.
OH, GOD... DAD...
WE HAVE TO GET BACK TO MY DAD!
WAIT!
UNGH
FSSS
WELL, MAYBE NOT GOOD FOR EVERYONE.
PROBABLY NOT VERY GOOD FOR YOU.

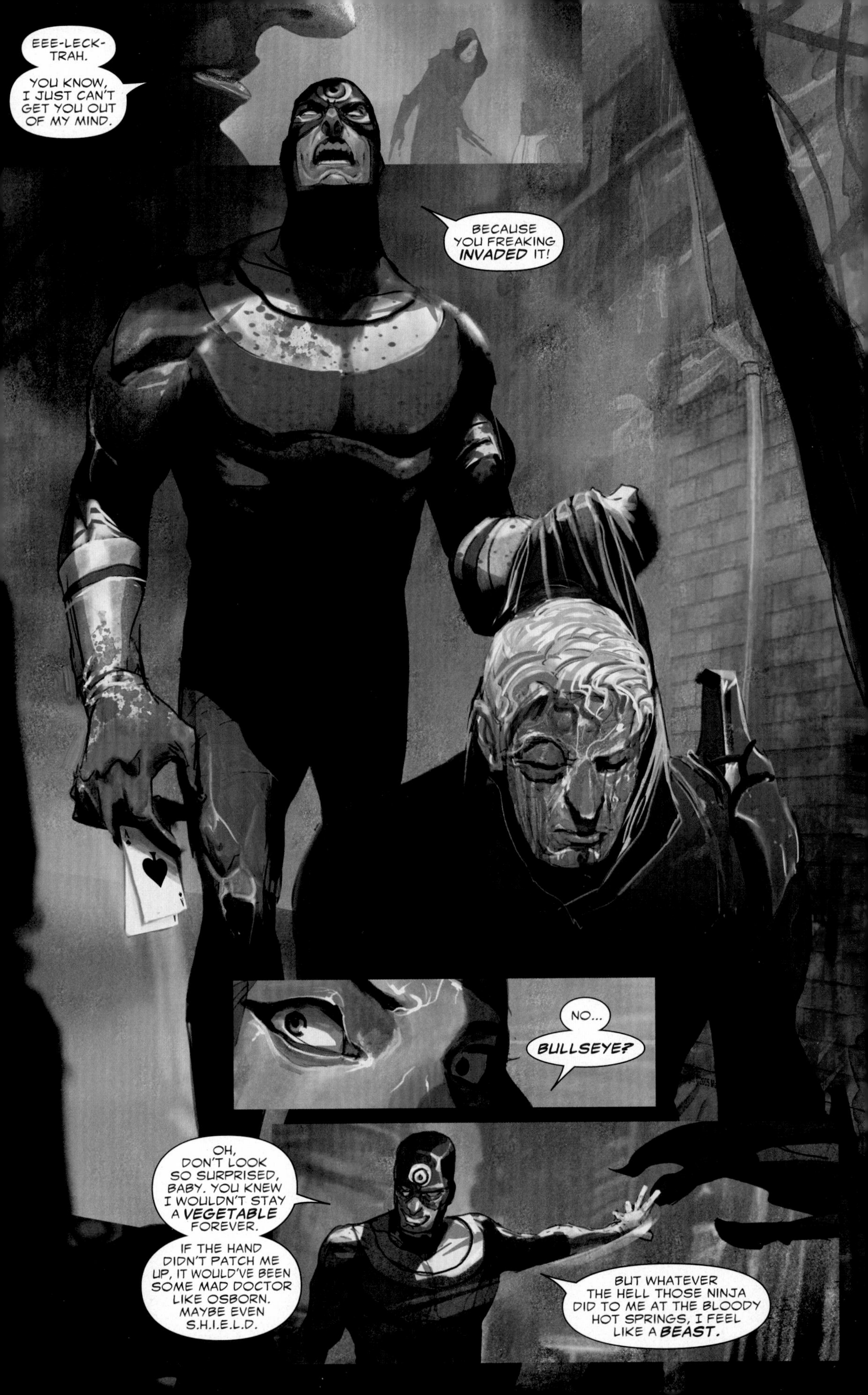
EEE-LECK-TRAH.
YOU KNOW, I JUST CAN'T GET YOU OUT OF MY MIND.
BECAUSE YOU FREAKING INVADED IT!
NO... BULLSEYE?
OH, DON'T LOOK SO SURPRISED, BABY. YOU KNEW I WOULDN'T STAY A VEGETABLE FOREVER.
IF THE HAND DIDN'T PATCH ME UP, IT WOULD'VE BEEN SOME MAD DOCTOR LIKE OSBORN. MAYBE EVEN S.H.I.E.L.D.
BUT WHATEVER THE HELL THOSE NINJA DID TO ME AT THE BLOODY HOT SPRINGS, I FEEL LIKE A BEAST.

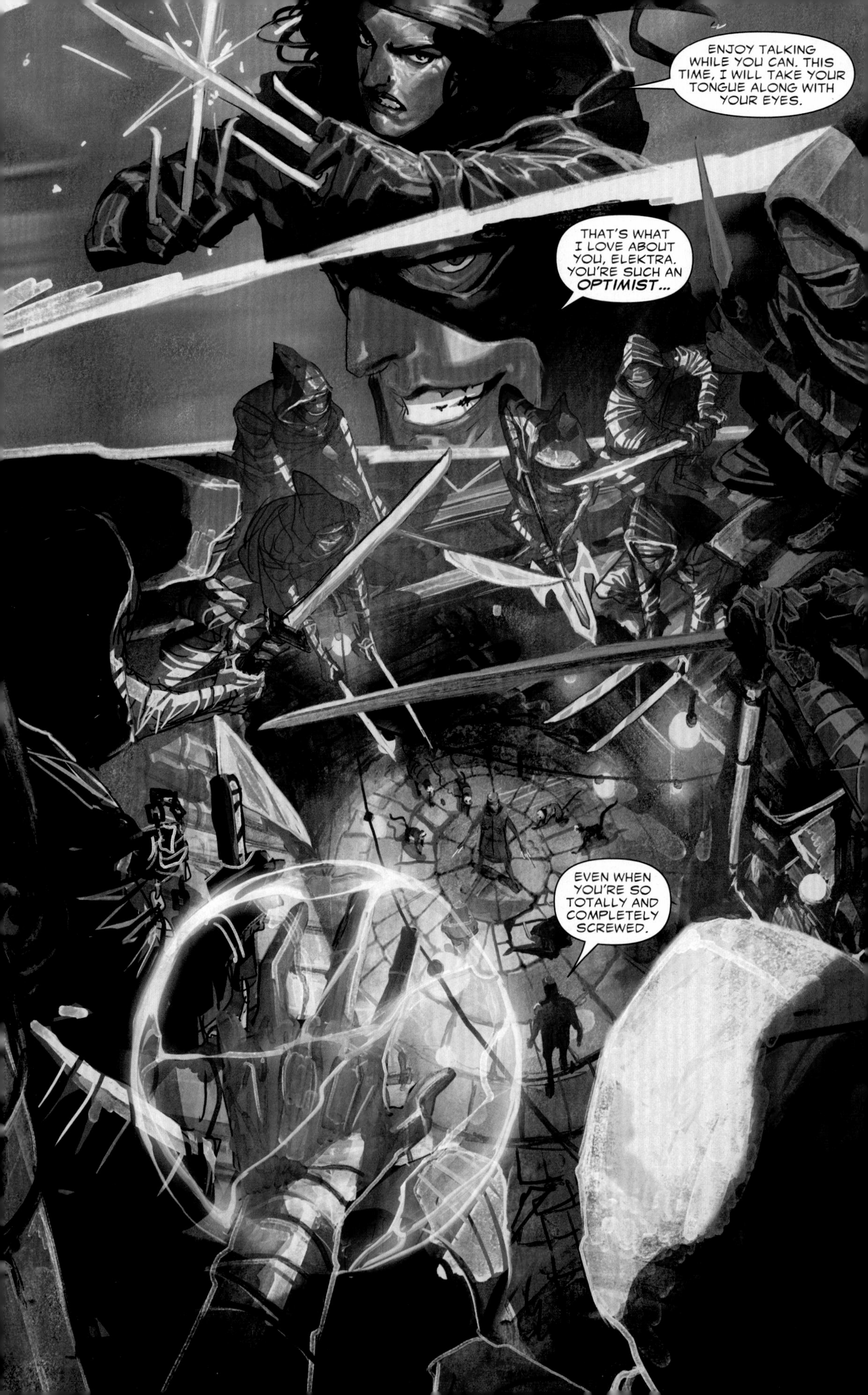
ENJOY TALKING WHILE YOU CAN. THIS TIME, I WILL TAKE YOUR TONGUE ALONG WITH YOUR EYES.
THAT'S WHAT I LOVE ABOUT YOU, ELEKTRA. YOU'RE SUCH AN OPTIMIST...
EVEN WHEN YOU'RE SO TOTALLY AND COMPLETELY SCREWED.

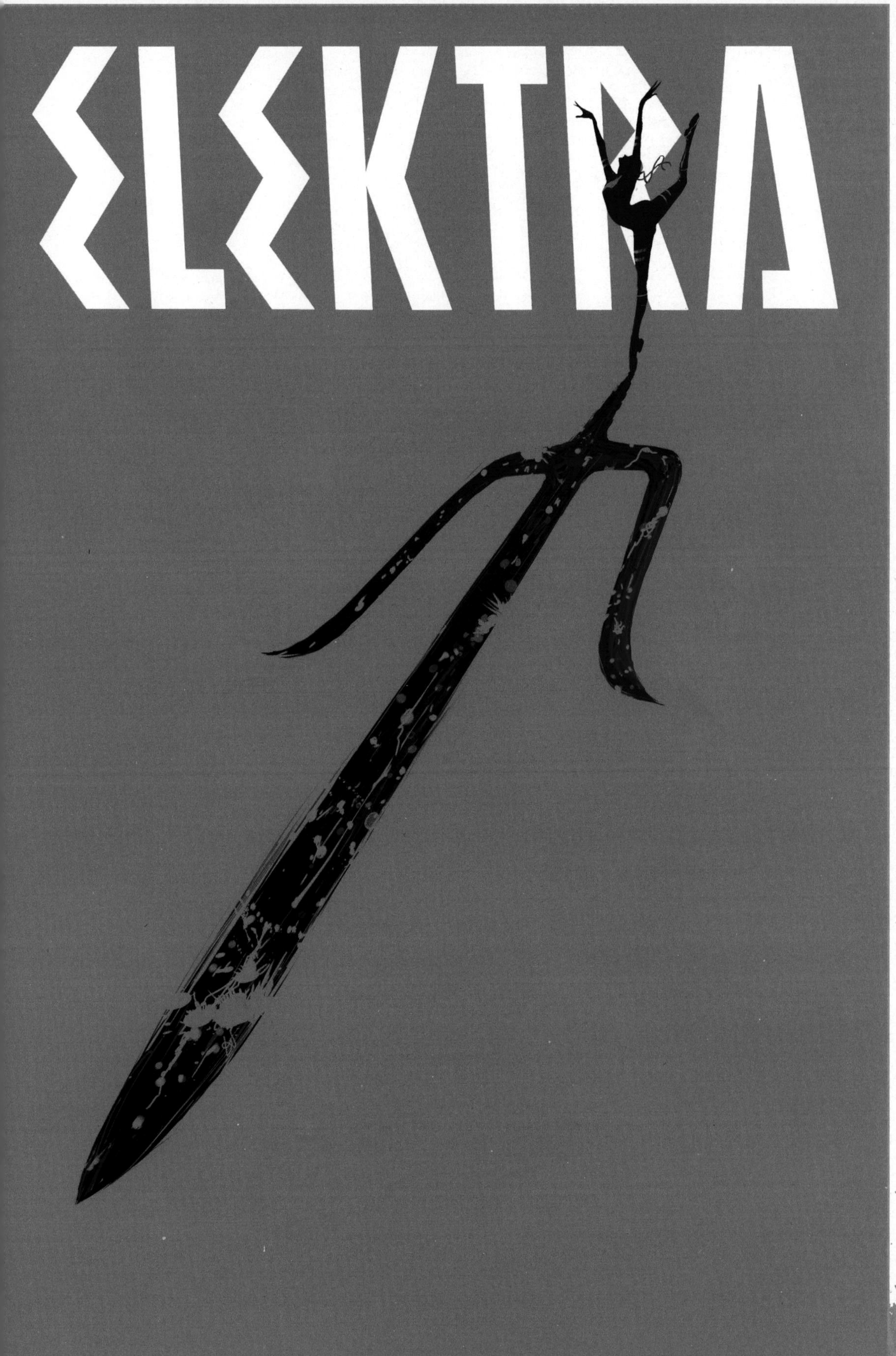
ELEKTRA

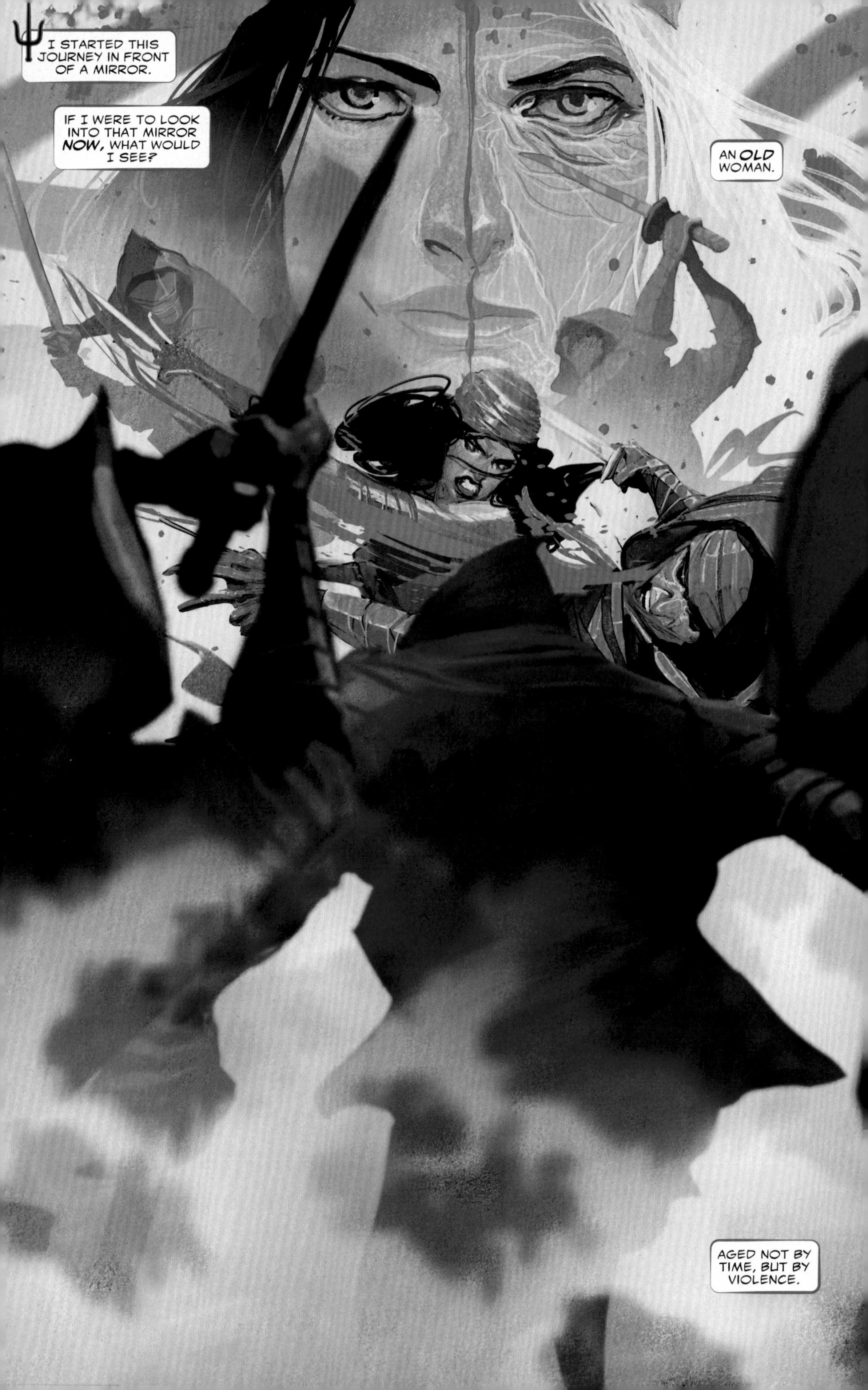
I STARTED THIS JOURNEY IN FRONT OF A MIRROR.
IF I WERE TO LOOK INTO THAT MIRROR NOW, WHAT WOULD I SEE?
AN OLD WOMAN.
AGED NOT BY TIME, BUT BY VIOLENCE.

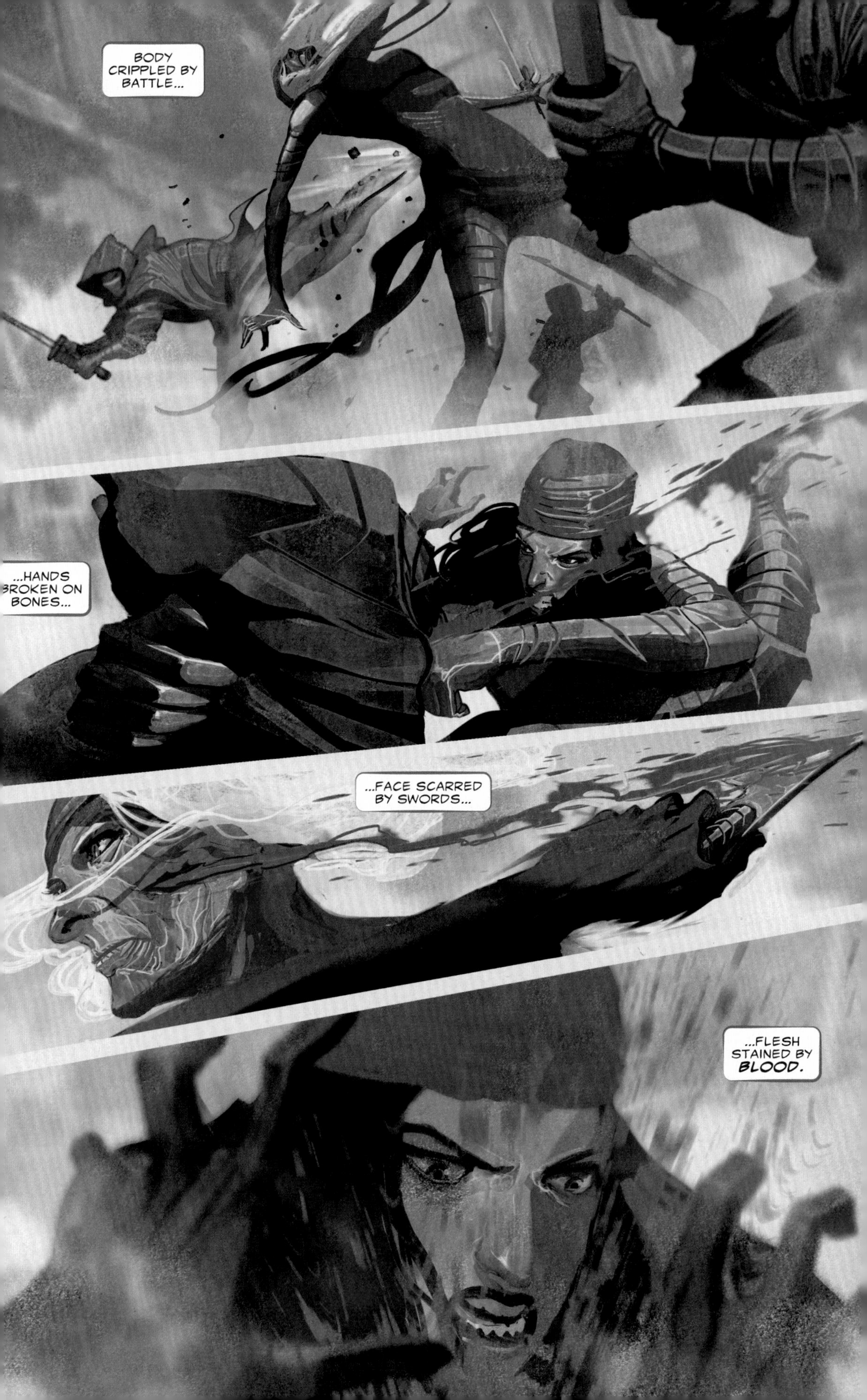

BODY CRIPPLED BY BATTLE...
...HANDS BROKEN ON BONES...
...FACE SCARRED BY SWORDS...
...FLESH STAINED BY **BLOOD**.

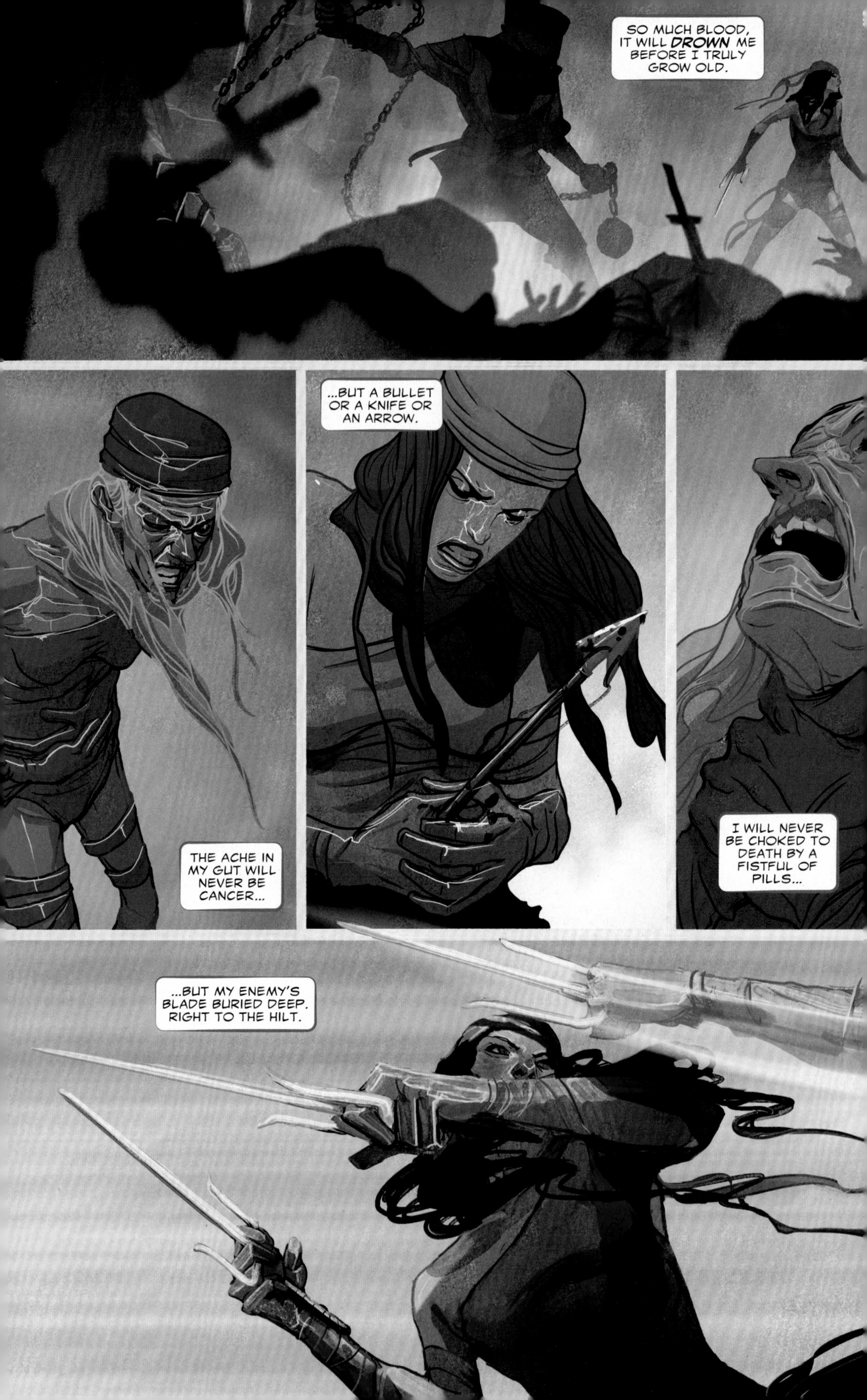
SO MUCH BLOOD, IT WILL DROWN ME BEFORE I TRULY GROW OLD.
THE ACHE IN MY GUT WILL NEVER BE CANCER...
...BUT A BULLET OR A KNIFE OR AN ARROW.
I WILL NEVER BE CHOKED TO DEATH BY A FISTFUL OF PILLS...
...BUT MY ENEMY'S BLADE BURIED DEEP. RIGHT TO THE HILT.

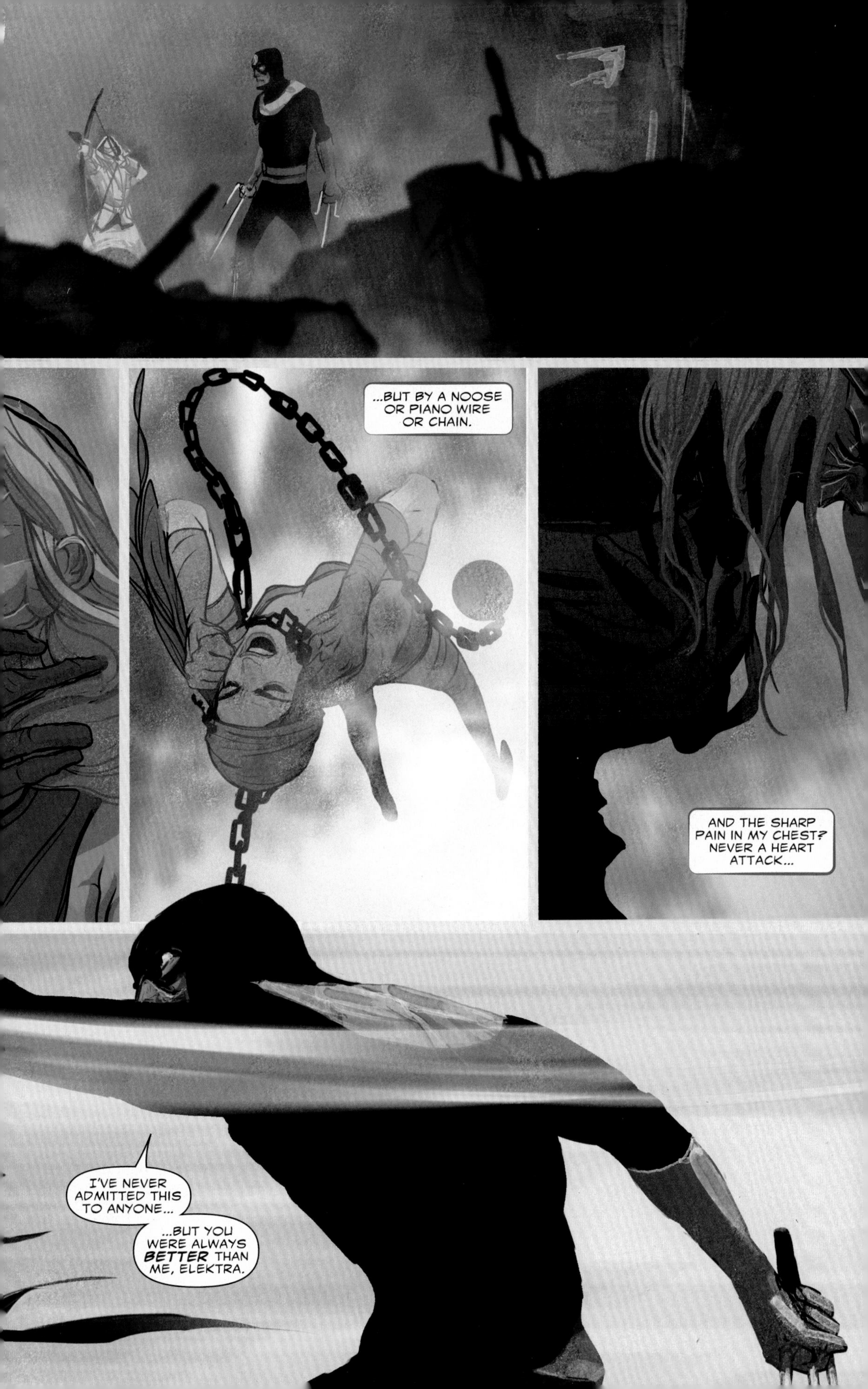
...BUT BY A NOOSE OR PIANO WIRE OR CHAIN.
AND THE SHARP PAIN IN MY CHEST? NEVER A HEART ATTACK...
I'VE NEVER ADMITTED THIS TO ANYONE...
...BUT YOU WERE ALWAYS *BETTER* THAN ME, ELEKTRA.

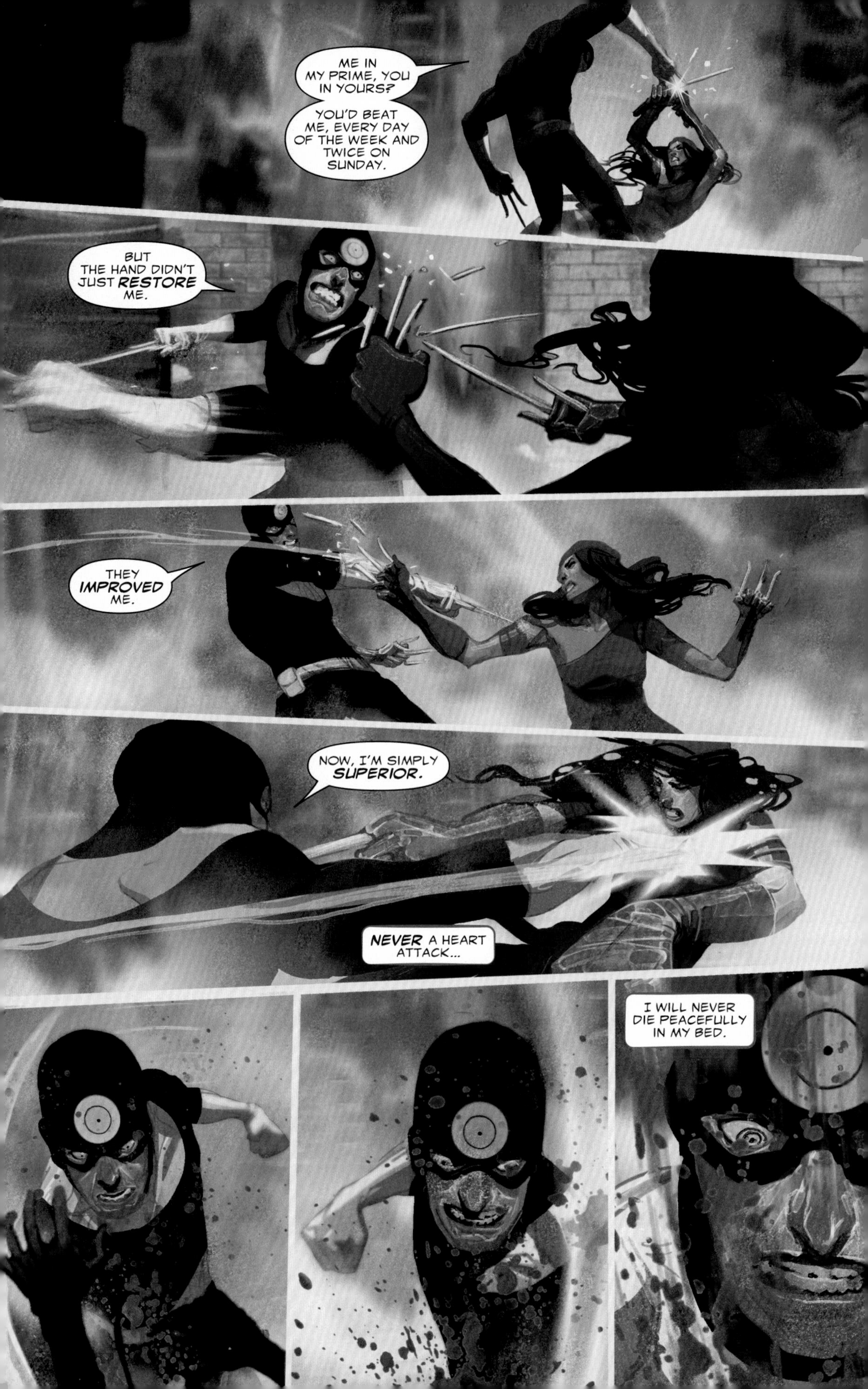

ME IN MY PRIME, YOU IN YOURS?
YOU'D BEAT ME, EVERY DAY OF THE WEEK AND TWICE ON SUNDAY.
BUT THE HAND DIDN'T JUST **RESTORE** ME.
THEY **IMPROVED** ME.
NOW, I'M SIMPLY **SUPERIOR.**
NEVER A HEART ATTACK...
I WILL NEVER DIE PEACEFULLY IN MY BED.

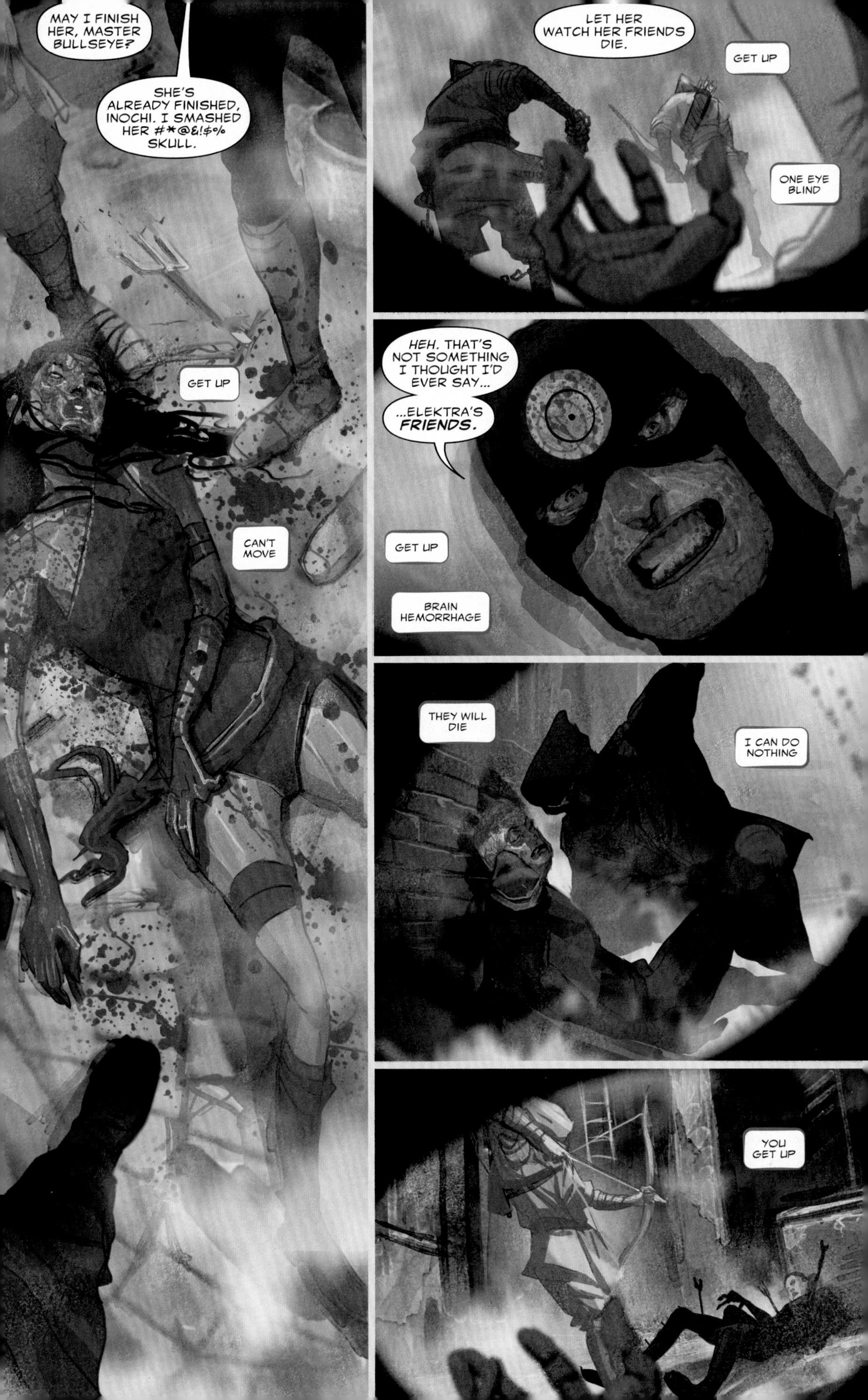

MAY I FINISH HER, MASTER BULLSEYE?
SHE'S ALREADY FINISHED, INOCHI. I SMASHED HER #*@&!$% SKULL.
GET UP
CAN'T MOVE
LET HER WATCH HER FRIENDS DIE.
GET UP
ONE EYE BLIND
HEH. THAT'S NOT SOMETHING I THOUGHT I'D EVER SAY...
...ELEKTRA'S FRIENDS.
GET UP
BRAIN HEMORRHAGE
THEY WILL DIE
I CAN DO NOTHING
YOU GET UP

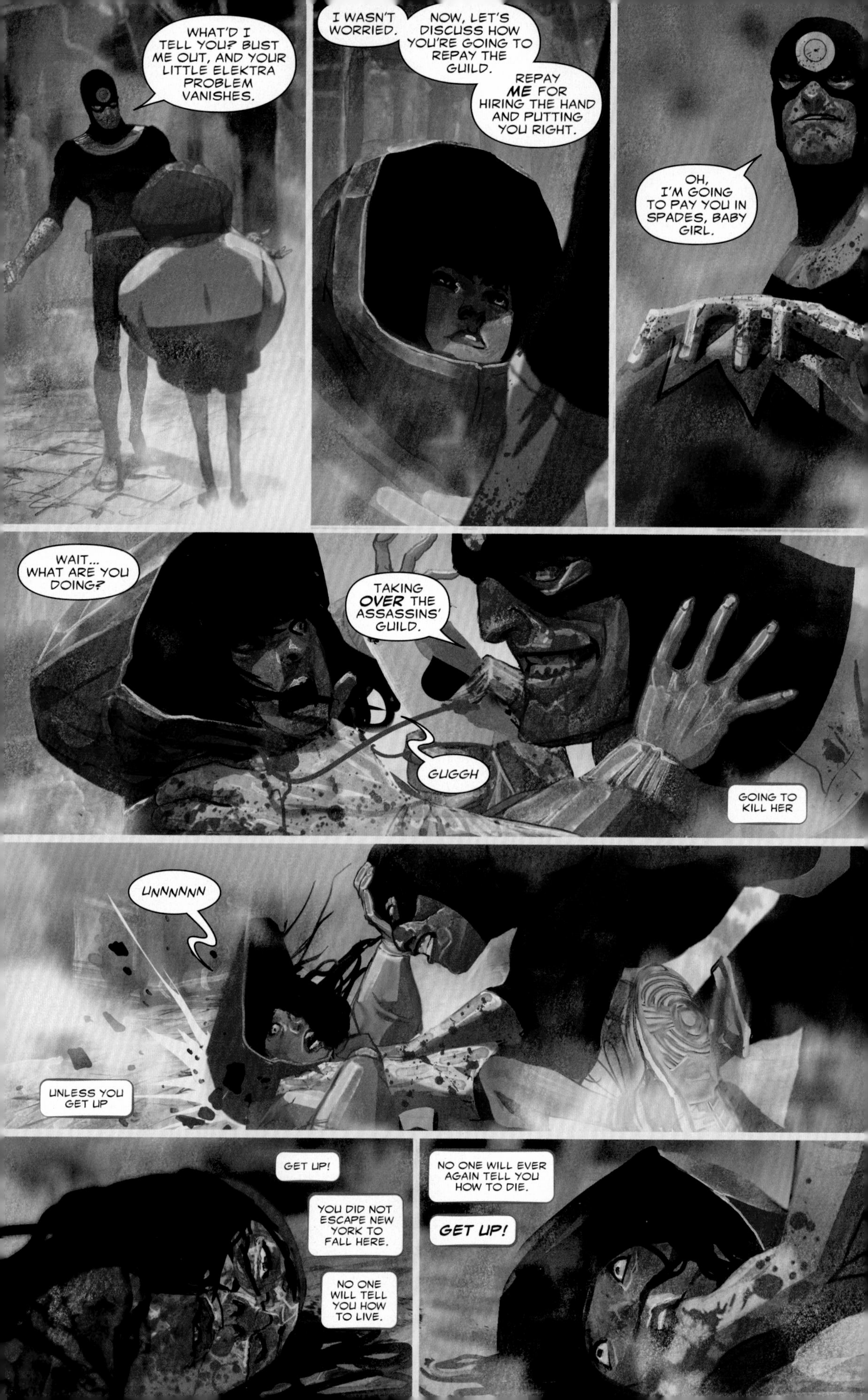
WHAT'D I TELL YOU? BUST ME OUT, AND YOUR LITTLE ELEKTRA PROBLEM VANISHES.
I WASN'T WORRIED.
NOW, LET'S DISCUSS HOW YOU'RE GOING TO REPAY THE GUILD.
REPAY ME FOR HIRING THE HAND AND PUTTING YOU RIGHT.
OH, I'M GOING TO PAY YOU IN SPADES, BABY GIRL.
WAIT... WHAT ARE YOU DOING?
TAKING OVER THE ASSASSINS' GUILD.
GUGGH
GOING TO KILL HER
UNNNNNN
UNLESS YOU GET UP
GET UP!
YOU DID NOT ESCAPE NEW YORK TO FALL HERE.
NO ONE WILL TELL YOU HOW TO LIVE.
NO ONE WILL EVER AGAIN TELL YOU HOW TO DIE.
GET UP!

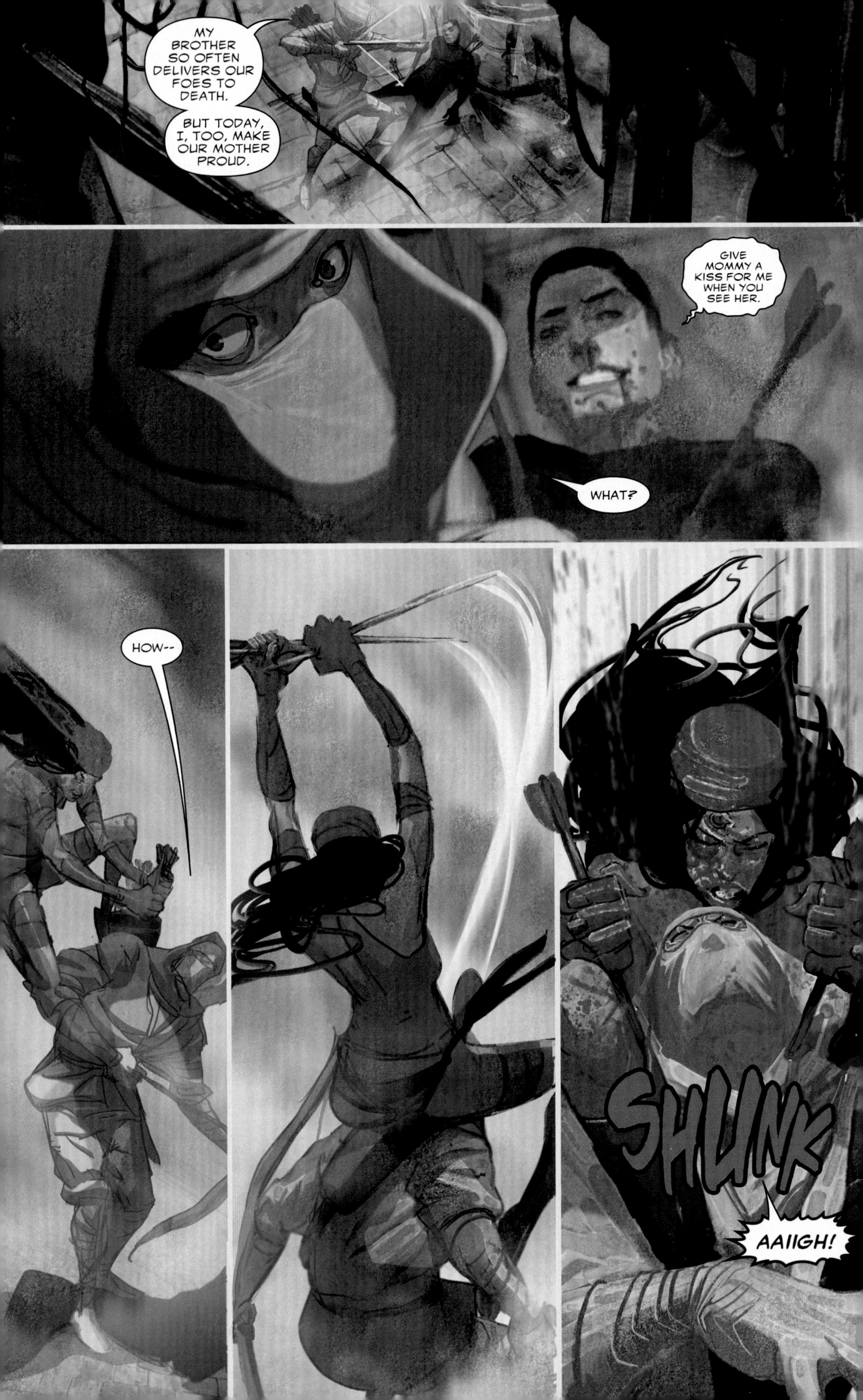
MY BROTHER SO OFTEN DELIVERS OUR FOES TO DEATH.
BUT TODAY, I, TOO, MAKE OUR MOTHER PROUD.
GIVE MOMMY A KISS FOR ME WHEN YOU SEE HER.
WHAT?
HOW--
SHUNK
AAIIGH!

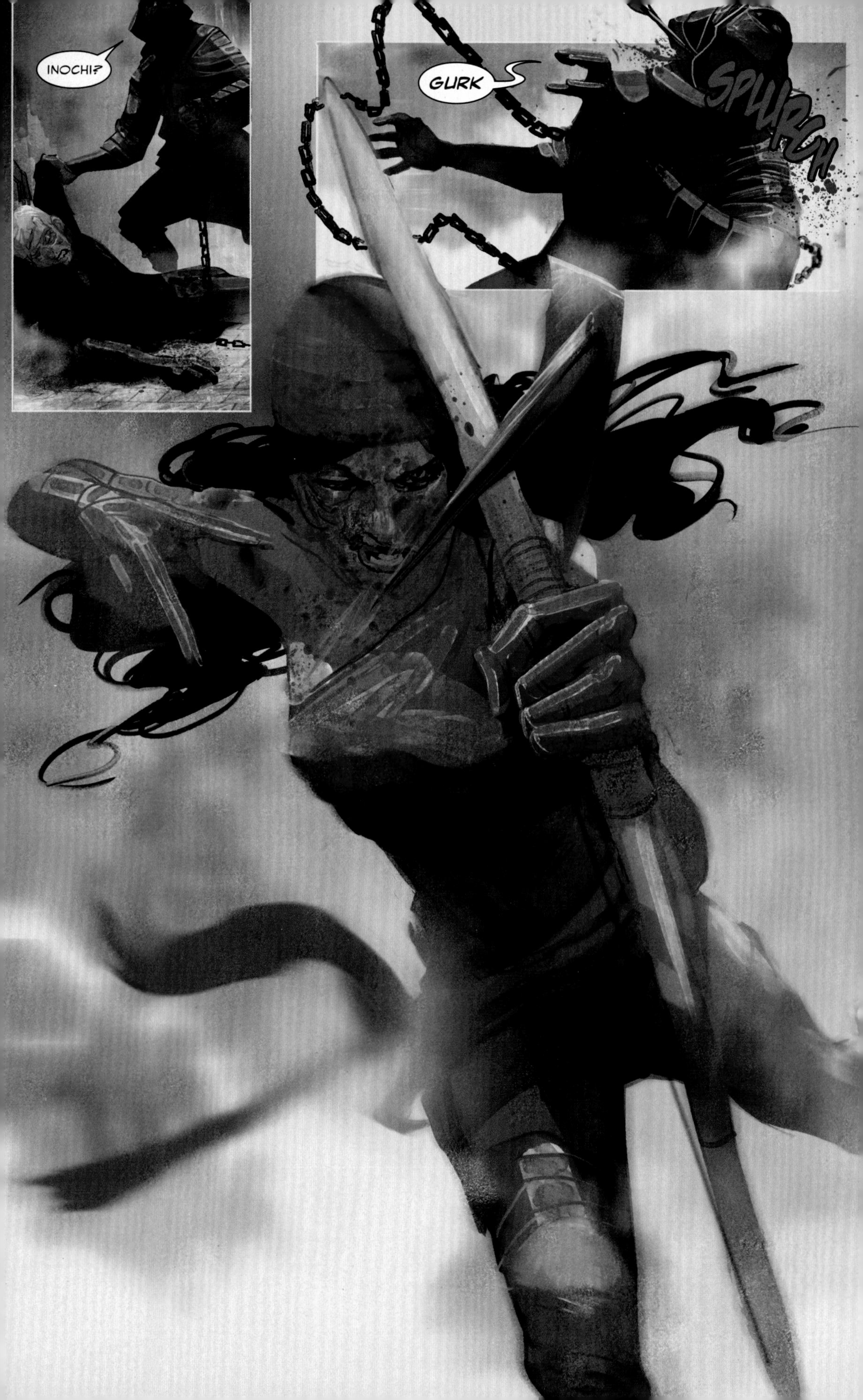
INOCHI?
GURK
SPLURCH

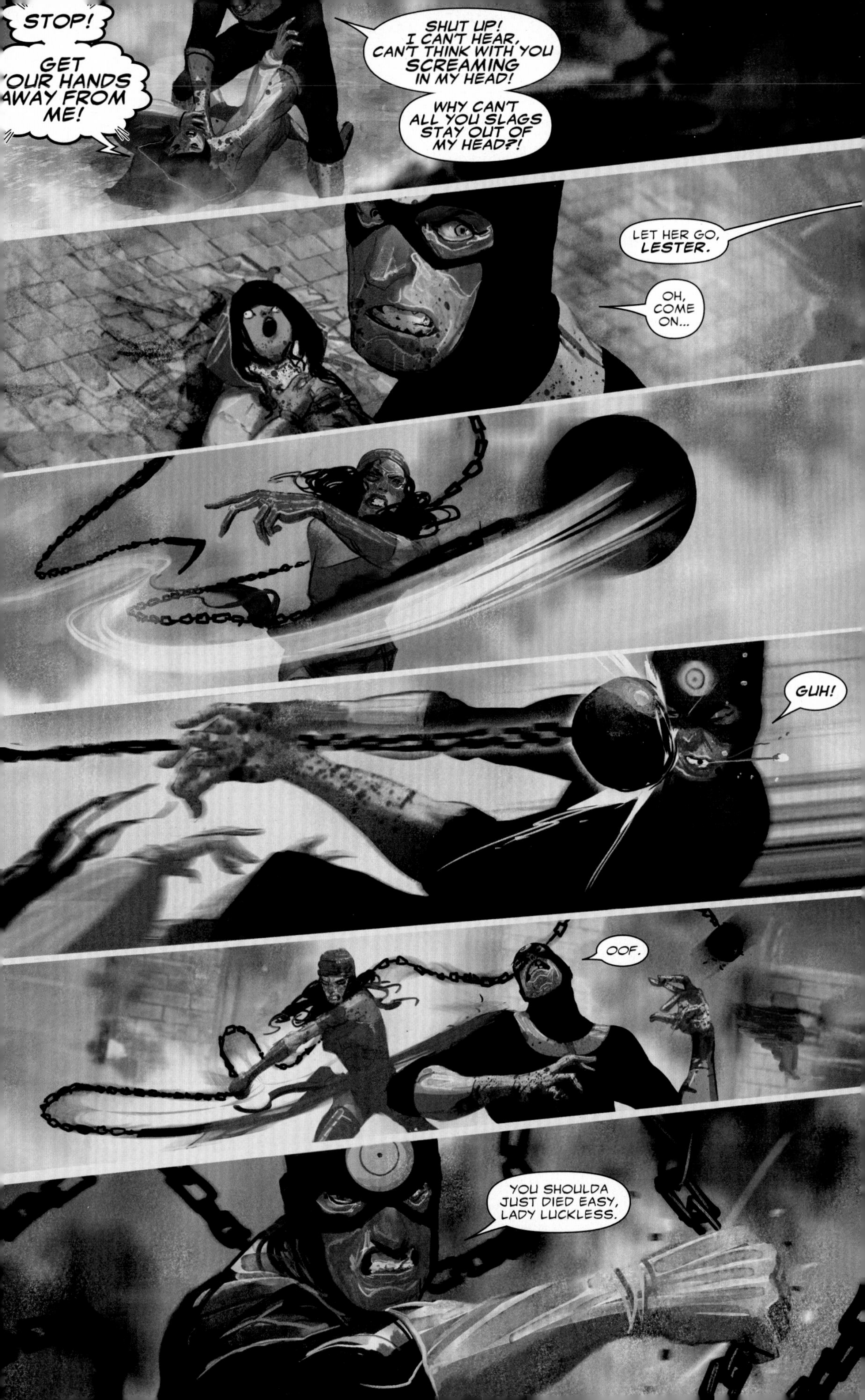
STOP!
GET YOUR HANDS AWAY FROM ME!
SHUT UP! I CAN'T HEAR, CAN'T THINK WITH YOU SCREAMING IN MY HEAD!
WHY CAN'T ALL YOU SLAGS STAY OUT OF MY HEAD?!
LET HER GO, LESTER.
OH, COME ON...
GUH!
OOF.
YOU SHOULDA JUST DIED EASY, LADY LUCKLESS.

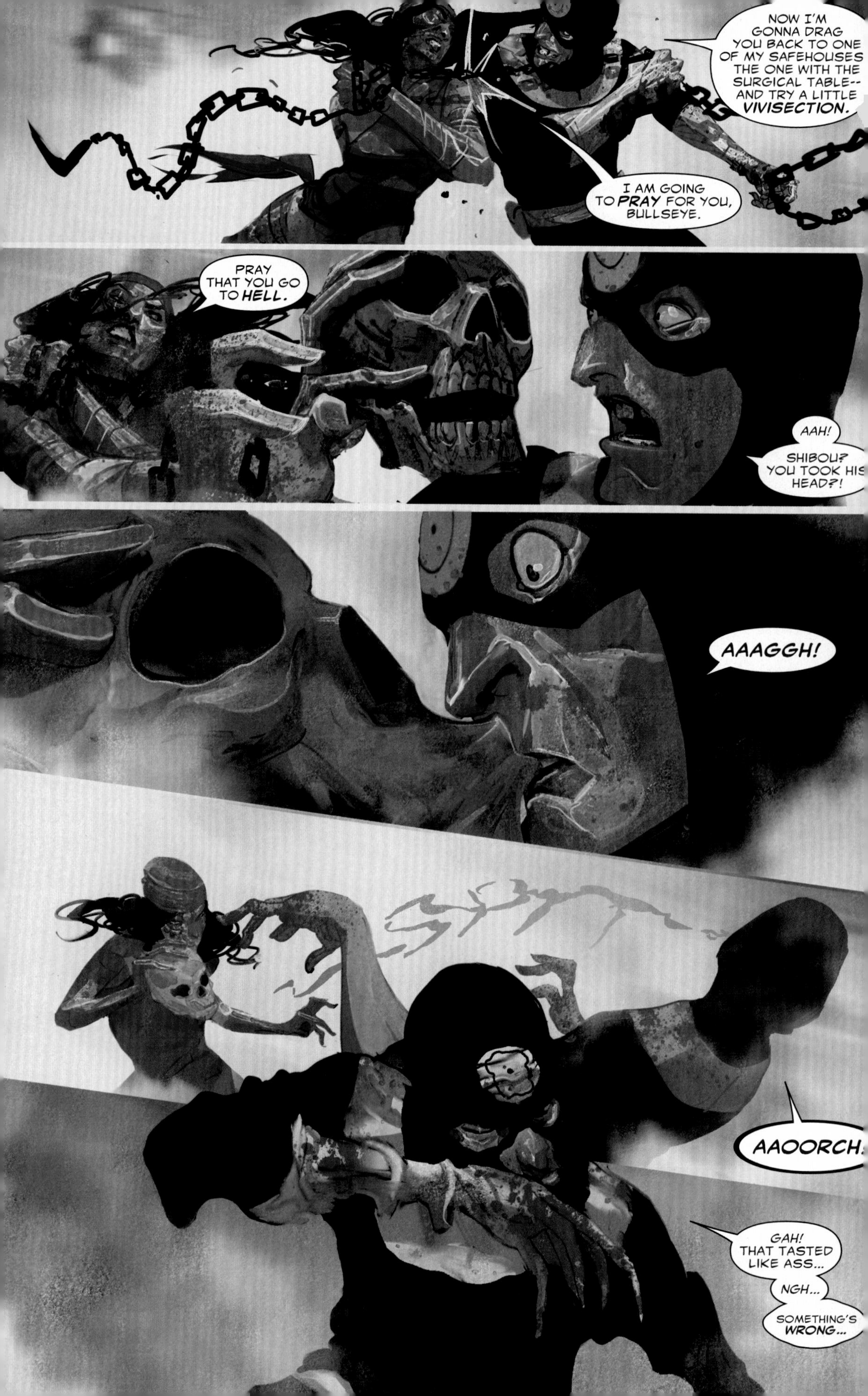
NOW I'M GONNA DRAG YOU BACK TO ONE OF MY SAFEHOUSES THE ONE WITH THE SURGICAL TABLE-- AND TRY A LITTLE VIVISECTION.
I AM GOING TO PRAY FOR YOU, BULLSEYE.
PRAY THAT YOU GO TO HELL.
AAH!
SHIBOU? YOU TOOK HIS HEAD?!
AAAGGH!
AAOORCH
GAH! THAT TASTED LIKE ASS...
NGH...
SOMETHING'S WRONG...

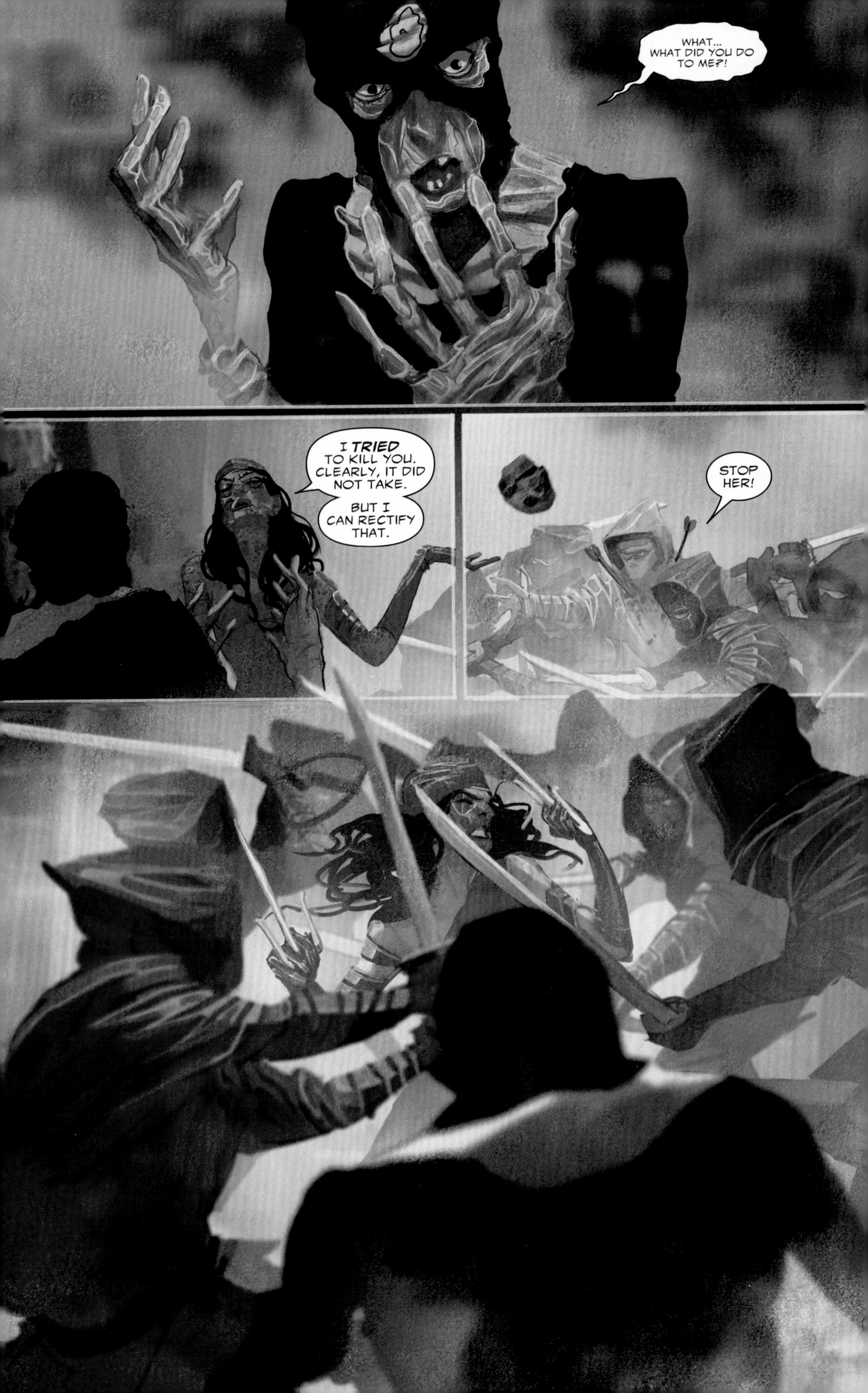
WHAT... WHAT DID YOU DO TO ME?!
I *TRIED* TO KILL YOU. CLEARLY, IT DID NOT TAKE.
BUT I CAN RECTIFY THAT.
STOP HER!

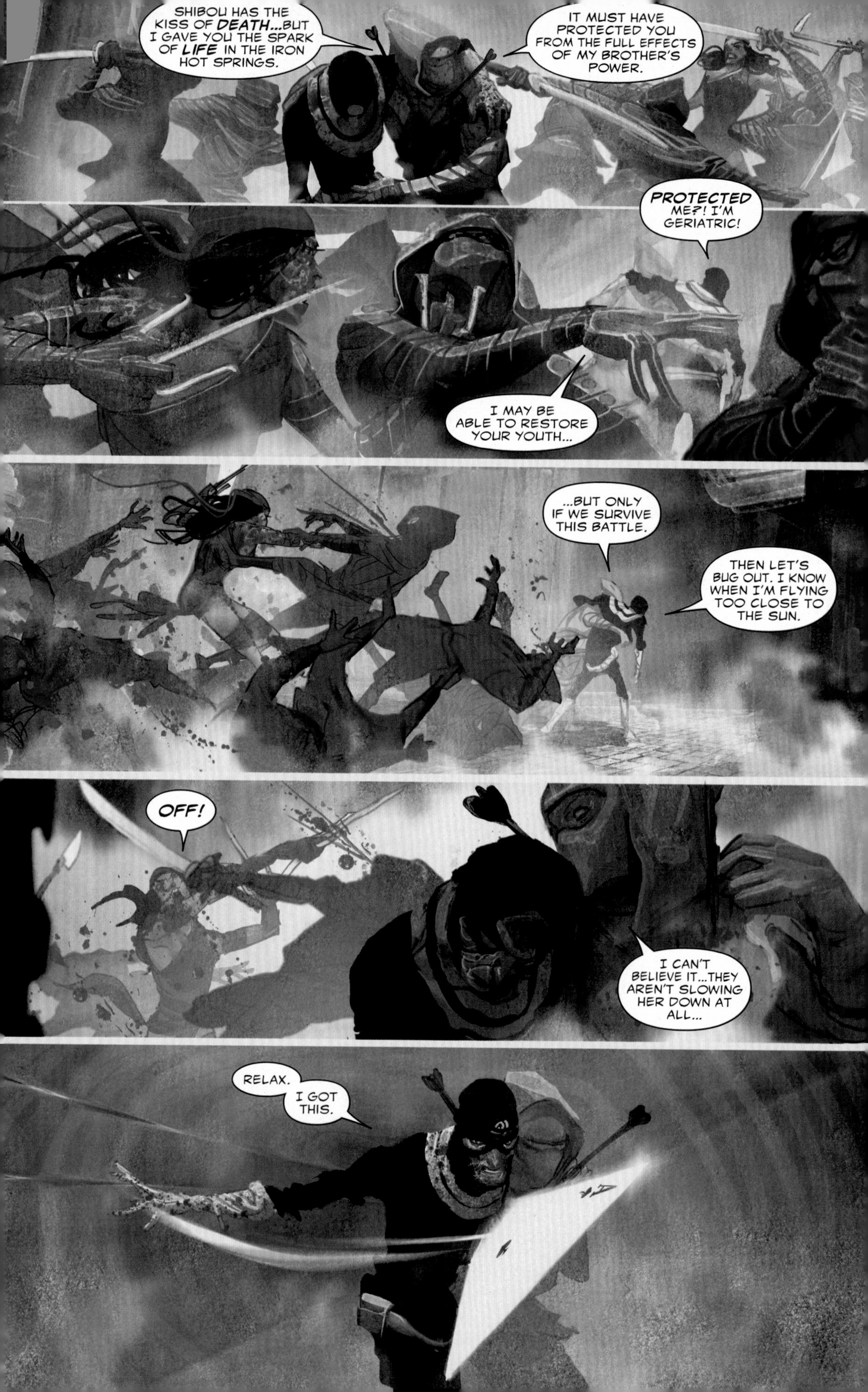
SHIBOU HAS THE KISS OF DEATH...BUT I GAVE YOU THE SPARK OF LIFE IN THE IRON HOT SPRINGS.
IT MUST HAVE PROTECTED YOU FROM THE FULL EFFECTS OF MY BROTHER'S POWER.
PROTECTED ME?! I'M GERIATRIC!
I MAY BE ABLE TO RESTORE YOUR YOUTH...
...BUT ONLY IF WE SURVIVE THIS BATTLE.
THEN LET'S BUG OUT. I KNOW WHEN I'M FLYING TOO CLOSE TO THE SUN.
OFF!
I CAN'T BELIEVE IT...THEY AREN'T SLOWING HER DOWN AT ALL...
RELAX. I GOT THIS.

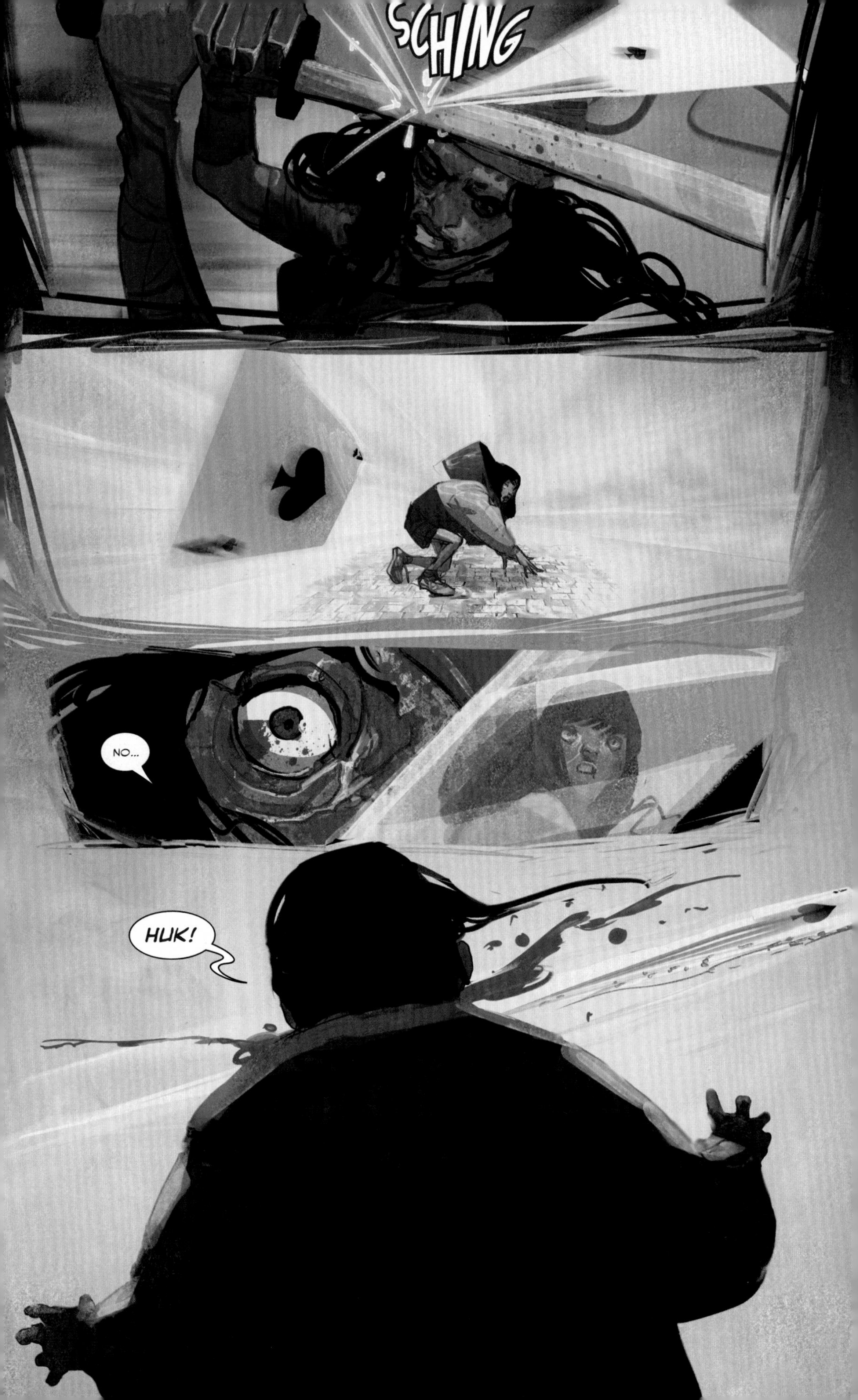
SCHING
NO...
HUK!

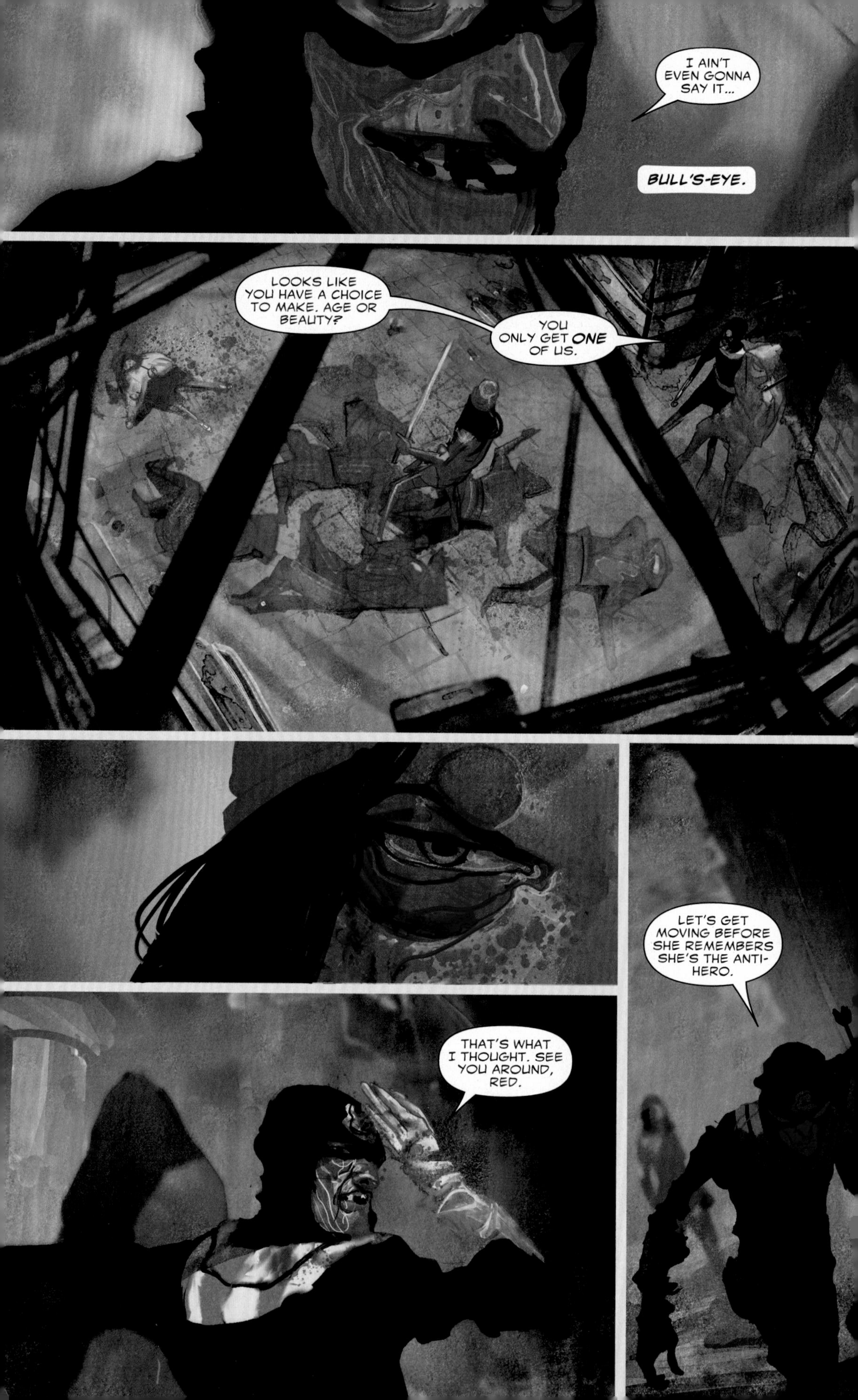

I AIN'T EVEN GONNA SAY IT...
BULL'S-EYE.
LOOKS LIKE YOU HAVE A CHOICE TO MAKE. AGE OR BEAUTY?
YOU ONLY GET ONE OF US.
LET'S GET MOVING BEFORE SHE REMEMBERS SHE'S THE ANTI-HERO.
THAT'S WHAT I THOUGHT. SEE YOU AROUND, RED.

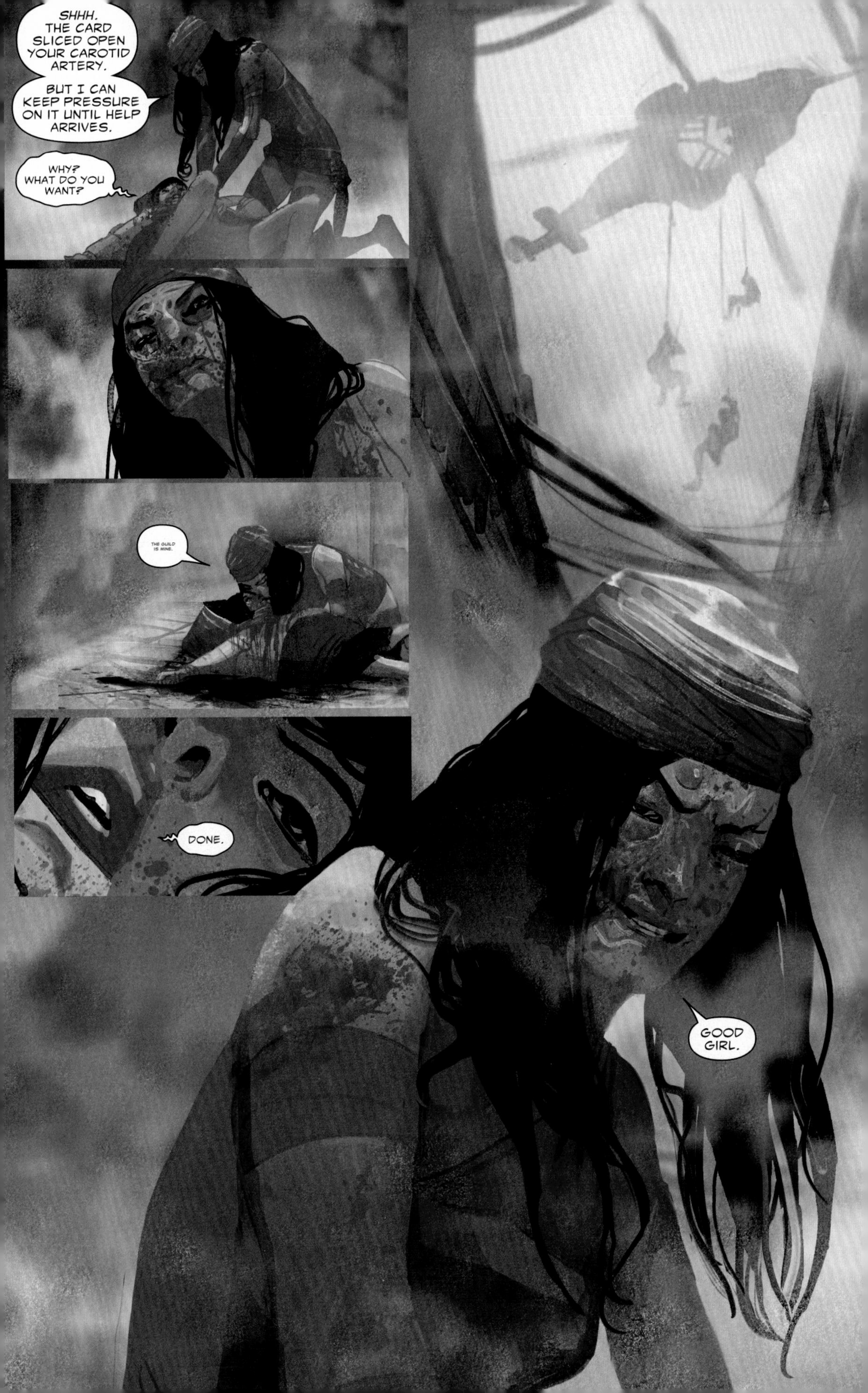
SHHH. THE CARD SLICED OPEN YOUR CAROTID ARTERY.
BUT I CAN KEEP PRESSURE ON IT UNTIL HELP ARRIVES.
WHY? WHAT DO YOU WANT?
THE GUILD IS MINE.
DONE.
GOOD GIRL.

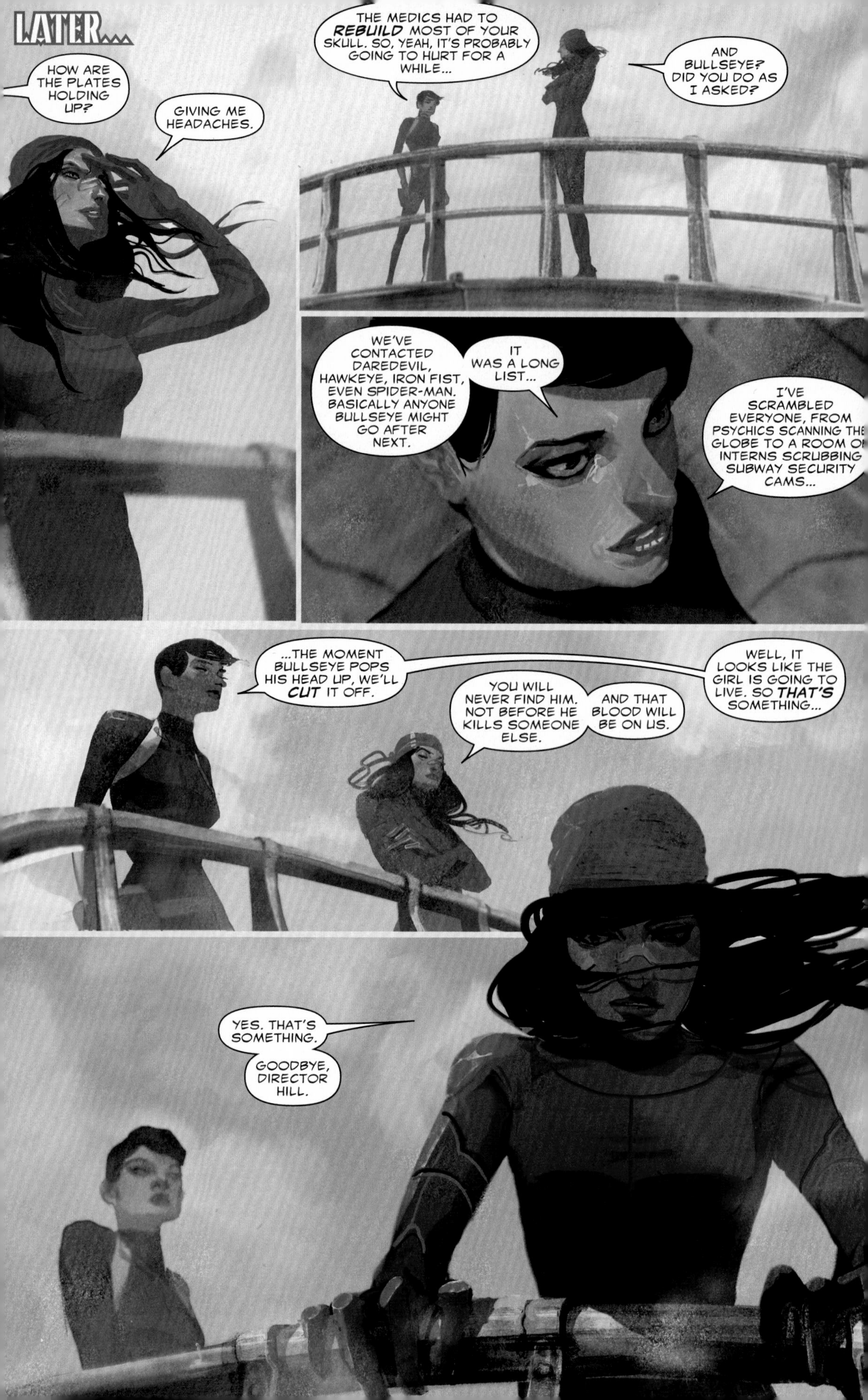
LATER...
HOW ARE THE PLATES HOLDING UP?
GIVING ME HEADACHES.
THE MEDICS HAD TO REBUILD MOST OF YOUR SKULL. SO, YEAH, IT'S PROBABLY GOING TO HURT FOR A WHILE...
AND BULLSEYE? DID YOU DO AS I ASKED?
WE'VE CONTACTED DAREDEVIL, HAWKEYE, IRON FIST, EVEN SPIDER-MAN. BASICALLY ANYONE BULLSEYE MIGHT GO AFTER NEXT.
IT WAS A LONG LIST...
I'VE SCRAMBLED EVERYONE, FROM PSYCHICS SCANNING THE GLOBE TO A ROOM OF INTERNS SCRUBBING SUBWAY SECURITY CAMS...
...THE MOMENT BULLSEYE POPS HIS HEAD UP, WE'LL CUT IT OFF.
YOU WILL NEVER FIND HIM. NOT BEFORE HE KILLS SOMEONE ELSE.
AND THAT BLOOD WILL BE ON US.
WELL, IT LOOKS LIKE THE GIRL IS GOING TO LIVE. SO THAT'S SOMETHING...
YES. THAT'S SOMETHING.
GOODBYE, DIRECTOR HILL.

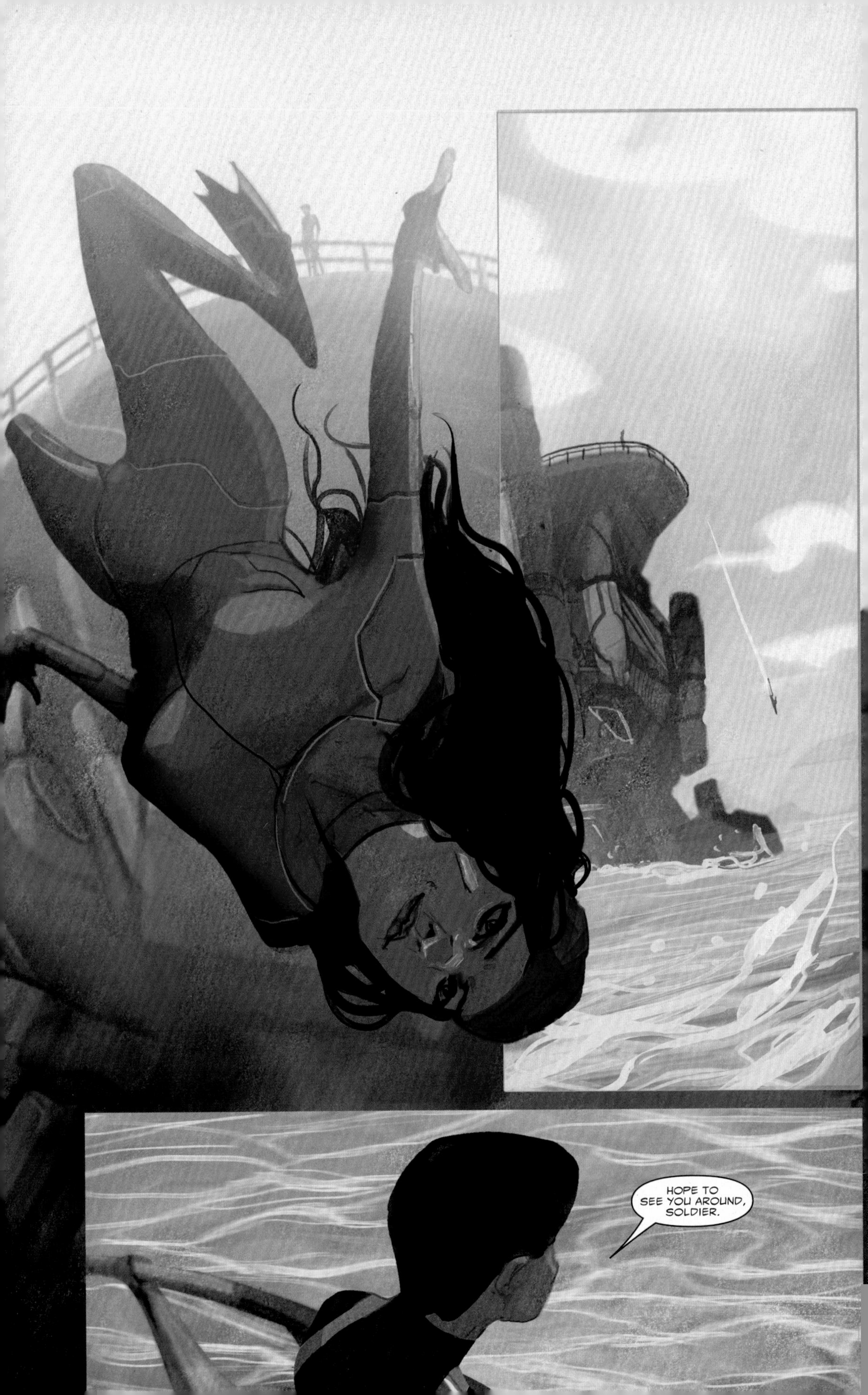
HOPE TO SEE YOU AROUND, SOLDIER.

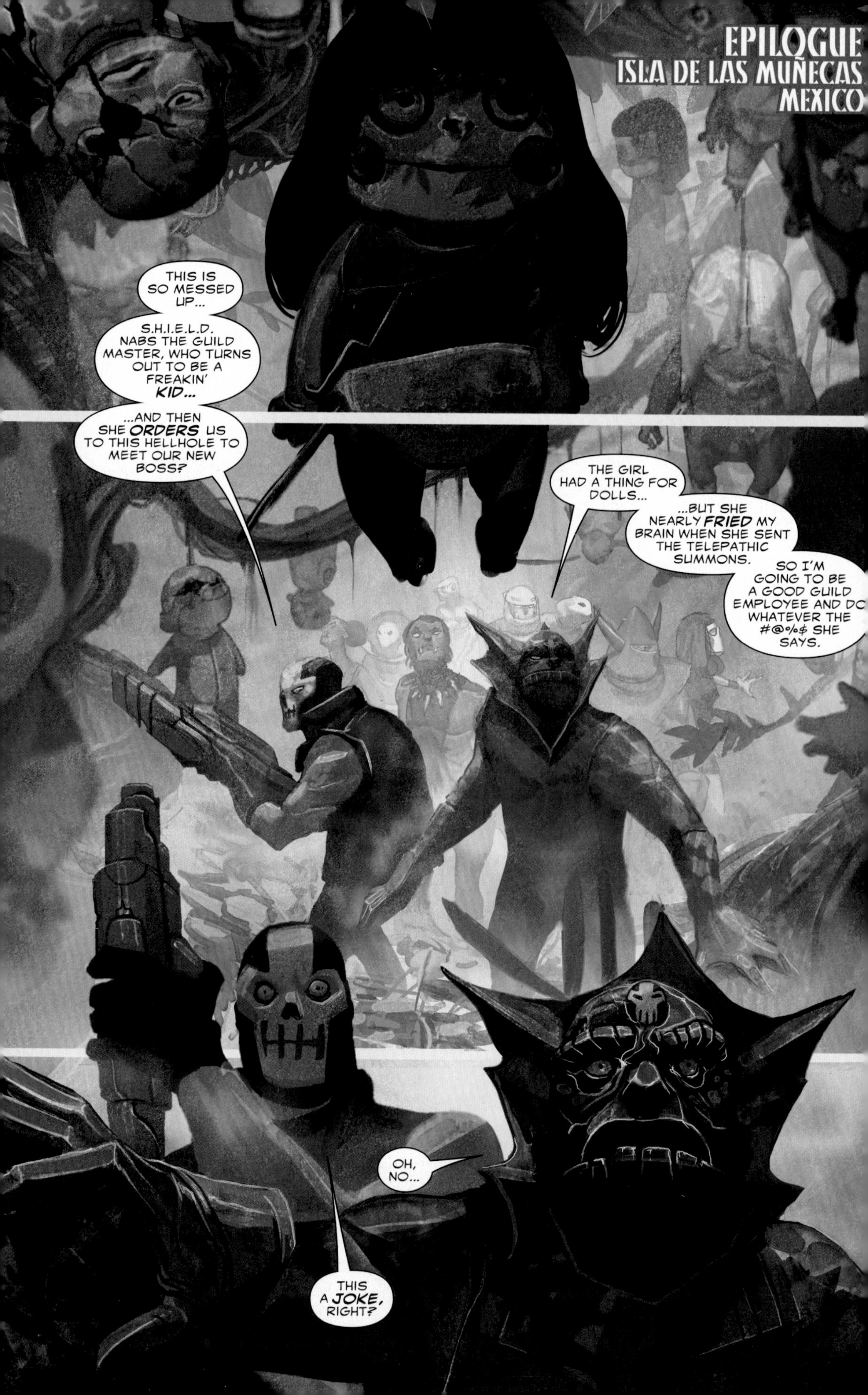
EPILOGUE
ISLA DE LAS MUÑECAS
MEXICO
THIS IS SO MESSED UP...
S.H.I.E.L.D. NABS THE GUILD MASTER, WHO TURNS OUT TO BE A FREAKIN' KID...
...AND THEN SHE ORDERS US TO THIS HELLHOLE TO MEET OUR NEW BOSS?
THE GIRL HAD A THING FOR DOLLS...
...BUT SHE NEARLY FRIED MY BRAIN WHEN SHE SENT THE TELEPATHIC SUMMONS.
SO I'M GOING TO BE A GOOD GUILD EMPLOYEE AND DO WHATEVER THE #@%$ SHE SAYS.
OH, NO...
THIS A JOKE, RIGHT?

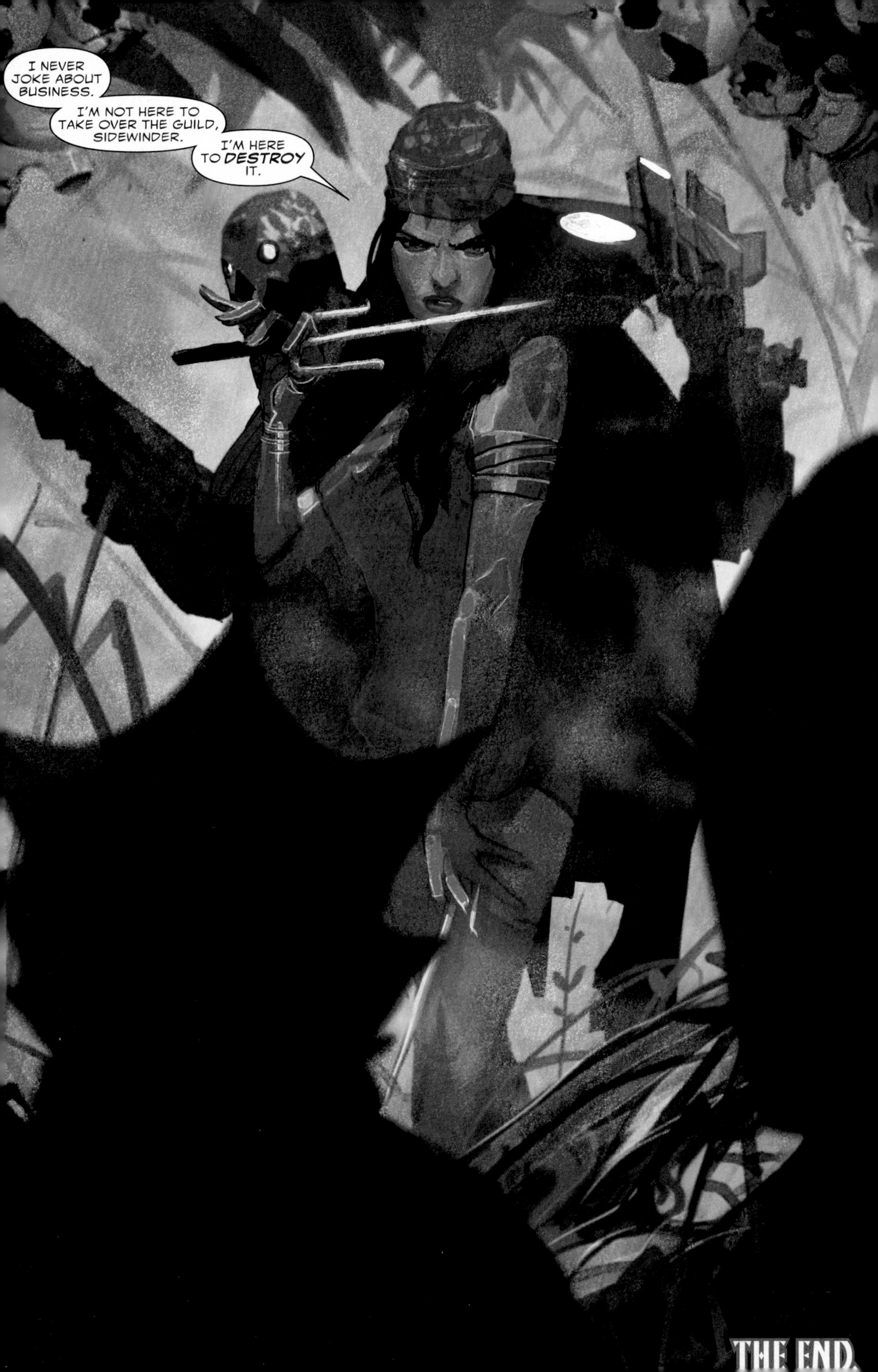
I NEVER JOKE ABOUT BUSINESS.
I'M NOT HERE TO TAKE OVER THE GUILD, SIDEWINDER.
I'M HERE TO DESTROY IT.
THE END.

When I first started this series, I wasn't really sure what to do with Elektra, what I might add to the character or how this new series could be different from all the amazing Elektra stories that had come before. All I really knew was that Elektra needed to get the hell out of New York and away from the stigma of being "Daredevil's dead girlfriend." I figured I'd just make everything else up along the way…and, somehow, it all worked out all right in the end, becoming the story and character I am most proud of writing. So, I just want to say thanks to Sana and Devin for leading me back to the heart of the story when I lost the plot; to Alex and Esther for taking us all to the Himalayas and New Orleans; and to Mike, whose breathtaking work always inspired me to be better with my own. And, most of all, thanks to all of you who read, love and understand Elektra, who were patient with the story as it unfolded and gave us time to find our voice. I wrote every panel for you.

Haden Blackman
February 2015

This book has been such an awesome ride! As a huge fan of ELEKTRA: ASSASSIN I was honored to carry on the legacy that is Elektra!

Thanks to Sana Amanat, Devin Lewis, Haden Blackman, Marco D'Alfonso, and Clayton Cowles for all their hard work and late nights to make this book great!

I'm so proud of what we have accomplished!

TEAM ELEKTRA GO!!

Mike del Mundo
February 2015

So we're finally here, almost one year after the launch date of Elektra, we are putting the series to bed…for now.

It's always a pleasure working with creators who just know what their vision is. Haden and Mike have brought such a sense of gravitas tempered with allure to Elektra's mission that it has kept us enraptured all the while. Elektra is that kind of character, her forceful vengeance becoming a thing of strange beauty. Strong, yet fractured, but always certain of herself and of her mission. That's why I've always been drawn to her—her complexity is relatable, and, for me at least, what makes her the most fascinating Marvel hero out there.

Thanks to all of you for sticking around with us. Being on books like this is what makes being an editor so gratifying. Thanks for reading.

Stay sharp.
Sana Amanat
February 2015

ISSUE 9 PAGE LAYOUTS

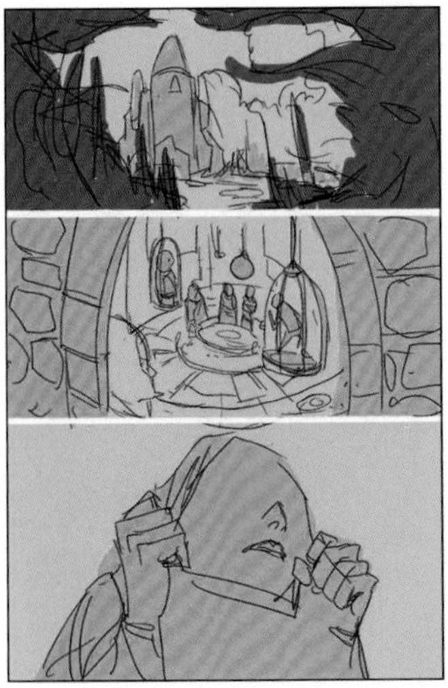

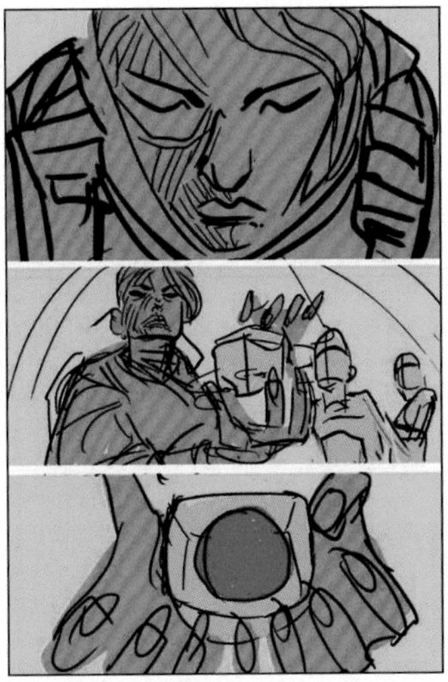

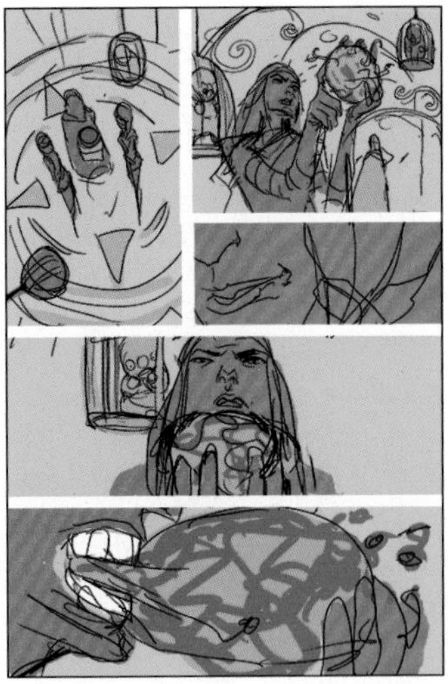

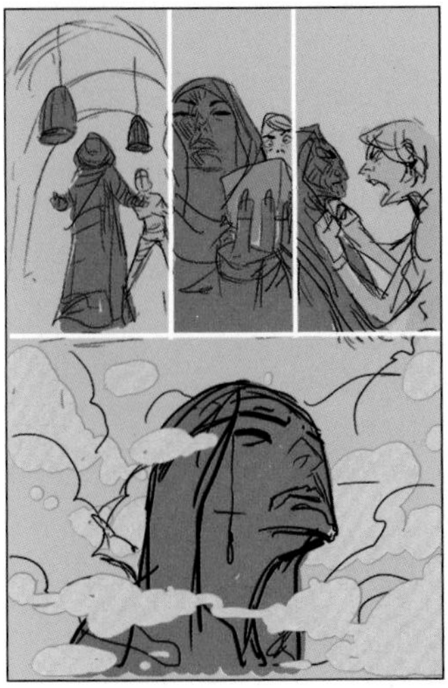

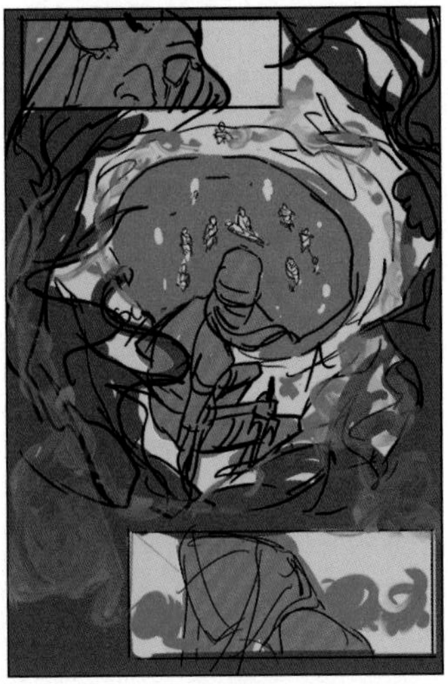

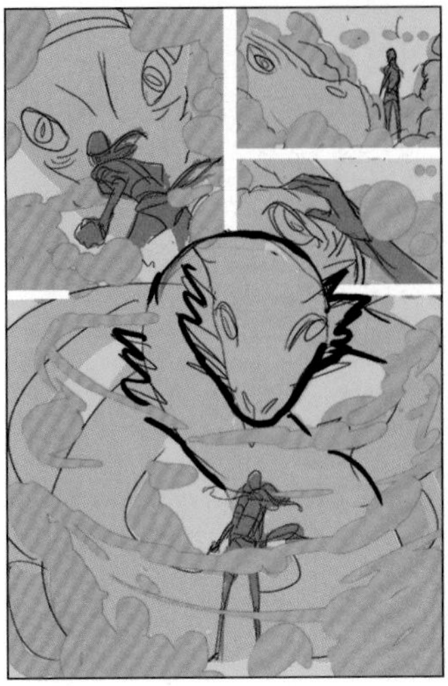

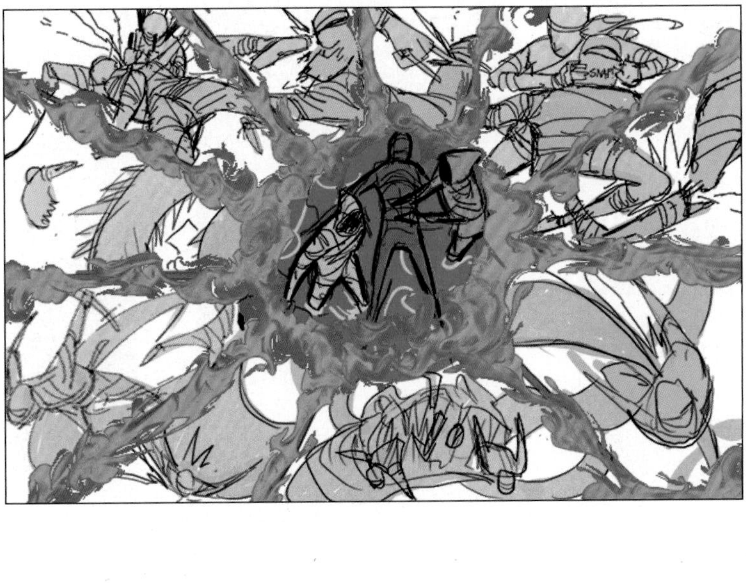

ISSUE 10 PAGE LAYOUTS

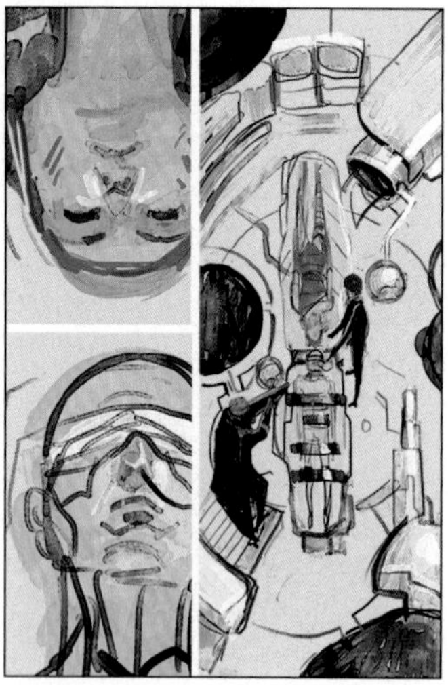
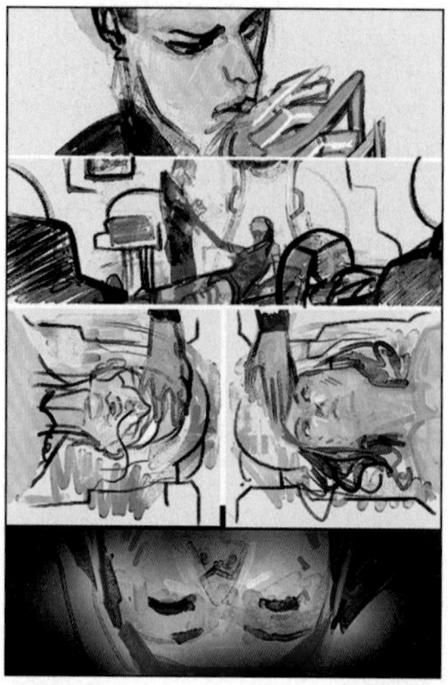
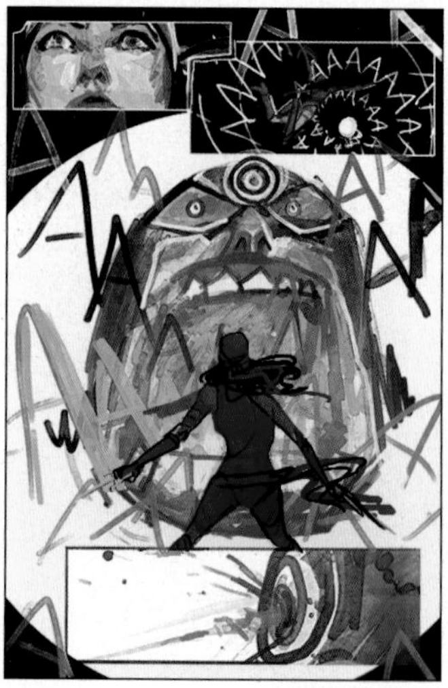
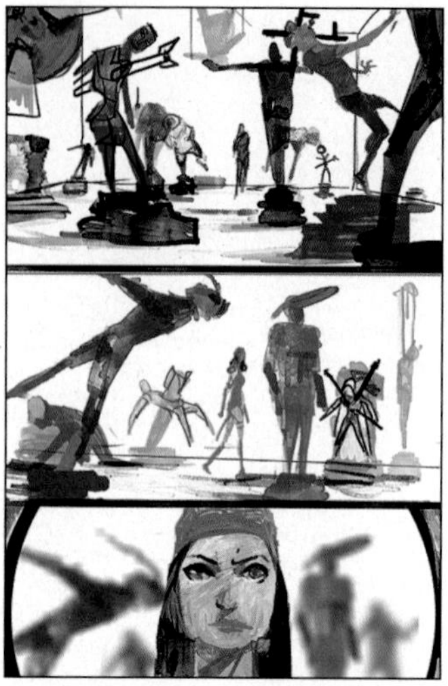
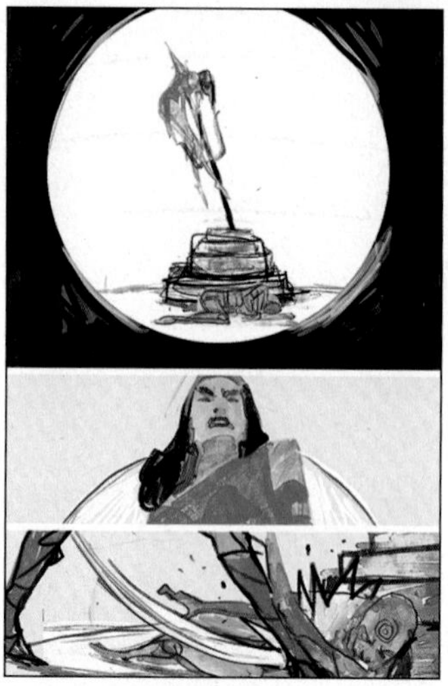
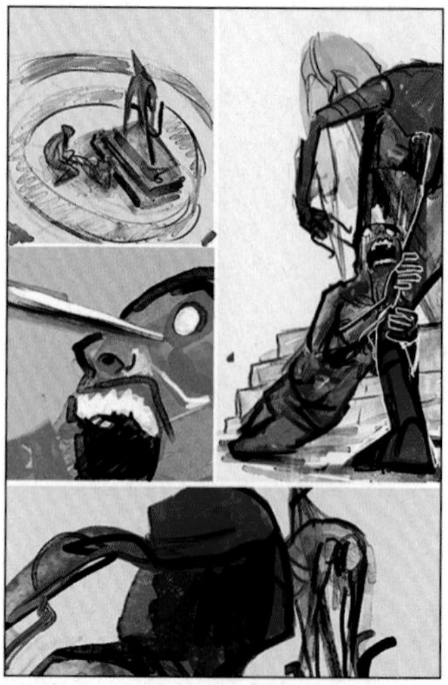
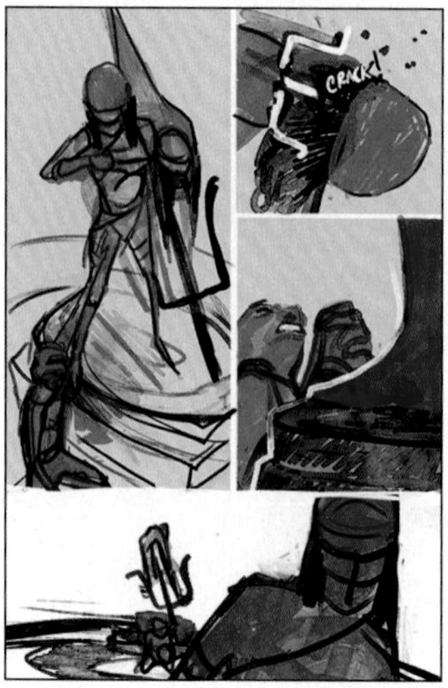
CRACK!
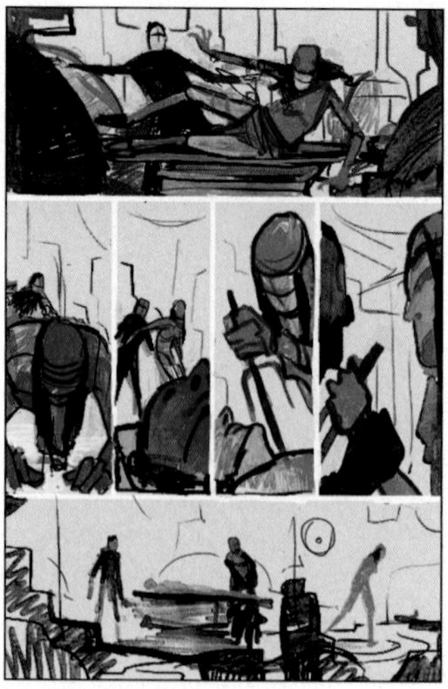
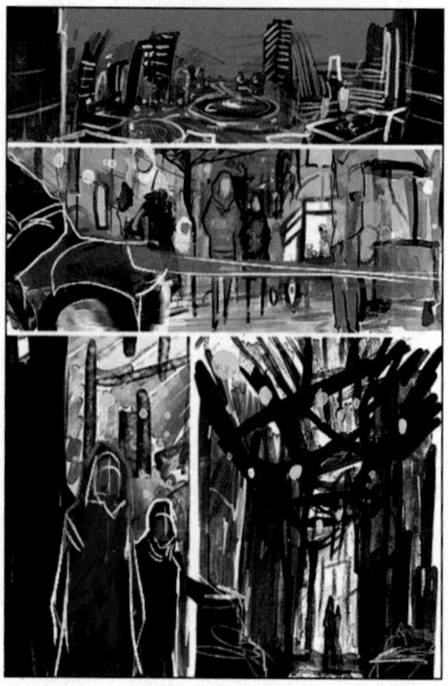